THE SECRET TEACHINGS

D1598700

Also by Harold Klemp

THE SECRET TEACHINGS

HAROLD KLEMP

MAHANTA TRANSCRIPTS
BOOK 3

ECKANKAR
Minneapolis
Eckankar.org

The Secret Teachings,
Mahanta Transcripts, Book 3

Copyright © 1989, 2022 ECKANKAR

Printed in USA

Compiled by Joan Klemp and Anne Pezdirc
Cover illustration by Roy Kerswill
Text illustrations by Signy Cohen
Spine photo and text photo (page 297) by Art Galbraith
Text photo (page xii) by Chris Morris

Second edition—2022

MAHANTA

This book has been authored by and published under the supervision of the MAHANTA, the Living ECK Master, Sri Harold Klemp. It is the Word of ECK.

Library of Congress Cataloging-in-Publication Data

Names: Klemp, Harold, author.
Title: The secret teachings / Harold Klemp.
Description: Chanhassen : Eckankar, 2022. | Series: Mahanta transcripts ; book 3 | Includes index. | Summary: "Author Harold Klemp, spiritual leader of Eckankar, shows, through stories and insights, how Divine Spirit works with each person in daily life, helping them master their spiritual destiny and find their secret key to happiness"-- Provided by publisher.
Identifiers: LCCN 2022011347 | ISBN 9781570434914 (paperback)
Subjects: LCSH: Eckankar (Organization)
Classification: LCC BP605.E3 K565 2022 | DDC 299/.93--dc23/eng/20220329
LC record available at https://lccn.loc.gov/2022011347

♾ This paper meets the requirements of ANSI/NISO Z39.48-1992 (Permanence of Paper).

CONTENTS

FOREWORD

The teachings of ECK define the nature of Soul. You are Soul, a particle of God sent into the worlds (including earth) to gain spiritual experience.

The goal in ECK is spiritual freedom in this lifetime, after which you become a Coworker with God, both here and in the next world. Karma and reincarnation are primary beliefs.

Key to the ECK teachings is the MAHANTA, the Living ECK Master. He has the special ability to act as both the Inner and Outer Master for ECK students. The prophet of Eckankar, he is given respect but is not worshipped. He teaches the sacred name of God, HU. When sung just a few minutes each day, HU will lift you spiritually into the Light and Sound of God—the ECK (Holy Spirit). This easy spiritual exercise and others will purify you. You are then able to accept the full love of God in this lifetime.

Sri Harold Klemp is the MAHANTA, the Living ECK Master today. Author of many books, discourses, and articles, he teaches the ins and outs of the spiritual life. Many of his talks are available to you on audio and video recordings. His teachings lift people and help them recognize and understand their own experiences in the Light and Sound of God.

The Secret Teachings, Mahanta Transcripts, Book 3, contains his talks from 1983–84. May they serve to uplift Soul to greater areas of consciousness.

To find out more about Harold Klemp and Eckankar, please turn to page 297 in the back of this book.

Sri Harold Klemp, the MAHANTA, the Living ECK Master visited the site of the ancient oracle at Delphi on a trip to Greece in 1983, traveling the globe to bring out the teachings of the Light and Sound of God to the people of today.

1
THE OTHER SIDE
OF THE ROPE

s we go through our many lifetimes, it's like being the eternal surfer. We become part of a wave. This wave is the Audible Life Current, the Sound Current, or the Holy Spirit. The wave is going back to God; It's going back home. And like the surfer, when you catch a wave—if you get to the crest and ride it right—you can take it all the way in to the beach. If you don't ride it right, you fall off; but if you're lucky, you can catch one of the other waves that are always coming in.

Like the surfer, when you catch a wave and ride it right, you can take it all the way in to the beach.

There have been waves of Souls before us, riding the Sound Current of Spirit back to God—thousands of waves going back through time, where Souls have tried in one way or another, with varying degrees of discipline or urgency or dedication, to find the Ocean of Love and Mercy. And when we finish our turn on the surfboard, there will be thousands more waves carrying countless Souls riding the wave of life.

I refer to Soul as the eternal surfer because many times we fall off. Just about everyone here tonight has fallen off the surfboard of this Life Stream before. We have come on the path to God through one of the Living ECK Masters in the past, but at some point we had had enough. For one reason or another, we began to look someplace else, thinking that maybe we had been misled. Perhaps there wasn't enough fanfare, not enough phenomena to hold our interest. Why not leave and go for something that promised more excitement than the true path to God?

So we got off the path. And in another life we came back, made it to the Second or Third Initiation, and then fell back down again. Later we found the Living ECK Master once more and very quickly gained ground.

This is why some people in this lifetime move very quickly to the higher initiations: They have earned it before—the hard way. This is not to say that someone who is new to the spiritual path has to fall the way we did in the past. But we have the right to fall; we have the right to fail. God gives us the right to learn, and we can do it any way we want to.

THE OTHER SIDE OF THE ROPE

I see two approaches to life: the active and the passive. A travel-magazine writer wrote a story about the day he and his daughter, who was a baseball fan, were trying to figure out how to spend the afternoon. The writer asked his daughter, "How would you like to go see the Texas Rangers play?"

"No thanks, Dad."

"Why not?" he asked.

"Because," she said, "I'd rather be on the other side of the rope."

He wondered if this was the latest slang or a new team slogan. "What do you mean?" he asked.

She reminded him of the previous summer when she and her little sister had gone to watch the filming of an episode of the TV show "Dallas." A rope had been put up around the set to keep the spectators back. They had stood with the rest of the crowd, watching the film crew run back and forth, really working up a sweat in the ninety-five-degree heat of the day. But even observing their discomfort, this little girl decided that if she ever had a choice, she would rather be on the other side of the rope, doing things instead of watching them being done. So when her dad asked if she would like to go and watch a baseball game, she explained that she really would prefer to *play* baseball.

Procrastination is a facet of attachment that holds Soul in the lower worlds. The point of this story is to inspire you to find out how to live life and enjoy it. When troubles come and we find ourselves in a karmic situation not to our liking, we say, "Dear Lord, please deliver me from this evil." It's a nice prayer; an easy way to hang on to the idea of old God with the white beard standing ready to take care of us. But it was we, in our ignorance, who disobeyed the laws of Spirit, thus bringing ourselves to this low state.

Being on the other side of the rope simply means going out to live life actively. When you are out of work, for instance, instead of sitting back and waiting for the next welfare check, you go out and look for a job. Why? Because you are interested in something more than leisure. As Soul, you owe yourself the experience of going out in life and getting the richest, fullest experiences you can.

The other side of the rope has even more angles. We can turn things over to Spirit, but even when we don't, the resulting experience is part of our lesson. Once we have recognized this, we can move on for now and, if necessary, catch the lesson later.

LIVING LIFE ACTIVELY AND CREATIVELY

A young man told me about an incident that happened several years ago when he went looking for a

This little girl decided she would rather be on the other side of the rope, doing things instead of watching them being done.

job at a little magazine that was just getting started. As it turned out, the editor needed a reporter to go out and gather information for certain articles she had in mind. She said to him, "Since this is a desert area, we want a story on the pitfalls of the unwary hiker who, ignorant of the laws of the desert, gets lost and succumbs to the trials and dangers—snakes and scorpions and all these things. Get me a story on this."

The reporter was new at this and didn't really know how to go about it. He decided to start by interviewing the town sheriff.

The sheriff was very cordial. He made an effort to help the reporter with his story, but finally he had to admit it: "You know, I really can't remember the last time we lost a man out in the desert."

The reporter continued to quiz the sheriff from other angles. He said, "What dangers could you foresee for a hiker?"

The sheriff thought about it for a moment. "Well," he said, "there are snakes and scorpions, and of course the danger of running out of water. But in spite of all that, I still can't think of anybody we've ever lost in the desert."

This man wanted to earn his living as a reporter. He was under pressure to write the article— but so far he hadn't been able to come up with a story. So, ever-inventive, ever-creative, he went to a restaurant and started talking with the townspeople, hoping to get a story with a little local color.

He asked several of the patrons, "When is the last time a man from this town was lost out in the desert?" A few of the old-timers came over and joined the group. Soon everybody was thinking real hard, trying to remember. Eventually they all agreed: They couldn't think of a single man who was ever lost in the desert.

The reporter finally gave up on that idea. But still being creative, he sat down and began to work

Ever-inventive, ever-creative, the reporter asked several townspeople, "When is the last time a man from this town was lost out in the desert?"

out another angle to satisfy the editor. He would write an entirely different article on hiking. In order to add his own perspective, he went hiking in the desert, and he wrote a story about the things that happened to him. This is what he brought back to the editor.

When he handed it to her, the editor read it and said, "This wasn't the assignment." He tried to explain that there was no story as she had originally stated it, but she wouldn't be swayed. "I can't use you," she said.

The young man had shown persistence and creativity in the face of insurmountable obstacles. The editor, on the other hand, refused to recognize that there was no story. By thinking more creatively, she could have considered the other opening that he offered: a story about hiking. For a number of reasons, this magazine folded within a short time.

RECOGNIZING OURSELVES AS SOUL

We squeeze what we can out of life. We do it through the ability to tune in to Divine Spirit, or the ECK, by chanting our sacred word. This is how we come in contact with It. Not that God lifts our difficulties and our burdens, but God shows us the way to get through them while learning the lessons needed to give us strength. In this way, we become strong enough to walk the road that takes us back home to God.

So when you ask me, as the Living ECK Master, to take your burdens, I can walk beside you and help you, but I won't carry your burdens forever. Gradually, as you get stronger, there comes a time when I give more and more back to you. The tears and the sorrows life gives us are for our own spiritual development and unfoldment. By development and unfoldment, I mean the growing

We squeeze what we can out of life. We become strong enough to walk the road that takes us back home to God.

recognition of ourselves in the true state—as Soul,
the divine spark of God.

Paul Twitchell didn't often go out of his way to
ask someone why they had decided to leave the path
of Eckankar, but one time he wrote a letter to a
woman who had been a very dear friend of his during the early days of Eckankar. He had helped her
with spiritual problems for quite some time, only to
find out that she chose to follow another master on
another path. When she told him of her decision, he
was very upset.

"Why are you leaving Eckankar for this particular path?" he wrote. "It's not a very high one. Even
if you leave Eckankar, I would suggest that there
are higher paths than the one you have chosen."

Less than a year earlier, he had helped this
woman's mother at the time of death. This particular
woman had been present. At the moment her mother's translation (death) occurred, she had seen Paul
in the Soul body taking her mother across to the
other side. This is one of the services provided by the
Living ECK Master to help those on the path to God
who have earned the right through their own efforts.

"You were there, in full consciousness," he pointed out to her. "Why would you leave Eckankar?"
And yet, this is another example of what I mentioned
earlier: a person who, in a later life, will come back
to find the Living ECK Master. This individual will
have another opportunity to find the Light and Sound
of God—to experiment and to test It—and then
decide if that will be the lifetime in which to reach
the recognition of the God State within.

*We are led
by the spiritual
hierarchy from
the lowest state
of spiritual
evolution to
the highest.*

SPIRITUAL EVOLUTION

We are led by the spiritual hierarchy from the
lowest state of spiritual evolution to the highest.
We are led gradually through the different religions,

through the different moral precepts, until we gain enough strength to come to an awareness of the spiritual laws. The moral precepts have to do with the emotional body of man—the Astral body—and this is a good step. This is what Moses was working toward when he brought the Ten Commandments down from the mountain.

When Moses went up the mountain, God said to him, "I'm going to give you these Ten Commandments to take down to the children of Israel." Then God revealed to him that in his absence, the people had made a golden idol. Moses couldn't believe it. He ran down the mountain, and when he got to the camp, he found the people worshipping a golden calf. He was so angry that he threw the two stone tablets that contained the Ten Commandments down to the ground and smashed them.

Moses later went back up the mountain and said to God, "You were right, but I lost the Ten Commandments." God said, "With my own hand, I'm going to put the very same words down again, and then you can take them back to the people."

Now here's a peculiar thing. Anyone who makes a study of the Bible will find that the first set and the second set of the Ten Commandments are not the same. There is a wide difference between them, and they were both supposed to be the same. Those of you who are of the Christian faith, or are new to the path of ECK and still trying to decide what really is so and what is not, can study the different versions of truth that have been brought out.

All in all, I'm sure the church hierarchy must have realized that it's impossible to give people ten of anything and hope that they will remember them. So the next step was to boil it down some more, and this resulted in the Golden Rule. And still, people can't seem to follow even that one rule.

Those of you who are new to the path of ECK, still trying to decide what really is so and what is not, can study the different versions of truth that have been brought out.

When you get to the Golden Rule, you're standing at the top of the worlds of moral precepts. This is the toe level of the full laws of Spirit, the spiritual laws of ECK. The moral precepts are preliminary, they are essential; but then you move on. The next step up the ladder is ethics. In ECK we don't look for ethics, because this isn't our goal, but as one develops in spirituality, his ethics also improve. They can't help but do so.

THE DANGERS OF CHANNELING

A letter that told an interesting story came to me from a woman who lived in the southwestern part of the United States. She and her husband weren't ECKists at the time this incident took place, but they were earnest seekers after truth. In their quest for spiritual growth, they joined a church group whose leaders channeled for entities from a very low area of the Astral Plane. This can be a danger for those who explore on the other side without the proper guidance.

An entity spoke through one of the church leaders and claimed to be Jesus. It introduced another entity named Emmanuel, who was to be the spirit guide for this couple. As the couple opened themselves more and more to this very low force, they strengthened the hold that this entity had over them, and it began to run their lives.

One day the entity said, "You have come to the point in your spiritual life where you will be permitted to give your home to the church."

One day the entity Emmanuel said, "You have now come to the point in your spiritual life where you will be permitted to give your home to the church. Ten of the church members will move into your house." Fortunately the couple had two houses. They vacated the larger house so the ten church members could take up residence, and moved themselves into the smaller one.

Pretty soon Emmanuel and the other entities spoke again. "You are coming along very well in your spiritual growth," they assured this couple. "Since you have two cars, you can drive the older, blue one and give the newer one to the church members." The couple said, "If this is what's needed for our spiritual growth, we are willing to drive the old blue car."

It wasn't long before Emmanuel said, "Since you are now part of our church, you may turn over your money to us. We will give you enough of a salary to purchase your food, and we will pay all your bills."

Soon the couple discovered that the church members who had taken their money did not pay the bills, and now their house was up for sale to satisfy the creditors.

One Saturday morning the couple talked it over, and they concluded that they had been absolute fools. They called up some friends and explained their problem, and the friends were able to back a loan so the couple could pay the bills and take their house off the market. The letter ended with, "We're older, but wiser." Their own experience was richer than anything I could have told them. My advice is, When you step onto a spiritual path, keep your hand on your wallet.

The couple's own experience was richer than anything I could have told them.

Proving ECK to Yourself

In ECK we are looking for the Light and Sound of God. You want proof that there is such a thing as the Word of God, which is heard as Sound and seen as Light. Taking my word for it is not good enough. The outer teachings are only to lead you to the inner—to the Inner Master—to prove ECK to yourself.

I received a letter from an individual who had just gotten his Fourth Initiation. This means that he had earned the privilege of coming to the Mental Plane after spending the proper amount of time going through all the other initiations that led to this one. He was curious as to whether a certain power came with it.

Sometimes the initiate will have a conscious experience with the initiation, and sometimes he won't. During one initiation, a person may have all kinds of manifestations of the actual Light and Sound of God; several years later, as he moves into the next initiation, he may get absolutely nothing. The reaction may be, Hey, this path isn't working! Something's wrong! He doesn't understand that it's a test.

The Holy Spirit isn't going to feed experiences to you on a silver spoon just to delight your senses. It won't send you one phenomenal experience after another to keep your interest. Life isn't like that. It doesn't put us in the receiver position, constantly waiting for life to do something for us. Somewhere we have to take the step.

This new Fourth Initiate heard a buzzing sound. He assumed a fly had gotten into his office, but he couldn't find it.

One day this new Fourth Initiate was at work, going through some inventory reports. It was very quiet in his office. As he studied the reports, his mind was half on the initiation he had just taken. All of a sudden he heard a buzzing sound. He assumed a fly had gotten into his office, and because he is a gentle-hearted Soul, he decided to open the door and let it out. But he couldn't find it. He got up and walked around his office, trying to figure out where this buzzing was coming from. It wasn't in the desk. It was off to the left: He thought the buzzing was coming from the file cabinet.

He figured the fly must have somehow gotten trapped inside the file cabinet, so he opened all the drawers and stood there waiting for it to fly out. Nothing flew out, but the buzzing continued. He was really puzzled by now because he could no longer tell exactly where it was coming from. All of a sudden another person walked into the office, and just that fast, the buzzing stopped.

He wrote in the letter: "I looked at the God Worlds chart in *The Spiritual Notebook*, and it says that a sound like the buzzing of bees comes from the Etheric Plane." The Etheric Plane is the high level of the Mental Plane. He said, "I believe there is a connection between the Fourth Initiation, the buzzing, and the Etheric Plane." This connection was proof for him.

THE PURIFYING SOUNDS OF GOD

What's so great about a buzzing fly, a buzzing bee, a buzzing anything? This is the Sound of God. It's the Voice of God coming to you in one of Its forms. It can come as the sound of a flute—we have a book called *The Flute of God*—or It may come in many other ways that most of you are familiar with, such as the sound of chirping sparrows. It's the sound of the atoms of God moving in the high worlds.

When you hear the Sound that represents a particular plane, it means that in the Soul consciousness, this is where you are. This man was at the Etheric Plane. It meant in these high worlds, Spirit was purifying his state of being and uplifting him in consciousness, but he didn't recognize or know it.

Sometimes people mistake the sound of thunder for a storm that's going on outside, but when they look out the window, there isn't anything happening. No rain, no flashes of lightning. What they are hearing is the Sound of God. If you have the opportunity to hear this only once in your lifetime, it's a privilege and a benefit; with the path of ECK, I try to see that you have an experience of some kind at least once a month. I don't say it will be Light once a month, or Sound once a month, but that you at least experience, in some way, an understanding of the presence of ECK. It may come through an intuitive nudge that tells you what business decision to make or which doctor to go to for a particular

What's so great about a buzzing fly, a buzzing bee, a buzzing anything? It's the Voice of God coming to you in one of Its forms.

ailment. Or when you feel run down, It may lead you to a nutritionist. These are some of the ways that Spirit works.

HOW SPIRIT USES US

Millie Moore is an Eighth Initiate in ECK. She was one of the early students of Eckankar when Paul Twitchell first brought the teachings out. We were talking this afternoon about the transition that occurred in October 1981, when I took the Rod of ECK Power, which is the leadership of Eckankar. I said to her, "I was aware that you knew this was going to happen as far back as 1974, at the Youth Conference in Tucson, Arizona." Millie was listening to me with great interest. I continued on: "Yes, I remember it very well. It was the first time I had been asked to give a talk in front of all those people, and I was really scared." The talk was on the Temples of Golden Wisdom, and because I was so nervous, everything about that whole weekend was etched in my mind.

I reminded her, "After this one session, I was standing out in the hallway when all of a sudden the auditorium doors opened and the crowd came out. One of the first people out was you. You came over to me, and you were really crying." She wasn't just sobbing a little bit, she was crying so hard that she couldn't talk. Then she put her head on my shoulder—now she was practically washing my shirt. It was embarrassing, because I didn't know Millie that well at the time.

I couldn't think of anything to say other than, "There, there, Millie. It'll be OK."

I couldn't think of anything to say other than, "There, there, Millie. It'll be OK." I didn't know what to do. Then she raised her head, and as I looked into her eyes, suddenly I realized that she knew what Paul had told me via the ECK-Vidya in 1970: I was going to have this job. Though I had been very discreet and never talked about it to anyone, I knew that she knew, and furthermore that she could see all the things that were going to happen in the years before I came to this job. She didn't say a word, but just kept crying her eyes out. It was very awkward.

When I finished telling Millie my story this afternoon, she just stared at me for a moment. And then she said, "I wasn't in Tucson in 1974."

I was taken aback. "But Millie, I hugged you. You got tears all over my shirt."

She said, "I've never been to Tucson until recently."

Later I asked my wife about it. "I was just talking to Millie," I said, "and by the way, wasn't she at the Youth Conference in Tucson in 1974? Do you remember seeing her?" She said yes. I said, "Did you talk with her?" She said, "No. When we were out in the hall, she came over, but we didn't really get to talk, because she was crying. And then she left." Then I told her what Millie had said. She said, "But I saw Millie too!"

Spirit sometimes uses us to form and manifest the seed of a truth that is going to ripen, often years later. There are going to be people who come up to you and say, "I've seen you before. You helped me years ago when I was in bad trouble, and now I have found the path of ECK."

ECKists usually learn to say nothing, because as often as not, they aren't aware that Spirit used their form; or if they were there physically, the human consciousness has been erased. Soul works on many different planes, at all levels and in all dimensions. It would be too much for the human mind to try to encompass this. Because the burden would be too great to handle, Soul—the true being that we are—wipes out the memory. The mind is only a tool, a blackboard that Soul can erase. You are going to find this too.

Spirit sometimes uses us to form and manifest the seed of a truth that is going to ripen, often years later.

LETTING GO OF LIMITATIONS

Millie said that back in 1970, she had gotten a call from Paul Twitchell. He said, "A young lady named Marge is coming in from Utah to work at the office. Until she earns enough money to get her own place, would you take her under your wing?" Millie said, "Sure."

Marge had just come on the path of ECK a short time before that. As she was getting used to her duties at the ECK office, she was also exposed to the teachings of ECK full volume in Millie's home, where several ECK Satsang classes were being held. On top of that, Millie and Marge talked about ECK into the wee hours.

Marge had been a good Mormon before this—a missionary. She was one of the cream of the crop, giving her whole heart to the teachings. But at some point she knew she had outgrown them, and she asked to be let out of the church. Now she was getting all this ECK instruction, so she was pretty careful about staying away from negative habits—like smoking.

One night Millie woke up to find Marge coming very quietly into her room. She didn't really want to wake Millie, but this was very important. She said, "Millie, I love and follow the teachings of ECK, and because you smoke, I don't know if I can stay here." It was a big trial for her. At that time, Millie and many of the initiates coming on the path were learning about the things that stood between them and spiritual unfoldment, and smoking was one of them.

Millie told a story about this: During a meeting several years ago, which Paul attended, one of the early initiates in ECK decided to lecture Millie on the evils of smoking—especially in the presence of the Master. Paul was a kind person in that he didn't like to see anyone embarrassed. While the initiate

One early initiate in ECK decided to lecture Millie on the evils of smoking— especially in the presence of the Master.

was giving his lecture, Millie reached for her cigarettes, and Paul slid the ashtray over to her.

Millie didn't just throw the cigarettes away, but she worked with Spirit to try to give up the habit. The Master knows and understands. He understands the halting steps you take. He also tells you to work with the Spiritual Exercises of ECK, which are found in the ECK discourses and books. Work with them. This opens the door for Spirit to come in and begin purifying you, lifting you above the passions and perversions of the mind which are responsible for the negative habits that ruin your health and affect your spiritual unfoldment.

As Marge went along, she came to realize and understand that she could stay in Millie's house even though Millie smoked at the time. It was a great lesson for her. Millie knew that if she kept on with the spiritual exercises, faithfully and with love and devotion, those blocks which were part of her makeup in the lower bodies—the Physical, Astral, Causal, Mental, and Etheric—would all be taken care of.

When you walk the path of ECK, do it on the other side of the rope. Do it on the side of the rope where you embrace life with both arms and with joy, not afraid of the sorrows it will bring. Do it with awareness of the love that Spirit is pouring into you, and know you are now becoming, in your own way, at your own time, a spiritual giant who is walking on his own side of the rope.

Know you are now becoming, in your own way, at your own time, a spiritual giant who is walking on his own side of the rope.

World Wide of ECK, Los Angeles, California, Friday, October 21, 1983

Like the fly, we take off without knowing the first thing about the laws of Spirit and head full-speed into an invisible barrier.

2
HOW TRUTH
IS TAUGHT

he topic that I would like to address this evening is, How truth is taught. In Eckankar we are quite aware of the different ways that ECK is taught: by the Master, by the Light and Sound, and in the dream state. Spirit works through us, but It also teaches through nature and through the lessons of history.

THE LESSONS OF HISTORY

The Greek philosopher Plato wrote an account of Solon, the Athenian statesman who lived during the golden age of Greek civilization, about 600 BC. The Greeks considered themselves to be very wise, but when Solon traveled to Egypt, he was told by the wise men of that country, You are children.

The Egyptian wise men then told him the story of a continent that had existed long ago in the Atlantic. They were talking, of course, about Atlantis, a country that had scientific wonders far beyond any of the inventions which we know of today. Their technology was so advanced that they

The Egyptian wise men told Solon, the Athenian, of a continent that had existed long ago in the Atlantic.

were able to colonize other planets. The orthodox mind of today considers such stories science fiction.

The very slender hold we have on historical truth is based on man's ability to write. In the absence of writing materials or skills, he has to pass down fables and stories to his sons about the greatness of past cultures that were destroyed.

The Egyptians told Solon of the different cataclysms that occurred periodically throughout the history of the world. In one case it might be a comet that passed close to earth, causing all life in the mountains and highlands to be scorched and burned. This time the people in the lowlands would be spared; they could survive by finding shelter in low caves. Then after many eons, another cataclysm would occur, allowing nature once again to cleanse itself of the impurities put out by man. A huge flood would hit the lowlands, not only raining down waters from above but opening the fountains of the deep, this time destroying the lowlands along with all the people and creatures that lived there. Again and again, nature alternated between one kind of destruction and another.

The Egyptians made an interesting point: After each one of these cataclysms, all the technical knowledge and advances made by man were wiped out completely. The survivors who had the knowledge to form the different steps and processes needed to develop complicated scientific operations were unable to get together. They were left with no way to communicate. Some perished, while others were forced to move to different areas in search of food. The greatest loss was that of the ability to write; thus, the record of the previous civilization became a legend that began with the father telling his sons how the country used to be. In the space of two generations, mankind was again at the dawn of civilization.

HOW TRUTH IS TAUGHT

The same thing happens with truth. When truth was found in the past, these same destructive forces were unleashed, and the truth that had been gathered for centuries was lost in the blinking of an eye.

So how, then, is the truth taught? The clearest, simplest way begins from the heart as a civilization is forming.

History proves there is no permanency in the civilizations of man, nor in the religions of man. The only permanence is in the inner direction that comes from the heart center. This direction is never felt more keenly than when man is forced to go forward and develop himself spiritually in the harshest, most primitive circumstances.

The only permanence is in the inner direction that comes from the heart center.

In time, though, the people again develop the mental abilities and become more and more intellectual but, in a way, less spiritual. So once again a great cataclysm occurs, and after the destruction, the Souls then incarnate in new bodies as they begin their lessons over again. The dawn of civilization revisited.

Eventually Atlantis was controlled by the priest-craft and black magicians who, through use of the black arts, abused and bent the spiritual forces down through the psychic realms. At this point a mistake was made. Due to someone's miscalculation, the forces were unleashed in a wild, unregulated manner, and Atlantis was destroyed. A simple mistake— a continent lost.

My daughter told me the riddle of the Sphinx, and perhaps some of you have heard it. It goes like this: What walks on four legs in the morning, two legs at noon, and three legs in the evening?

The answer is man. He crawls on all fours as a baby, walks upright on two legs in adulthood, and uses a cane in his old age.

This is very similar to the cycles of man's history. Man in his consciousness stumbles along as the infant, grows into a strong adult who brings about the golden age of a civilization, and then wanes.

In the spiritual works of ECK, we are looking for a higher permanence than the physical body and human history. Soul yearns to leave the limits of time and space that encompass the events of the earth. To leave behind the karma which binds us here, to gain liberation of Soul, to gain the attributes of God: wisdom, power, and freedom. But these are only the attributes, and they come after one has unfolded to God Consciousness. We start out as the child, ignorant of the laws of Spirit.

Soul yearns to leave the limits of time and space that encompass the events of the earth.

LEARNING THE LAWS OF SPIRIT

My daughter and I went to a fast-food restaurant recently. People sometimes wonder what a Living ECK Master eats, while I often wonder when I'm going to have a chance to eat. And when you've got a child in grade school, I'm afraid it's not all brown rice and green veggies.

As we sat there eating our hamburgers, all of a sudden we heard a fly buzzing around. It kept flying back and forth, the way flies do, and every once in a while it would work up speed, probably anticipating a long flight, and go smacking into the plate-glass window. The fly would hit this invisible barrier which was completely beyond its comprehension, bounce off, and fall down on the sill. Then it would gather up strength, take off in the air, head for another plate-glass window, crash, bounce off, and start all over again. I just sat there, shaking my head.

Sometimes I try to get away from the spiritual lessons long enough to have a hamburger, but rarely is it possible. I pointed out to my daughter, "We're just like that fly. We take off without knowing the first thing about the laws of Spirit and head full-speed into an invisible barrier. We get banged on the head, fall down, say ouch, and cry."

As far as I can tell, the fly just gets back up, takes off, and does the same thing over again. Man, of course, is far beyond the fly. We pray or blame God. Sometimes we just say, "God, I don't know where this came from, but please take it from me."

Someday, if the fly is lucky enough to grasp the grand concept of a door, it's going to bide its time until a customer walks in or out. I've often thought of directing the fly, but in a restaurant where other people are trying to eat their food, it just isn't polite to chase after a fly.

We are trying to learn the laws of Spirit, and until we do, we make karma. And as long as we make karma, we have troubles—because we're learning. No person on this earth has all the answers, including myself, because as soon as he does, it's time to go.

Someday, if the fly is lucky enough to grasp the grand concept of a door, it's going to bide its time until a customer walks in or out.

Giving Up to Life

There was a college student who had been on the path of ECK for some time, but the different tests that were thrown at her seemed so difficult that she decided to step back from the active path. She kept on with the spiritual exercises, but for her it was the period spoken of by St. John of the Cross as the dark night of Soul. During this time she felt no assurance whatsoever that there was any such thing as Divine Spirit or a power greater than herself.

She had her heart set on gaining admission to one of the large, prestigious universities to get her master's degree in communications, but because it was so expensive, she had to apply for a government loan. A few weeks later, even though she was an excellent student, she was told by the registrar that this loan had been denied. At this point, she just threw up her hands and said, "Well, this is it. Without that loan I can't afford it." The registrar said,

"Let's wait a few more days and see what happens."
But she had given up trying.

By giving up to life, no longer buzzing around
blindly, she allowed the creative centers within her
to open up. She opened up as Soul, so the ECK could
come in.

A few days later, the registrar called her with
some news: Instead of the government loan, she had
been able to obtain a stipend for her, which meant
money to help her through school that did not require
repayment.

She realized then that once she gave up to
Spirit, the plans that she had carefully laid out for
herself were fulfilled. She said, "This is the first time
in a long time that I've had any assurance in the
power of ECK." This incident was her proof that
there was power to Spirit.

I'm not saying that anytime you want more
money, you need only do the spiritual exercises, throw
up your hands and say, "I give up," and then all of a
sudden you'll get more money. This isn't what the path
is about.

The path of ECK is for spiritual unfoldment,
which simply means learning ways to make ourselves
a clearer vehicle for Spirit. Through all the lessons
we face every day, this is all we are trying to do.
Spirit will work with each person, with each one of
you, in a way that is right for you.

Spirit will work with each person, with each one of you, in a way that is right for you.

THE ECK WAY TO PRAY

An executive of a computer company was put in
charge of a department that was about to fold because
it was not carrying its own weight. After a year on
the job, the contracts for his department tripled.

I got curious. "What did you do to make this
happen?"

He said, "Before I do anything or make any decision at all, I pray to God."

There are a lot of people who pray to God in the wrong way. They want others to do things *their* way, so they use prayer to control others and bring about their own wishes. It's like a basketball team praying together before a game: "Dear God, please help us win." Meanwhile, on the opposite side of the court, the other guys are busy doing the same thing: "Dear God, help us win." What kind of prayer is that?

On the other hand, the computer executive said that when he prayed to God, he would say, "I am aware of the situation and the problem, and I want your help in whatever way you see fit." He actually has the attitude of the ECKist: You look to see what you, yourself, can do to make the thing work; how you can overcome your own problem. You are learning, unfolding, getting experience to become a mature Soul—someone fit to be a Coworker with God. This is how the man worked. It was a clear prayer.

You are learning, unfolding, getting experience to become a mature Soul—someone fit to be a Coworker with God.

There is nothing wrong with prayer, but the kind of praying that is done by most people is wrong in that it tries to control others, to make them come to one's church or to believe in one's savior—things like this. If you want to say that anything in the works of Spirit could be wrong, it would be that type of prayer. It's wrong because by using it to control others, one is playing with black magic.

Going through Life with Open Eyes

The people who study the biblical works have had truth told to them by such people as the ECK Masters, Buddha, and even by Christ. But over the centuries, as the sacred scriptures are translated, retranslated, interpreted, and reinterpreted, finally there are only little bits of truth left from the original teachings. At this point, for most followers the holy scriptures become a matter of faith—not studied faith but blind faith. As if there is some merit in going through life with your eyes shut.

These people may appear very devout in their beliefs, displaying their Bible in a prominent place in their home—but not necessarily reading it. They would rather make a show of going to church on Sunday and let the minister take care of reading the Bible. After all, that thing is big. With small print. And with television programs and VCRs, there are a lot more interesting things going on. Anyway, you can occasionally catch movies on television that are based on the Bible.

Jesus said there were some among his disciples who would not die until they saw the kingdom of heaven. And then he said, "The kingdom of God cometh not with observation: Neither shall they say, Lo here! or, lo there! for, behold, the kingdom of God is within you." So two points were made: the kingdom of heaven is within you, not somewhere out there; and there were some standing there who would see the kingdom of heaven before they died.

Centuries have passed, and many people, misunderstanding his words, are still waiting for that great day. He said that the Kingdom of God is within you, and those who misinterpret the meaning are waiting for the clouds to part and the trumpets to blow. Furthermore, they shout from their pulpits that if you don't believe the horrendous lies told by the priestcraft over the centuries through the twisting and distorting of the sacred words, then you will go to hell and be lost forever. This is a grip of fear placed upon the heart of man, designed to keep him in spiritual slavery for as long as he will stand for it.

This is a grip of fear placed upon the heart of man, designed to keep him in spiritual slavery for as long as he will stand for it.

What I have to offer you are simply the Spiritual Exercises of ECK. Found in the books and discourses of ECK, they show you how to come in contact with the Light and Sound of God: the Voice of God, Itself. To see the Light and hear the Sound is to experience spiritual upliftment that pulls you into the worlds of knowing. Here you become aware, consciously, of the divine laws of Spirit and can use this knowledge to wend your way through life, stepping carefully among the rocks that have been thrown there to stub your toe. And in so doing, you ride this great wave which in ECK we call the Audible Life Current. This huge wave flows back to the heart of God.

By doing the Spiritual Exercises of ECK, Soul learns how to ride this wave through all the hardships, the disappointments, and the sorrows, until It can rise above the traumas of life and ride this wave back to the heart of God.

A Soul that is able to do this stands forth in glorious Light, but he walks quietly among men, unknown. The ignorant and the spiritually blind can never see his spiritual stature. But his greatness does not depend upon the opinions of his fellow men, because his whole life depends on God.

By doing the Spiritual Exercises of ECK, Soul learns to ride this wave through all the hardships, disappointments, and sorrows, back to the heart of God.

HOW DREAMS TEACH US

A pilot for a commercial airline found that he had a very severe malignancy. One night he had a dream that fit with his life. He saw an airplane that was painted red, white, and blue, and he had the sensation that he was flying in it and yet was above it, like Soul in the body. He saw himself in the pilot's seat, but for the first time in his experience, he was also standing back as Soul, observing the scene as well as participating in it.

Without warning, the plane went into a dive, heading straight toward the earth. He was certain that was the end. His life flashed before his eyes. But just when it seemed that the plane must surely crash into the earth, it suddenly nosed up and started to climb.

This man, though not an ECKist, had an experience in the Soul consciousness. He saw how quick and easy it was to approach the veil of death and, more importantly, that life continues. After the plane pulled up, it went into a victory roll and flew off into the sky.

The pilot described it as a resurrection. He said this experience in the dream state gave him more confidence than he had gotten from a lifetime in his religion. He was able to step forth as Soul, shake the fear, and see that death isn't even as substantial as a curtain. Realizing through his own experience that life continues, he found himself happy and uplifted.

Truth in the area of health matters is also taught through the dream state. These benefits come to the ECKist who has learned how to do the spiritual exercises and has made some degree of advancement on the spiritual path. The Inner Master will come and take him into some other world to give him instruction in an area that needs improvement, so that he can walk around a physical problem and avoid a serious illness.

In one instance, a woman visited the inner planes with the MAHANTA, also known as the Dream Master. The other planes generally are not seen as clouds and floating ethereal things, but as places that look very much the same as they do here. Often the auditoriums are similar to this one, though usually larger because the inner worlds are larger.

This woman walked into a large shopping complex with the Dream Master. Together they entered a store and went up the stairs to a section that contained shelves lined with a colorful array of glass decanters for sale. Each one was filled with colored sugar water to make the display more attractive to the eye. She made her selection, and as they walked downstairs to the checkout counter, the Dream Master took the decanter from her and poured the liquid into a potted plant.

The manager, wearing a very impressive tuxedo, stood by the checkout counter watching the shoppers.

The pilot said this experience in the dream state gave him more confidence than he had gotten from a lifetime in his religion.

It was a very high-class store; even the salesclerks were dressed in fine clothing.

The woman said to the clerk, "I'd like to buy this glass decanter."

The clerk said, "But what did you do with the liquid?"

The Dream Master replied for her: "I dumped it in a potted plant upstairs."

The manager got extremely upset. This was not in keeping with the style of the store. He and a couple of the clerks ran upstairs to see if any damage had been done to the plant, but when they came back downstairs, he said it was all right. The Dream Master stood there while she paid for the decanter, and then they left.

When she first woke up, she wondered what this dream was all about. Later she interpreted it to mean that sugar was bad for her, no matter how attractively it was packaged. The Dream Master illustrated this for her as a product in a store where everything was marketed with the greatest degree of class. A certain aura of respectability had been given to this food by placing it in expensive glass decanters. But because it was actually bad for her health, the Dream Master dumped it out to show her that she had no use for it. She had been having health problems that she suspected were connected with sugar, and thus she was able to understand why the Dream Master used this example.

If you learn how to work with the Dream Master, you can have a healer in your house, on call every night; or a prophet, someone to tell you the future. This is how the Inner Master works.

If you learn how to work with the Dream Master, you can have a healer in your house, on call every night.

How Nature Teaches Us

Truth is taught by the Master through dreams and in many other different ways. In *Stranger by the River*, Rebazar Tarzs points out to Paul Twitchell that truth is also taught by nature. A woman who experienced this method of teaching wrote to me with this story.

One day when she was outside with her daughter, all of a sudden a ladybug landed on the little girl. The child began to recite that little poem, "Ladybug, ladybug, fly away home. Your house is on fire." And they laughed about it.

They stayed out in the sun a while longer, and pretty soon, one by one, a whole bunch of ladybugs came along. In a short time her daughter was covered with them. They still thought this was pretty cute, again recited, "Ladybug, ladybug, fly away home. Your house is on fire," and continued to lie out in the sun.

When they finally returned home, they realized the little girl had gotten a tremendous sunburn. The ladybug had come to show them that the little girl's house—her physical body—was burning. But they had been so caught up in the ladybug rhyme that it never occurred to them that truth was being taught through nature.

I encourage those of you who are not having experiences in the dream state to keep your eyes open. Look around you, because once you are linked up with Divine Spirit through the initiations of ECK, Spirit begins to work—to uplift, to strengthen, and to straighten out your life. The only reason one often doesn't notice is because he is walking around with his eyes and ears shut, too busy crying about the injustices that have come to him in life. When something happens to him, he'll proclaim it's somebody else's fault, certainly not his own.

In ECK we learn very soon that no matter what

Through the initiations of ECK, Spirit begins to work—to uplift, to strengthen, and to straighten out your life.

happens to us, the purpose is to teach us more about the laws of Spirit.

World Wide of ECK, Los Angeles, California,
Saturday, October 22, 1983

The worship of Moloch is an example of the priestcraft practicing black magic at its worst.

3
THE WORSHIP
OF MOLOCH

he purpose of the Living ECK Master is not to destroy religions, but to enliven them. I try to prompt you to become stronger in your own religion, to become a student of the highest order—the cream of the crop in your faith. It isn't that I want to convince you to become an ECKist, because I don't; but if my words make you think, make you go back and study your Bible and learn more about your relationship to God, then I feel I have done what I'm here for. I don't expect you to agree with me, but perhaps it will cause you to think and question, rather than blindly accept something just because it was given to you by an authority.

I try to prompt you to think and question, rather than blindly accept something just because it was given to you by an authority.

QUESTIONING AUTHORITY

Several weeks ago I listened to a radio talk show which had a well-known astronomer as the guest. He talked about some of the unusual phenomena of the celestial worlds, and one of them had to do with the harvest moon. When it rises in the east, just as it's breaking above the horizon with an orange-gold cast, the moon looks huge. Then an hour or two later, as it rises higher in the sky, it looks smaller.

"And yet," said the guest astronomer, "if you take a camera and photograph the moon as it rises over the horizon, and again a few hours later when it appears to be at the top of the sky, you will find that it is exactly the same size in both positions."

The explanation sometimes given is that as the moon comes over the horizon, you're looking along the surface of the earth where the air is dense. The air acts as a magnifying glass and makes the moon appear larger.

The astronomer said that's fallacy. "It seems larger due to perspective," he said, "your points of comparison. When the moon first comes up over the horizon, it's seen next to trees, barns, and buildings. This point of reference shows the size of the moon as huge in comparison."

He's a popular astronomer, and I respect him. He may be right about the moon. But I'm still curious. It's on my list of things to do before I leave this life: I'm going to check out his theory for myself.

No matter who the authority is, check it out for yourself. Don't be sheep.

No matter who the authority is, check it out for yourself. Don't be sheep.

A YEARNING TO KNOW TRUTH

I've always had a yearning inside to know the truth. When I was in preministerial school, I read the Bible very carefully. As I studied and noticed apparent discrepancies, I asked my professors for an explanation. They didn't have any answers. "There are some things we don't understand," they said.

I had a question about Adam and Eve and their sons. Adam and Eve had two sons, Cain and Abel. The brothers had a dispute—Cain was jealous because his gift to God of fruit and vegetables was scorned, while for some reason God liked Abel's offering of meat. This made Cain so angry that he killed Abel.

Now you've got three people in the world: Adam, Eve, and Cain. So God puts a mark on Cain's head and says something like, "This is to mark you so that when you walk, and men see you, they will know the deed you have done but will not kill you."

My question was, What men?

What struck me as even more amazing was this: After Cain kills Abel—leaving only three people in the world, Adam, Eve, and Cain, who now has a mark on his head—Cain then goes off to the land of Nod. And what does he do? He takes a wife.

I was curious. Where did she come from? I had some good questions but got no answers. Instead, with a lot of authority, my teachers would puff themselves up and say, "Now see here, young man."

ROBERT INGERSOLL'S CHALLENGE

There was a man who was quite prominent at the end of the nineteenth century. His name was Robert Ingersoll. He was known as the great agnostic of his day. An agnostic is someone who doesn't feel he can know if there is a God. Even though Ingersoll had been raised the son of a preacher, he had questions.

He was a great orator who spoke to more people in the nineteenth century than any other man alive at that time. One time in Chicago, his appearance not only filled a hall that seated ten thousand, but left another thirty thousand people still standing outside. He addressed such controversial topics as abortion and the protection of children who, in those days, had to go to work at a very young age. But his most popular lectures were on religion and his view of God.

A lawyer who spent most of his life in Peoria, Illinois, Ingersoll was a friend of presidents and chiefs-

Robert Ingersoll, known as the great agnostic of his day, was a great orator who spoke to more people than any other man alive at that time.

of-state; he was well-known, liked, and respected. Yet, he would challenge anyone in a discussion about the Bible. It made the ministers of his day quite angry that anybody would dare challenge their authority and point out the discrepancies found in the Bible. This took place in the late eighteen-hundreds, during a time of great religious revival. The people were so frantic in their worship, that in addition to their regular evening prayer meetings, some would use their lunch hour for praying. Not only that, they tried to make everybody else join their faith; they would not let anyone alone to practice his own belief.

Ingersoll's studies of the history of different saviors who came to earth revealed some very interesting parallels.

Ingersoll's studies of the history of different saviors who came to earth revealed some very interesting parallels. For instance, even though both Krishna and Buddha came centuries before Jesus, Ingersoll found these similarities: It was claimed that each one of these saviors had a virgin mother, with God as his father. Furthermore, at the birth of each one, it was alleged that the people heard celestial music. In Krishna's case, shepherds watched in the fields. All fasted for forty days, all were killed for spreading their message, and all were resurrected.

For a long time, the early church did not assign a date for the birth of Christ. They finally decided on December 25, which Ingersoll said was the common date attributed to the births of Krishna and Buddha. For the ancient Romans, late December was when they held the festival of Saturn—a time of feasting, a lot of food, and all kinds of licentious living. This holiday symbolized the birth of the sun. Winter was here, the sun was young. At its youth in the spring, seeds were planted; and then in the fall, after it had grown hot and aged, the harvest was brought in.

So Ingersoll's question was, Did Christianity borrow its ceremonies, rituals, and festivals from the pagans? Questions such as this totally outraged the ministers of the day. How could he have the audacity to say such a thing?

THE WORSHIP OF MOLOCH

The Tiger's Fang describes Paul Twitchell's journey through the other worlds, guided by his teacher, the ECK Master Rebazar Tarzs. In this book is a chapter entitled "The Worship of Moloch." This means worship of the personality. It's too easy to let someone else tell us what to think, what to believe. If there is a spiritual leader, there need to be followers, but when they fall into worship of the personality, they have stopped their spiritual growth.

"Do you know what the worship of Moloch is?" asks Rebazar Tarzs. Paul says no. Rebazar explains that Moloch was a pagan god back in the ancient days of Israel, long before Christ. He was symbolized by the head of a huge, metal monster set on a platform that stood higher than the treetops.

Rebazar Tarzs then opens a scene to Paul so that he can observe the worship of Moloch. He sees steps leading up to this platform that holds the big brass head with gaping jaws. Fire roars from openings into which the people throw jewels and money. Around the edge of the platform, white-robed priests stand guard over the virgins who dance, naked except for their headdresses. Every so often one of them leaps into the mouth of this brass monster and disappears into the flames, screaming. This, Paul is told, is an example of the priestcraft practicing black magic at its worst.

This chapter points out that no matter how far we go, we must always be careful about our spiritual values and balance.

Later in the chapter, Paul asks the ECK Master Fubbi Quantz, "What happens if a man should see God and fail in his duty?" The answer that is given is for every one of us as initiates, no matter how high we go.

The worship of Moloch means worship of the personality. It's too easy to let someone else tell us what to think, what to believe.

Fubbi Quantz answers, "He would never have completely seen God. He might get very high on the ladder of spiritual success and fail. This is the source for the legend of the fallen angels. It is the same thing as the man who fails as a surgeon, a philosopher, a scientist. Is he not worse than the ignorant if he has envy, hatred, and malice in his heart? He becomes dangerous, and although the spiritual hierarchy might exclude him, God is always willing to help him return to the path again.

"He might become the leader of the enemies of Light, and his lack of integrity would exclude him from the society of saints. But it is really only the weight of his guilt that holds him off."

And he continues, "He can call upon the Kal power to seek to justify himself by deeds. He can use his intelligence to smother Light, if that is ever possible, to identify himself with all negation and attract to himself all those too unwilling to resist or too stupid to prevent him. See the picture of Moloch here?"

Fubbi Quantz goes on: "How can you tell when the Kal power is greater in one man than another? He thinks vice is a virtue and virtue is a vice."

He goes on to say, "How can you tell when the Kal power is greater in one man than another? You may say to him, 'Bless you,' and he will try to use the blessing as a stick with which to beat you. If you say to him, 'This is truth,' he will start working his mind at once to prove it isn't so. If you say, 'Love your enemies,' he will go to work to make some enemies, including you first, in order to have someone to love. Show him money, and he begins to think how to get that money from you. Make peace in your household, and he will proceed to try to break it up. He thinks vice is a virtue and virtue is a vice."

This applies to all of us. There is no person who can ever become so secure in his stature that he is beyond the laws of ECK.

SIMPLIFYING TRUTH

As Paul began giving talks on ECK, many people said, "Can you please put something in writing so that others will have the benefit of these teachings?" Since people in our time and culture are not able to go off to an ashram or travel long distances to hear each talk, Paul decided to put the ECK teachings in written form.

He wrote what he considered the essential directions, the things Soul needs to know in order to take the first step to God. This first series of ECK discourses at that time was called *Soul Travel—The Illuminated Way*. Then he sat down and wrote another series, and this he called *The Secret Way*.

Paul soon discovered a peculiar thing: Many people found these discourses too complicated; they couldn't understand what he was saying. So he started writing again, and this time he got even deeper in the truths. He wrote another series, *The Precepts of ECKANKAR*, which he considered very simple. But again he was amazed to find that there were still some people who were having difficulty understanding it. So he tried again. This time he wrote *The ECK Satsang Discourses*.

First he attempted to give out the truth as he knew it, and then, in the way of the ECK Masters, he had to try to simplify it. This is what I am doing. Many times I work long hours on a talk to make it as simple as I can. The same with my writing. What we try to do is take the etheric, amorphous mass that floats around in the ethers and turn it into something you can use right here; something that will help you take the first step to God.

What the ECK Masters try to do is take the truth and turn it into something you can use right here; something that will help you take the first step to God.

HAVING YOUR OWN EXPERIENCES WITH THE LIGHT AND SOUND

Paul wrote the discourses so that others could have their own experiences with the Light and Sound of God.

This woman
heard the sound
of flutes but, at
the time, didn't
realize this was
not someone's
radio.

A seventy-eight-year-old woman wrote to tell
me how she came in contact with Eckankar. She
was riding on a train in London, and a businessman
sat down next to her. He pulled a copy of the *ECK
News* —a newspaper that we used to distribute—out
of his briefcase and settled down to read for a while.
This woman kept glancing over at the paper, trying
to read it along with him. In the meantime, she
heard the sound of flutes, but at the time she didn't
realize that this was not someone's radio. The music seemed to fill the whole train compartment.

She became very curious about the subject matter
of the newspaper and asked the man if she could read
it. He said, "This is my only copy, but if you'll give me
your address, I'll be glad to send you a book about
it." Just then the train pulled to a stop at the next
station. As the man got up and started to go out the
door, she saw a light appear above his head. Thinking
it was her imagination, she didn't say anything about
it. And within a short time, she forgot all about him.

But he hadn't forgotten about her. True to his
word, a couple of weeks later he sent her *The
Spiritual Notebook*, by Paul Twitchell. She had
studied other paths for a long time, but after reading this book, she said, "These are the teachings I
have spent forty years looking for."

Last summer the new ECKist traveled to Holland
to attend the European Seminar. At the end of the
first day, she didn't feel like taking the train back
home, but she hadn't reserved a room for the night,
and the hotel was completely booked. She mentioned
this to a woman she knew, and her friend said, "I'm
in a room with two beds. You can stay with me." So
rather than making that long trip home and then
taking another train ride to return in the morning,
she gratefully accepted the offer. "Incidentally," her
friend said, "we're a couple of floors directly beneath
the room of the Living ECK Master."

The next morning she mentioned her good fortune to a new acquaintance she had made in Holland. He said, "How did you sleep last night?" She said, "I slept fine, except for the roar of the cargo planes which kept me awake for a time." The man said, "But there were no cargo planes flying last night." He explained that due to severe government restrictions of the airspace, only three flights per day were allowed in this corridor, and none at all during the night.

Later, while reading *The Far Country*, she saw a passage that described a particular Sound of ECK. It is as if you were standing between two buildings that are close together. Then a train runs past, and you hear the roar as it comes echoing through. She said, "This was the sound I heard, but I didn't know It was the ECK. I was just two floors below the room of the Living ECK Master, but I wasn't aware that the MAHANTA Consciousness was trying to get through to me." The important point is that she did eventually recognize what it meant: Spirit was coming in to open her up.

STEPS OF SPIRITUAL GROWTH

I received a letter from a man who had just become a father for the first time. It was a joyous time for him and his wife as they experienced the ups and downs of new parenthood. This Soul had come into a new body, and they looked forward to watching It go through the whole learning cycle as It grew.

The new father was reminded of a story he'd heard once. A master was walking with several of his disciples. They passed a bungalow where a mother was placing her new baby on a blanket in the sun. The infant lay there waving its tiny hands and wiggling its little feet in the air. One of the

A master, walking with several disciples, passed a mother placing her new baby on a blanket in the sun.

Lying down
next to the
infant, the sage
began to wave
his arms and
kick his feet
in the air,
gurgling and
cooing like
the baby.

disciples said, "Master, what is Self-Realization?" The sage answered by walking over to the blanket and lying down next to the infant. To the shock of his students, he began to wave his arms and kick his feet in the air, gurgling and cooing like the baby.

This master was trying to say, I can't tell you in words. You'll have to experience it. It was his way of saying what is also written in the Christian Bible: "Except ye . . . become as little children, ye shall not enter into the kingdom of heaven."

Self-Realization is the first real step into the kingdom of heaven. It takes place in the first of the spiritual worlds which lie beyond the heavens of the Christian, Buddhist, and Indian religions.

The Darshan, meeting the Master, can take place in the waking state as you view the form of the Living ECK Master of the times. And when I leave this position, there will be someone else to fill it. Even though that's years in the future, I'm already making plans. And I'm already preparing the people around me. I tell them, "This is a vortex that runs at a very high speed. Are you getting yourself ready, so that when I step aside, you're not going to have things collapse on you?" I try to stress this: Start making plans now for the next step.

For now, we must work together to bring the message of ECK out in a way that hasn't been seen for thousands of years.

As ECKists, we like to get together to enjoy the friendship and companionship of others who think like we do, and who have experiences similar to our own. This gives us the opportunity to talk about these things to someone who won't make fun of us.

I would like to thank you for coming. I appreciate it when people want to hear about the works of ECK. As you ride home, you carry the Light and

Sound of Divine Spirit with you. And you have the love and protection of the MAHANTA. Baraka Bashad.

World Wide of ECK, Los Angeles, California,
Sunday, October 23, 1983

The Inner Master is really only one of the faces of
Spirit, which might also be seen as one of the other ECK
Masters.

4
WHAT YOU ALWAYS WANTED TO ASK THE LIVING ECK MASTER

: This opportunity reminds me of a joke I once heard. Two sailors were out in the middle of the ocean, and one turned to the other and said, "Look at all that water out there!" The other guy said, "Yeah, and that's only the top of it!"

I don't know how deep we're going to get in terms of fathoms, but there are a lot of questions that some of you may have always wanted to ask.

Q: Sri Harold, what exactly is the Living ECK Master? And what distinguishes what you do from any other kind of spiritual leader?

HK: To put it simply, the Living ECK Master is the spiritual leader of Eckankar. I work on the outer with talks, books, and discourses. If you want them, I make sure they are available.

I also work as the Inner Master, to link up Soul with the Light and Sound of God. These are the two things Soul needs in order to find Its way back to God.

To put it another way: Look at all that water!

Q: Sri Harold, what distinguishes what you do from any other kind of spiritual leader?

43

THE FACES OF SPIRIT

Q: How can the Master be with all the chelas at one time?

HK: This is usually the kind of question where I like to ask the audience, "Would anybody like to answer this?" There are always plenty of raised hands, because we all are tuned in to the ECK, or Spirit—sometimes referred to as the Holy Ghost or the Audible Life Current.

Some people see me as the Inner Master, but it's really only one of the faces of Spirit, which might also be seen as one of the other ECK Masters. When this divine power is able to manifest in your inner vision during contemplation, you will see a reasonable likeness of myself. We then do things together, one-on-one, so that you can learn about the things that are important to you.

If you were to ask me, Do you remember when we were together last night? I may or may not. Sometimes I remember and you don't.

During contemplation, we do things together, one-on-one, so you can learn about the things that are important to you.

WHAT IT MEANS TO BE THE LIVING ECK MASTER

Q: What does it mean to you to be the Living ECK Master?

HK: This is interesting. A few years ago, Patti Simpson wrote a letter in which she commented on her observations of Paul Twitchell. At one time, about 1970, he became very interested in how the MAHANTA Consciousness was working through him. He asked Patti to have a tape recorder going at all times. There were occasions when he was aware that Spirit, or the MAHANTA Consciousness, would use him to move here and there, do this and do that. At other times he was not conscious of how It was using him. He wanted to make a study of it, in the same way a scientist would study some strange, unusual phenomenon in the world.

This is what I am doing. To me it's an adventure. I had to get used to how things suddenly became different, and this is not something you can easily describe to another person.

Last night we were riding back to the hotel with Millie Moore, and she told us about a conversation she had with Paul. She mentioned to him a particular inner experience she'd had which showed that she had been conscious on one of the high planes of God, in one of the far worlds. When Paul heard this, tears came to his eyes, because he knew that she had experienced something which was beyond words. As soon as he realized Millie had seen his tears of happiness, he shook his head and said, "Ahem, let's go on to something else." He didn't want her to see that he cared as much as he did that she had gotten this high spiritual realization. He was very happy for her, but he didn't want to let on.

It's the same with myself. I work as carefully as I can with you, in one way or another—by story, by example. If you have the interest, I try to give you the inspiration to go find out about it for yourself.

Words come from the Mental Plane. The reason there are so few things written about the higher planes beyond the Mental—the Fifth, Sixth, Seventh, Eighth, and so on—is because they are the worlds beyond words. There is no way to speak about them. All you can do is have the experience. All I can do is show you the direction or help you along in your own direction.

When you get your own enlightenments—and there are more than just one—I'm happy for you and with you. I've cried with people, too, but I don't often show it. It's just something you can't talk about.

When you get your own enlightenments, I'm happy for you and with you.

THE LAW OF ECONOMY

Q: Has your personal life changed since you became the Living ECK Master?

The Law of Economy merely means you get the most mileage out of every gallon of gas.

HK: There is something that I have been watching and studying for years, and it's one of the laws that is rarely mentioned. It's called the Law of Economy. The principle is referred to in some of the ECK books, but without that title. It merely means you get the most mileage out of every gallon of gas. I get better mileage than I did before, but I still think it isn't running as fast as it could or as far as it could, because there is always another step.

My life has changed quite a bit. In 1981, the hardest part was just accepting the position—the Rod of ECK Power. The next hardest thing was my first visit to the ECK office in Menlo Park after the seminar at which my new position was announced. I had to take two or three deep breaths before I could even walk in the door. As far as I was concerned, I was still myself, but in a different job. I had been at one end of the production line, and now I was at the other end. And I hoped this change wouldn't cause the people I had known as friends to suddenly back off and build walls.

I'm not particularly fond of being called "Sri" by those who are in ECK. It's all right, maybe even necessary, for going out in public. Newspapers like an authority. If there's a news story, the media feels the audience can benefit if it names an authority. "This is Dr. So-and-So, the eminent physicist from This-or-That Laboratories." And so when the reference is made to me as Sri Harold Klemp, I consider it a title that helps people understand that I am the spiritual leader of Eckankar. But I didn't want the office staff to build walls. In ECK we respect each other very much, but we never get into the worship mode, because I'm no greater than you are.

LEVELS OF CONSCIOUSNESS

Q: Does Soul ever evolve to the point of becoming a miniature SUGMAD, capable of creating Souls and sending them down to the lower worlds for experience?

HK: Soul goes through many levels of consciousness, beginning with some of the lower life-forms. Sometimes I tease my daughter. She likes little things like snails and fuzzy caterpillars that turn into moths. We'll be walking down the street, and I'll say, "Ants are so small. I can't feel the way they do, and it makes me wonder: Do ants have feelings?" Other times I'll tease her, "Do children have feelings too?"

But let's say the adult ant is talking to a young ant. The adult is wise; having very great consciousness, he knows all about man, those huge beings that thunder by with heavy, earthshaking footsteps. The usual ant knows nothing but left, right, forward, backward. Basically they are not very advanced in consciousness compared to man, and the adult ant realizes this.

Let's say the adult ant is talking to a young ant.

And so he tells the young ant, "Someday we will evolve in consciousness to a point where we can create great vehicles that will allow us to do more than just trudge forward, backward, or sideways. It will be a great vehicle that will travel many miles faster than you could ever imagine. There will be times when you can fly like a bird. You will be able to see pictures of the past, present, and future. You will see all the corners of the world." The little ant probably says, "Gosh, Dad, what are you talking about?"

It's the same way with us. Although we attain God Consciousness, we don't ever become God. We become one with Spirit, and in so doing, we reach the God Consciousness and become a Coworker with God.

There are levels of awareness so far beyond us that if I tried to talk about them, you wouldn't understand.

There are levels of spiritual development that are beyond understanding at this stage.

Somebody once asked a prophet who had the ability to see the past, "I would like to know how things were in ancient Lemuria. What happened there?"

The man said, "Do you know the language? Do you know the values of the people of ancient Lemuria? Do you know how they thought? What was important to them? What was considered life-threatening? Do you know the kinds of things they did to build themselves spiritually? The culture and language were too different for you to be able to relate to their thoughts," he said, "so I can't tell you, because you wouldn't understand. It would be a waste of time for both of us."

Somebody once asked a prophet, "I would like to know how things were in ancient Lemuria. What happened there?"

LOOKING AT THE HEART OF PEOPLE

Q: How do you think people expect the Living ECK Master to be? What is your personal experience in this sense?

HK: You probably mean what I am versus what people think I am, or should be. Some people, for instance, are worried that I'm watching them when they undress at home at night.

Back when I was still in preministerial school, I had the ability to look at the heart of people, to look through and see what they were. Most people didn't know it, because I'd just listen quietly as they talked and tried to put one over on me. While they were being pompous at my expense, I would sit there and see the mortality in them. I would see them from birth to old age, the time when most of the follies of youth, such as ambition and vanity, would be gone. I never said anything, but I just sat there and quietly watched the people, let them go on with their little trips; and eventually they got tired and left.

One of my friends caught me at it. He said, "You know, it's unnerving. It's scary. It's as if you can see through us." When I realized that it was noticeable, I became more discreet and careful.

We talk about the five perversions of the mind, yet we are here to learn how to let Soul get in control of our lower selves. We're up and down. Some days we're doing great, other days we're not. But the worst thing we can do is feel guilty and start criticizing or blaming ourselves, saying, "I have sinned." An interesting definition of sin comes from the Greeks: *hamartanein.* It means to err, to miss the mark. Rather than implying an afterlife spent in hell, it simply means to miss the mark. So when I see people conducting themselves in certain ways, it doesn't bother me a bit. I've seen a lot of it, and to me there isn't anything that's shocking.

Here is a question for you: Is it possible to get so many experiences in life that you become jaded, dull, and bored? It should never happen. It would mean that you are refusing the avenues of growth to which Spirit is leading you.

The Cycles of Life

Q: I assume you're subject to all the human things that affect the rest of us—depression or any of the mental passions that might want to creep into your consciousness. How do you deal with them?

HK: Even before I took this job, it always took a whole lot to get me down. For some reason, I'm a pragmatist; I see things very practically. Something either works or it doesn't. When I do get down, I bounce right back, because when things get really bleak, I know they've got to get better. It has to get better because life runs up and down, in cycles. It's day, it's night, and then it's day again. If it's bleak now, I know it has to get better.

When I do get down, I bounce right back, because when things get really bleak, I know they've got to get better.

HARMONY AND BALANCE

Q: Since God-Realization is a goal that is attainable in this lifetime, how would you describe some of the attributes of this state of consciousness?

HK: Anything you can say to describe the attributes of God-Realization sounds like dead, tired words. But I would say harmony is among the best of them. Harmony in this sense is not necessarily something that shows out here. It means working toward integrating my personal mission with the greater mission, so that it all fits together for the benefit of everyone.

Besides the service you give to ECK, it is important to have your own life. You need both for balance.

The ECK Masters have two missions as they support the Living ECK Master. There is a personal mission that keeps them interested in the microcosm; and when they are working in the macrocosmic state of consciousness, there is the greater mission of helping with the teachings of ECK. So besides the service you give to ECK, it is important to have your own life, your own goals, to plan your vacations, and to pursue your own ambitions. You need both for balance.

World Wide of ECK, Los Angeles, California,
Sunday, October 23, 1983

This cartoon illustrates how our lack of awareness of a basic law can complicate a very simple thing.

5
THE SECRET
TEACHINGS

he secret teachings are not secret
because they are hidden away somewhere
or because I'm keeping them from you.
They are secret because until one is ready
for these teachings, he couldn't see them even if
he tripped over them.

EXPERIENCES IN SURVIVAL

As we are learning the spiritual laws of ECK,
sometimes we make mistakes. But eventually we
learn what we have to do, in keeping with these
spiritual laws, to make things work better. We learn
all sorts of different things in life as part of our
experiences in survival. One ECKist told me this
story about his adventures as a Boy Scout.

One evening while attending the annual Scout
jamboree, some of the boys in his troop decided it
would be a lot of fun to play a trick on the other
troops that were camped throughout the area. Soon
after everyone else had settled in for the night, the
boys crept outside and proceeded to loosen all the
ropes from the stakes that held up the other tents.
Before long there was total confusion: tents were

*Eventually we
learn what
we have to
do, in keeping
with these
spiritual laws,
to make things
work better.*

collapsing all around them; everybody was hollering and running all over the place.

The pranksters ran back to their own tent and stayed up half the night, laughing about this funny thing they had done. They thought they had really put one over on the others. The problem was, they had overlooked one small detail: They didn't think to loosen the ropes on their own tent, so theirs was the only one still upright.

The pranksters, laughing about this funny thing they had done, had overlooked one small detail.

As a result, the boys were up most of the next night too. They had to stand guard for hours, warding off the Scouts that kept creeping to their tent to loosen the ropes. This experience taught them that if you're going to pull a prank like that, it's best to make yourself look like one of the victims. In their effort to be clever, they had managed to overlook that little angle.

ARE WE REALLY SO SMART?

In living life, we often get to thinking we're so smart. But it seems that the more intellectual one becomes, the harder it is for him to see the spiritual essence of God—the Light and Sound.

He learns the laws of man and figures he knows a shortcut, a way to get into the underground workings of life. You do whatever you feel you have to, to survive. But somewhere along the way, life requires full payment for everything you extract from it. Whatever we do is balanced out with the law of life. This is not at all bad; as we go through these different phases, we learn what works and what doesn't.

There's a cartoon that illustrates how our lack of awareness of a basic law can complicate a very simple thing.

In the cartoon you see two men and a four-wheeled cart. One of the men is in front, working up a lot of sweat as he tries to pull the cart along. The other guy is in back, working just as hard to push it. The cart they are pushing and pulling has four square wheels. Oddly enough, the cart is loaded with four more wheels, only these are round. They have the right wheels, but they are in the wrong place.

That cartoon is an example of the intellectual man groping around in the spiritual worlds. He has absolutely no understanding of the laws, so what does he do? He makes fun of something he is unable to understand because it is beyond his sight and hearing.

Those who have experience with the Light and Sound of God are not usually orthodox church members who attend services regularly every Sunday. Instead, they may be the people of Malaysia or Africa, places where the ancient religions of animism are taught. These beliefs are misunderstood by the people in the West, who view them as the worship of nature spirits. But this is not so. Many of these people know about the Light and Sound. They see the Blue Light of ECK, even without knowing we call It that. They are aware that the Light and Sound will come to them in times of trouble and help them out.

SELF-SURRENDER

What does self-surrender in ECK mean?

What does self-surrender in ECK mean? It means giving up all your cares, worries, and troubles to the Inner Master, to Spirit. In a way, the leaders of each major religious teaching do the same thing for their followers, passing their cares and troubles on to Spirit. But it should only be done until one can learn how to do it for himself.

The Inner Master, which is a part of the teachings of Eckankar, is not a physical being. It is someone you see in the inner planes during contemplation or in the dream state. He may look like me, he may look like another ECK Master, or he may even look the same as Christ. All it is, really, is the merging of the Light and Sound of God into a matrix, into a form which appears as a person. This, then, becomes the inner guide which steers a person out of the pitfalls of karma, the troubles we make for ourselves through ignorance of the spiritual laws.

Soul Travel is the ability to move into the inner planes in the spiritual consciousness and bring back something that is of use to you here and now. This technique is used by inventors and writers, whether they realize it or not. Ideas, themes, story lines—they all come from a common source.

I found the teachings of ECK through a little advertisement by Paul Twitchell. It said, "I can teach you Soul Travel." I had visions of zooming out of the body at will. Like so many others new to the path, I had a lot of misconceptions.

MYTHS ABOUT ECK MASTERS

Some time ago I got a letter from an individual who said, "I recently heard about the path of ECK, and I was very excited by the teachings. Then I saw your picture—and you wore glasses! It seemed to me that no Master would have to wear glasses." Then he said, "Pretty soon I resolved myself to the concept that maybe it didn't make any difference if a person wore glasses, because there are records of some of the other spiritual masters who had physical problems too." So he made his peace with the fact that I wore glasses because of nearsightedness. Next thing he sees is a picture where I'm not wearing any. "What a relief," he said. "He cured himself. I was right all along." Then his faith in God was shaken once more when he learned I was wearing contact lenses. I don't know what he'll do if he finds out I sometimes get dirt in them.

Millie Moore, one of the Eighth Initiates in ECK, worked very closely with Paul when she first got into the teachings of Eckankar. In those days she, too, thought that ECK Masters didn't get sick, or

I got a letter: "I recently heard about the path of ECK, and I was very excited by the teachings. Then I saw your picture— and you wore glasses!"

if they did, there would be some miraculous cure to take care of the whole problem.

One day Paul called her up and said, "I promised to take my wife to a dinner show in Las Vegas, but I'm not feeling very well today. I would appreciate it if you could accompany her this evening." Millie arrived at the proper time and knocked on the door. When it opened, there stood Paul—all bundled up in his bathrobe, a towel wrapped around his neck, and smelling to high heaven of Vicks Vaporub. Millie really didn't know what to make of it. Finally she concluded that it was OK that he used Vicks to get rid of a cold.

The hardest thing a spiritual teacher has to do is get the foolish notions out of people's heads about what is spirituality and what is not.

There are many myths surrounding ECK Masters. For instance, people are often curious about the kind of food they eat. Years ago there was a picture of Paul Twitchell in which he looked very austere, as if he had been fasting for thirty days. This led some people to believe that if they ate nothing but brown rice, they would become very spiritual.

What does an ECK Master eat? Paul Twitchell, who was born in the South, ate what he considered to be good Southern food. The fact is, God doesn't care what you eat—whether you're a vegetarian or whether you eat meat.

SPIRITUAL TRUTH AND HEALING

There is a lot said about spiritual truths and about healing and everything else. Much of what you hear is foolishness, much of it is plain common sense. It is up to us, through the knowledge of the spiritual laws, to figure out which is which.

I've tried many fasts: water fasts, the different lemon-juice fasts, the rice fast. You can do these things

What does an ECK Master eat? Paul Twitchell, who was born in the South, ate what he considered to be good Southern food.

as long as you don't use them to control other people or to change their minds. This happens when people go on fasts to stop the use of nuclear power, for instance. They are being foolish. They take on a lot of karma, and it doesn't do them any good. Some have lost their eyesight after a couple of weeks of this kind of fasting, yet they think they've done some great thing for mankind. All they've done is hurt themselves.

After trying a lot of these different diets, I found that the best reason to fast is for cleansing. If you can find a good cleansing diet, do it for a short period of time, under a doctor's direction. There can be all kinds of dangers involved, and on your own, you can unbalance the minerals in your body. It's bad enough when it happens with vitamins, but with minerals it's a very serious thing. And once you're thrown off-balance, instead of experimenting with minerals from the health food store, you're better off to have the proper tests to determine what your body is not assimilating.

If you had no mechanical expertise, you'd never dream of lifting the hood of your car and blindly going to work on it. Yet, in a sense, this is what people do to their own bodies. Without knowing what's involved, they randomly plunk vitamins into themselves. I did, and sometimes I still do. But when my best efforts all of a sudden don't work, I go to a doctor. I can go through an extensive inner search of myself and figure out what I'm lacking, what my body isn't accepting at this point, and what balance is required; but it's a slow process. It's often easier and quicker to just go to a doctor who has a particular talent in nutrition or another area of medicine.

God created the lower worlds as a place for us to learn. We go ahead and do whatever we want to—and we pay the price. This is the divine Law of Cause and Effect. The lower worlds are like a big room with only one exit door up on the ceiling. As you come into the classroom, the instructor says,

> The lower worlds are like a big room with only one exit door up on the ceiling.

"The purpose is to try to get out any way you can, but there's one rule: Don't look up."

SPIRITUALITY AND MORALITY

Spirituality doesn't necessarily mean leading a good moral life. Some people lead a very moral life, but they are so conceited and vain about it, you can't stand to be in the same room with them. Just being moral doesn't make them spiritual. I wouldn't want to go to the same heaven that they did.

Back in the 1930s, there was a story circulating about a preacher named Father Divine. It was claimed that every so often a huge number of bills would appear in circulation. When the treasury agents tried to trace them, the trail led to Father Divine and his mission. There wasn't anything wrong with the bills—the serial numbers were all right; they weren't stolen. The problem, according to the story, was that this money came from the *Titanic*.

The treasury agents began to follow Father Divine and observe his activities very carefully, but they never saw him doing anything unlawful. An occultist later speculated that periodically, when Father Divine needed money for the mission—not for himself—he had the ability to go to the sunken ship and get some of the money.

The claim was that Father Divine had the ability to work with the imaginative faculty. There are also accounts of others, such as several Catholic saints, who were able to generate money when it was needed to supply food for the people. They had the ability to go beyond the sight and hearing of the intellectual man and perform miracles in a natural way. They understood the laws of Spirit—how to work with them, not bend them.

How could they do it? First of all, if one is able to tap into this source, he can't use it for himself. Heal-

In the 1930s, a story circulating claimed that every so often a huge number of bills would appear in circulation.

ing is another example of that. When I need healing, there are ways I can go about it; but I feel the best way is to avoid the need for a healing by trying not to get sick. There are certain things about our health we can control, such as experimenting to find out the foods that work for us and the foods that don't. If I eat the foods that don't work right, should I complain?

BRINGING LIGHT AND SOUND INTO YOUR LIFE

All that the spiritual teachings can ever do for anybody is to show them how to make contact with the essence of God. Some call It the Holy Spirit, the Holy Ghost, or the Comforter. You can even call It the God stuff. But whatever words you use, it means this unformed essence of God which comes as Light and Sound. You, as man, become the converter of It so that you can use It in your daily life. You can use the Light to show you where the pitfalls are and the Sound as a directional signal to show you the way back home to God.

The spiritual exercises are to bring the Light and Sound into your life. Several of these are described in the ECK books, such as *In My Soul I Am Free* and *ECKANKAR—The Key to Secret Worlds*. But like anything else, just because a technique is given about how to do something, it doesn't mean everyone will be successful at it.

In some respects, a spiritual exercise is similar to a cake recipe. Two different people use the same recipe, but one cake turns out well, and the other one doesn't. It's much the same with the spiritual exercises. Why? Because some people care more than others.

I was recently talking with a lady who has the ability to see the ECK Masters with her physical eyesight, even though they are someplace else. Others who hear about this might feel badly and think,

A spiritual exercise is similar to a cake recipe. Two different people use the same recipe, but one cake turns out well, and the other doesn't. Why?

*I must be failing in my spiritual life, because I don't
have the ability to see the ECK Masters.* This is not
so: we each have talents. This woman could see them
with such clear vision that she actually mistook them
for physical beings—until they disappeared on her.
It's quite a surprise to be around a person like this,
who has developed her inner eyesight in other lives.

There really isn't a quick and easy road to
heaven. In the teachings of ECK, we talk about the
three steps to find the kingdom of heaven here and
now. The first step is to find the Spiritual Traveler,
who has experience in the other worlds and can
help you out when you get in trouble. Secondly, you
need to find the Word of God, the Sound. This is
the Music of God, or the music of the spheres. Then
comes spiritual liberation.

THE INNER TEACHINGS

A woman who was very perceptive about colors
told me a story. She worked in a motel, making beds
and cleaning rooms. Her husband liked her to
work—they needed the money—but it upset him
when she couldn't be home on his days off. When
he came home from being on the road, he wanted
to spend time with his wife.

In a situation like that, it's a little bit hard to
constantly go to the scheduling supervisor and say,
"My husband wants me to change my schedule again
this week." It's not easy to keep switching the
schedule, because this affects the vacation and
weekend plans of the other employees.

This woman needed to figure out a way to
maintain a peaceful marriage and still keep working, to be independent. She started to notice how
her supervisor was dressed each day, and soon she
came up with a solution to her problem. She would
ask for a schedule change only on the days when
her supervisor wore pink, yellow, or some kind of

*This woman
started to notice
how her
supervisor was
dressed each
day, and soon
she came up
with a solution
to her problem.*

light-colored clothing. But she'd never bring up the subject when her supervisor's apparel was a dark color, such as brown with lavender stripes. She came to learn that on those days the supervisor wasn't feeling particularly good about herself.

The lady who told me the story thought she was just making a casual study of colors, but she had gained this knowledge through the inner teachings, the secret teachings. The ability had come to her so naturally, it never occurred to her that there was anything unusual about it. Yet it came about because of her need for survival.

This is the role that trouble plays in our lives. In general, if one has everything he wants materially, there's too much competition for his attention. This leaves little time for the higher things, such as developing the ability to move into the inner worlds. And why is this ability to travel to the inner planes or heavens important? Very simply, it's because this knowledge helps you overcome the fear of death.

Why is this ability to travel to the inner planes or heavens important?

HELP IN OVERCOMING FEAR

What you have in life doesn't matter as much as your attachment to it. If you have a happy family and a lot of possessions, how soon could you regain your balance if life took them away from you? Would you be utterly crushed? Sure, you can cry for a couple of weeks, but there comes a time when you put away your mourning clothes and say, There must be a reason I'm still alive.

This was the case with Job of the Old Testament. He had large herds, rich fields—all the good things in life. And then one day God and Satan had a little contest to see how much it would take before this man broke. What would it take to crush him?

Satan said, "It won't take much, God. You just let me take away all his property and his family, and you'll see. You think this guy is really one of yours? You watch." God said, "OK, I'll put my money on him." And so God let Satan go ahead and take away everything. Job was wiped out. And to make him even more miserable, he was covered with boils and sores.

Job went through a spell in which he cursed God, but at some point during this experience, he was able to accept the burdens and still keep his face to God. This story is a wonderful example of a man who rolled with life. There is something truly noble about a being such as that.

All a true spiritual teaching can give you is assurance of the eternal nature of Soul: that you live beyond the death of the physical body; that you are Soul, and you live forever. A sword can pierce the body but never Soul. And if you know what you're doing, when you leave this body it's not much of a change. It's very much the same as when you tour another country with an experienced guide.

A spiritual traveler who has been to the Far Country and knows the customs can lead you around the place where the Lords of Karma keep their tollgate. There's a line for the people who are subject to the Law of Karma. When they leave this life, they have to go before the Lords of Karma and take the punishment. It's not given in a mean way, but so that one can learn from the mistakes he has made. He then goes to classes or to some other setting, often on the Astral Plane, which is the next plane up from the Physical Plane. It's not a bad life unless he has committed some heinous crime, and in that case, he may experience a purgatory or hell. But it's not forever: There is no eternal damnation of Soul. If you've done a couple of bad things, you might pay for it, but it won't last forever. But be assured the scales will have to balance. This is the law of life—the law of God.

Job is a wonderful example of a man who rolled with life. There is something truly noble about a being such as that.

USING LIGHT TO HEAL YOURSELF

In your spiritual exercises there are two things you can use for healing. One is the orange light, and the other is the blue light. You may wish to experiment with them. Some people are successful in this kind of healing, and others are better off seeing a doctor. It depends on you.

The orange light is mostly for the physical body. Go into contemplation in your usual way, whether you sit up or lie down. Using the imaginative power, which is the God Force, or the seeing power of Soul, shut your eyes and visualize the Audible Life Stream. This is the pure white Light of God, a composite of all the colors. Now visualize a ray coming off of It. It's very much like using a prism to see the spectrum of colors.

The ray you see is orange, which applies to physical health. With your eyes closed, visualize this orange stream coming through you. Just let it flow to the area in your body that is diseased, afflicted, or injured. You can do this for twenty minutes. This is a healing technique, but you do it only for yourself. Don't go out and blast orange light at other people.

The blue light is another way of healing, but it is for the inner bodies—the Astral, Causal, Mental, and Etheric. These are the bodies of the psychic worlds below the Soul Plane. Here again, you use a technique similar to that of the orange light. And I'll repeat this: Do it only for yourself, never for another person.

Close your eyes, and visualize the blue light coming into the heart center. This light is known as the Blue Light of the MAHANTA. The MAHANTA Consciousness is the highest state of consciousness known to man. The blue light is for the calming and healing of the inner man—your emotions and your mind. Along with this technique, get plenty of physical rest.

The blue light is for the calming and healing of the inner man—your emotions and your mind.

The blue light is not something that is created out of the ethers from some source alien to yourself. It comes from your own God Worlds, and you are now becoming aware of it.

Let this healing Light of God come in and work on the area that you feel needs help. Or just let It flow into the Spiritual Eye. As It washes and cleanses the impurities, It will start to uplift you from the materialism and karma that you have created for yourself through ignorance of God's laws.

How Truth Comes

These are the secret teachings, but they aren't secret for the person who has the diligence and the self-discipline to simply sit down and do the Spiritual Exercises of ECK. They're simple. Try them, and experiment with them. Try different techniques. You might visualize yourself saying to God, "I have a great desire for truth. Can you show me truth and lead me to it?" There are ways, then, that truth will be opened up to you.

It's better if you don't get a big flash, such as in the experience of cosmic consciousness, because it can knock you off your feet. You could spend the rest of your life trying to regain your balance, going around unfit for the society of man. It's best that truth come in a way you can handle. It might be through a book, or maybe a friend will come up to you and say, "I heard about this particular teaching." It may be Eckankar, or it may be another teaching. It makes no difference.

Be perceptive enough to accept that which God gives you. And recognize that Spirit works harmoniously, in an indirect manner, so that your senses will not be shocked.

Tonight when you go to sleep, you can try some of these techniques to see if you will have an experience

The secret teachings aren't secret for the person who has the diligence and self-discipline to do the Spiritual Exercises of ECK.

with the Inner Master. In some small way to begin with, either in the dream state or in full consciousness during the Spiritual Exercises of ECK, you can ask to know reality outside of this physical world. If you are not acquainted with the works of ECK, ask God, "Show me Thy ways, O God. Teach me Thy path." It may take a couple of weeks or a couple of months, but if you are sincere, the Divine Being will surely show you the way.

If you are sincere, the Divine Being will surely show you the way.

Melbourne Regional Seminar, Melbourne, Australia, November 5, 1983

The simplest and best way to express the Light of ECK is not through a long discourse on philosophy, but with a simple smile of gladness that we have found the Light and Sound of God.

6
TWO FINGERS
TO BOREDOM

The title of the talk this morning is "Two Fingers to Boredom." There is a saying that if you live the spiritual life, you'll never suffer boredom.

My daughter, who's in elementary school, has occasionally made the mistake of saying, "Dad, I'm bored." It has been quite a while since she said it. Every time she did, my lecture to her was the same: "You know, the reason you're bored is because you aren't taking the opportunity given you to grow. What do you want? Shall I do it all for you?" When we are bored, it's simply because we are refusing to grow.

The other day I came across a guideline for measuring boredom. If you want to determine to what extent somebody is a bore, you put up one forefinger here and the other forefinger there. One finger represents where the person thinks he is, and the other finger shows where he really is. The farther apart they are, the more of a bore the person is.

I had a friend once who always had big dreams. He was always making some grandiose plan, but he never did anything. As he'd talk about his big dreams and plans, he would be looking at himself from *here*, and I would stifle my yawns and see him from *there*. But as we go along and get experience in life, lessons which Spirit gives to us in this university of hard knocks, the gap between the two fingers narrows. This means we're coming closer to being our True Self.

When we come to the point where the fingers are perfectly aligned, then you have what is called God-Realization. A preliminary step to this is called Self-Realization. This is when you have your dreams lined up and in tune with your actions.

Until you have your dreams aligned with your actions, you are not fulfilling your destiny. If you can dream something, you can do it. Talking isn't going to get you there. And the interesting thing about doing is that it gets you to the point where you are constantly doing.

THE PATH OF PERSONAL EXPERIENCE

ECK is not the intellectual path where we sit around and make more and more plans. ECK is the path of doing—the path of personal experience. It's a marriage of plans with action.

If you come from a religion which bases its whole authority on faith, you have nothing to give you real assurance that what you believe is true. If you want good business advice, you don't go to someone who hasn't ever started his own business or gambled his own money on his decisions. He may have plenty of ideas about how you should handle your money, but you'd be very foolish to listen to him. Why place your faith in an untested product? Somewhere along the line, you've got to look for somebody who has experience, who has walked that path before. And if you can find that person, then there is a fair chance that the advice he gives will be something you can draw on with a reasonable amount of assurance.

ECK is the path of doing— the path of personal experience. It's a marriage of plans with action.

The same is true in the spiritual arenas. The role of the Living ECK Master is to give you spiritual guidance; he has walked the path before. If there is something you want to know about your spiritual life, and you want to gain the experience to find out for yourself, then you can listen to this guidance. But be sure to prove it for yourself. Take any advice you get from anywhere with a grain of salt.

Healing and Karma

If any of you have comments or questions, I'd be willing to address them.

Q: Sri Harold, would you say spiritual healing has to do with one's karma? Let's say I practiced a healing technique, such as using the orange light for a particular ailment, and it didn't work. Could it mean the condition is something that I have to go through? Or that I don't believe enough in the technique?

HK: There are many things that can happen when you use such a technique. If you put the orange light on a physical problem, within a short time somebody might walk up to you and recommend that you go see a particular doctor or acupuncturist, or give you some idea you would never have thought of before. This may be one way in which Spirit heals you. So often when we start on a spiritual path, we somehow try to deny life here in the physical; but in the physical world, all the different methods of healing are also from the ECK, from Spirit. Often a doctor can explain to us why we got sick.

Illness isn't always caused from the karma of past lives which has been built up from incarnations ago. Sometimes it's a very simple matter of karma right here in this life—daily karma. If sugar is the cause of a health problem, we can decide whether we want to keep eating sugar. If it's salt that gives

In the physical world, all the different methods of healing are also from the ECK, from Spirit.

In many cases
health matters
can be handled
very simply by
adjusting our
food habits.

us headaches, we can choose to keep using it and put up with the headaches forever. It's our choice. Some of us are more sensitive to foods that other people can eat without any problem. So, in many cases health matters can be handled very simply by adjusting our food habits.

If the condition doesn't go away, it could be for several different reasons. First of all, it may not be the way we're to be healed. Or maybe we haven't perfected the technique for doing this kind of healing. Just because I have a desire to play the flute, that doesn't mean I have the ability. It could be that I haven't had the training, or I don't have the discipline to take the training. It's that way with healing too.

If you are really interested, you begin using the technique of the orange light or the blue light by visualizing it going through you. You just visualize it at first. This is how it starts. As you build the inner matrix, eventually it prepares the way and opens the door for the light itself to actually come through as you are in full consciousness.

Sometimes there are burdens we have to carry for our spiritual unfoldment, and as much as we'd like some kind of relief from a physical ailment, there isn't going to be any. There are things I carry, too, that I'd like to be rid of. But I wonder just how happy many of us would really be if all of our problems were taken away. Then we truly would be bored.

Q: In my work as a naturopath, I'd like to recommend the orange-light technique for people whom I think would be receptive to using it in conjunction with herbs and other physical treatments. Is it OK to pass that on to other people and suggest that they can use it for themselves?

HK: Yes, it is. As a practitioner yourself, you understand that it's best not to direct the light to someone else. That would be bending the Light of

Spirit, or the Light of God. Manipulating Its direction is using the psychic powers, and that is not what we're interested in on a spiritual path.

How God Cares

Q: What did you mean when you said that God doesn't care what we eat?

HK: God doesn't care in the way we think God cares. God knows when the sparrow falls, but God doesn't stop the sparrow from falling, because it's part of the divine plan. Knowing that Soul has no beginning or ending, God does not share our concern about the death of the physical body. God is concerned about the welfare of this spiritual being that we are.

Furthermore, God has not only created the many different kinds of foods but has given man the knowledge of how to prepare them and eat them.

Tolerance for Other Paths

Q: The God that you are talking about doesn't sound like the God in my religion. Could we be talking about different Gods?

HK: Possibly—but only in the sense that God is perceived differently by each religion and path. The God of the Catholics is not considered the same as the God of the Hindus. It's not that their Gods are different, but that the people who belong to a particular group see God from their own viewpoint. The different religions represent the different states of consciousness of Soul that exist side by side on earth. Each one is valid. Because God has provided all of these paths, we don't advocate intolerance or try to stifle the experience of another person.

Many paths in Western civilization have spun off from the Catholic Church, which was built from the

God is perceived differently by each religion and path. Each one is valid.

early experiences of the apostles. Their insights were developed from the Judaic experience, which in turn was built upon earlier experiences with the Light and Sound, such as Moses and the burning bush. The consciousness of man moves along several different directions, and these directions are formalized into the different religions.

People join the religion most suitable to them, because it is right that they belong there. For this reason, we must have a certain amount of tolerance for each other. This is why we don't have the right to put down a religious path simply because it differs from our own. To do so is to mock the plan of God, which allows for so many different ways of expression.

The plan of God allows for so many different ways of expression.

THE VARIOUS LIGHTS FOR HEALING

Q: I have a very sick mother who had a nervous breakdown. I have tried for quite a while to heal her by calling on the power of the great white light, which I heard about from another master. You specified the orange and blue lights for healing. Why the orange or blue instead of the white light?

HK: White is an all-embracing light, and from it you get the different individual currents, like the blue, green, or yellow lights. Each has a specific function. I was addressing the functions of physical healing through the orange light and healing of the inner bodies through the blue light, which is more calming, soothing, and restorative. The white light is also very good because it is the wholeness of the lights.

HELPING OTHERS

Q: You said this technique is not to be used for healing others, and I don't understand why.

HK: It can be used with their permission. The point I was trying to make yesterday is that healing done for other people without their permission, such as through prayer, is wrong. Why did God give them the sickness anyway? When you step in and start praying to God to take it away, you're trying to do God's business. Why would man be so vain?

But with that person's permission, it is OK. A mother will want to take care of her child, of course. But in the case of healing a parent, you want to be sure that it's the parent's desire to be healed.

Q: If you do direct some sort of light or energy at another person with their permission, what is the karmic link?

HK: That is a good question. I'll use an analogy: Suppose a man walks by carrying a big sack of flour, and you can see he's stumbling under the burden. "I can help," you say, and he accepts your offer. He takes the front of the sack, and you grab the back. But bags of flour have dust, and as soon as you take on part of his burden, you're probably going to get flour dust on yourself. It's nothing you can't brush off, though.

We've all helped other people. The problems usually occur when our emotional body is out of control. Until we understand that the laws of God are exacting, we won't realize that the burdens we carry are precisely those which we have made for ourselves.

We can help each other in compassion and sympathy, but we may get some of the dust on us. I have. Sometimes it has taken a terrible toll on my health, and that's how it is. But I did it knowingly. On the spiritual path, no matter what we do, we do it knowingly. Rather than going on belief or faith, this is the path of knowing.

Sometimes we are willing to take risks. I think a risk of the heart is one of the finest things for the

We can help each other in compassion and sympathy, but we may get some of the dust on us.

spiritual unfoldment of Soul that could ever happen. It is because of the love factor that we can afford to take risks sometimes. And we certainly learn as we do it.

TRUE SPIRITUAL HEALING

Q: I wanted to share something with you. Yesterday I had a bit of an upset stomach, so I tried visualizing the orange light in that area. Last night I got the best night's sleep I've ever had. I certainly feel much better this morning. It sure worked for me.

HK: I'm glad it worked for you. But remember, it's not a cure-all that will keep us healthy for the rest of our lives.

Many people today believe that the healings Jesus did back in biblical times were permanent. But if that were so, those who were healed might still be alive today.

A true spiritual healing first heals the spiritual condition that caused the symptom to appear in the physical body.

A true spiritual healing first heals the spiritual condition that caused the symptom to appear in the physical body. But this does not belie the fact that sometimes the body simply wears out. Just because a doctor has cured you of a number of illnesses doesn't mean you won't die someday. Nor does it mean that because you do die, the doctor was no good. When we have fulfilled our mission here, it's time to go on to another classroom, to another mansion in the other worlds.

PSYCHIC HEALING

Q: I used to know a lady who did psychic healings for a fee. During the two or three years I knew her, she was often in a cast—with two broken legs and a broken hip. Would that sort of healing bring on more karma?

HK: Yes. You've seen something important. Many healers don't know how to pass karma off into the stream of Divine Spirit. There's a knack to this. Until you learn how to do it, you take on karma.

Due to a lack of spiritual awareness, she probably never understood why these physical problems happened to her. But she'll come to understand it, the same as anybody else. That's what this world—this university of hard knocks—is for.

In the meantime, she has perhaps done a lot of good. And sometimes, unknowingly, she has also done a lot of harm, because she has taken lessons away from people which they needed for their own spiritual development. In our ignorance, we sometimes meddle like this in the works of God. It's vanity, but we in the human consciousness don't let a small thing like that stop us. We often just charge right ahead.

THE ORANGE LIGHT

Q: I would like to know if I can use the orange light to heal my four-year-old daughter, who has a serious physical problem. Medical attention was received, but it was very unsatisfactory. Since she's too young to be aware of how bad the problem is, can I use the orange light to cure her without her permission?

HK: You have to understand that when you use the orange light, it may not bring a miraculous healing such as the reshaping of limbs or anything like this. But it may lead you to a better doctor.

Q: Could you explain how to bring the orange light into focus?

HK: To focus the orange light, you shut your eyes, very gently put your attention on your Spiritual Eye, and then simply visualize it. Some people think visualization is an empty fantasy, but it's not. We couldn't

To focus the orange light, you shut your eyes, very gently put your attention on your Spiritual Eye, and then simply visualize it.

imagine something unless there was a reality to it. And because you can imagine the orange light, it is there. You're just not seeing it clearly yet.

You then visualize the orange light flowing like a river through the afflicted part of the body, healing as it washes around.

You then visualize it flowing like a river through the afflicted part of the body, healing as it washes around. Do this for about twenty minutes, and then stop. Don't try to push it. Just let it be. Stay very much aware, because Spirit might come up with an answer from some direction you never imagined, which probably will not be an instantaneous or miraculous healing.

A LITTLE BLACK DOT

Q: In contemplation, I've seen the Blue Light and other colors. I've also seen a little black dot. If you could say something about what that means, it might be helpful.

HK: This means that you now have the ability to focus your attention—which is the first step. Paul Twitchell often mentioned that you could visualize this black dot on the ceiling. Now that you have gotten to this preliminary step, it ought to be very easy to develop into the expanded consciousness and move into the next higher states. It's a very good step.

THE STARRY WORLD

Q: Sometimes I might see four or five little dots of light in the inner vision. They look like stars. Is this the same kind of light that you have been talking about?

HK: Many times this represents the initial stage of the Light of God on the Astral Plane, which is one of the preliminary heavens. It's known as the starry world, and you reach it before you come to the true Astral Plane. It looks like a fantasy land with sparkling lights—prettier than anything on earth.

This is the first indication that Spirit is starting to move in and bring upliftment of the spiritual consciousness. Gradually you will find that your viewpoint changes about a lot of things. You'll notice more tolerance and openness to life in all its expressions. And it's good. In a way, while still a youth, one becomes like the elder who has gained a broader vision and the mellowness of character that comes from experience.

THE LIGHT AND SOUND OF GOD

Q: When I do the spiritual exercises, I see this Blue Light and hear the Sound. Sometimes while I'm at work or walking down the street, I'll suddenly see such a bright light that I have to stop whatever I'm doing and sit down. I can't walk at all. More than once I've wondered if I should see a doctor.

HK: It's the same kind of light that Saul saw on the road to Damascus. The miracles haven't stopped.

Your comment leads to an interesting point. In the development that follows the original teachings of a spiritual master, the people who follow in that master's steps aren't able to duplicate the extent to which he was able to see the Light or hear the Sound of God. So they revert to dogma and doctrine as their authority. The light has gone out, and only glimpses are left. The first thing they do is say that the age of miracles is past; it existed only during the life of their founder. Because the followers themselves don't have the ability to lead anybody to the Light and Sound, they have to say there is no longer any such thing. This is merely one of the fallacies which tries to keep Soul in the lower worlds.

When you have this Light and Sound of God, you can even learn how to adjust It so It doesn't interfere

Gradually your viewpoint changes. You'll notice more tolerance and openness to life in all its expressions. And it's good.

to the point where you have to sit down. You can tune It down a bit by learning how to work with It.

The ECK teachings have been brought out again because there are many of us here who have had experiences that no one in an orthodox teaching could explain. Nor could the doctors. So now you have an alternative: to just go through life thinking you're strange, or to accept the fact that you have actually been touched by the hand of God. You believe this no matter what others think they know about you. It's a very wonderful thing and usually shows a degree of spiritual development that occurred in previous lives. When this knowingness comes out while one is still a child, it's an example of the continuity of Soul through many incarnations.

When this knowingness comes out while one is still a child, it's an example of the continuity of Soul through many incarnations.

Q: Did Jesus, as a Second Initiate of ECK, use the same light that you are talking about?

HK: He did. There are many different forces available to people who have some knowledge of these divine laws of Spirit. There are even brotherhoods outside the path of ECK that have knowledge of the different phenomena, such as levitation. But these involve working with the forces on a lower level in the psychic planes. Using a lower manifestation of the spiritual force, they turn or bend it to move matter.

Jesus followed the path of cosmic consciousness, which focuses on the Light of God. In ECK we are also interested in the Sound. Those on any path which has developed from the cosmic consciousness wait for the Light to come around them and fill the heart. This was the case with Jakob Böhme, the German shoemaker. It's the same passive state which the religions of India practice in their meditation. Unlike contemplation, which is the active approach to God Consciousness, meditation is a passive state. There is the intellectual path, the cosmic consciousness path, and the spiritual path. One leads to the next.

Jesus worked with the different manifestations of Spirit. The apostles saw the Light of Divine Spirit and heard the Sound of the rushing wind at Pentecost. The Sound of ECK can be heard as a rushing wind or, as described in *The Far Country*, the way a passing train would sound if you were standing between two buildings that were close together. Other times you might hear what sounds like large airplanes flying over.

These are just the Sounds of Spirit as heard on the inner planes while in a higher state of consciousness.

A World of Pure Light

Q: Someone mentioned that we cannot trust our sense mechanisms in determining the real world—that the so-called real world is not real at all, but completely illusory. Is it possible that even the inner experiences that ECKists have with the Light and Sound are illusory?

HK: In the most absolute sense, anything we can see, touch, or feel is completely illusionary. For instance, while physical objects seem solid, the scientist knows they are made up of loosely connected atoms. If we were small enough, we could walk through them. Physical matter seems real to us because it feels real to this body, but in the absolute sense, it is not.

Water seems like a real substance, but it changes when the speed of the atoms is slowed down. It becomes ice, which appears equally real. By speeding up the atoms through heating, it turns into steam and disappears. So in the absolute sense, it's all illusion.

On the other hand, we stub our toes on furniture, rip our clothes when they snag on a nail, and when we get injured, we feel pain. Soul can't feel it, but the physical body can. It's just a matter of how well we learn to work with the illusions and how much importance we attach to the things that are here.

Are the spiritual experiences also illusory? The books that we read are part of this world of illusion, but we can use them to help us take the first step to the inner experiences, which for a while may also be illusions. But there is a point we are trying to reach which goes beyond this illusion. The reality there is pure Soul and what we call the Audible Life Stream, or the pure Music of God. Soul's dwelling is purely a ball of white Light. That world of Light would have no meaning to our senses, because it is an existence without shadows.

This lower world of illusion is something the mind can understand and cope with. We perceive the contrasts—highs and lows, mountains and valleys, hard and soft, heat and cold. But beyond pain and suffering as we know it here, beyond cause and effect as we know it here, there is a world of pure Light, and this is our goal.

There is a world of pure Light, and this is our goal.

The lower worlds exist to give us spiritual experience so that one day we can become Coworkers with God. Not to become one with God, as the Eastern religions believe, but to become a Coworker with God.

THE EXPERIENCE OF GOD

Q: For me, the Light and Sound are very real, and I understand that when the Light and Sound blend, they form the Inner Master. Once I see the form of the Inner Master, will that mean I won't be able to experience the other manifestations of the Light and Sound anymore?

HK: Not necessarily. Spirit doesn't limit Itself to any one manifestation. It might show up as Light or

Sound, or you may have a vision of the Inner Master. And then for a while, you may have none of these.

Maybe all you'll have is a very high sound, so high in pitch that it's almost as if you have to stand on tiptoes to hear it. Or you may hear one of the other Sounds of ECK that fills your consciousness to the point where it overwhelms you. Some people can't even hold a conversation while this is going on. But that's only because they haven't yet learned how to work with this purifying force of Divine Spirit as It is coming through.

You'll catch the knack and learn how to control these things. Those who can't—such as the mystic who has a little cosmic consciousness and then leaves mankind and goes off somewhere to nurse his own glory—become totally useless here on earth. They do nothing for the upliftment of their fellow man.

There is no set pattern; you can have the experience of God in many different ways. The people who have these experiences often try to put them into words. Many times the closest they can come is in the form of poetry. One ECKist sent me some good poems about his experiences. The first one is about the Tejas, which means the glory of the ECK. This usually refers to the gaze of It. Even though the second and third are written as two separate poems, they actually are part of the first one.

Maybe you'll have a very high sound, so high in pitch it's almost as if you have to stand on tiptoes to hear it.

Tejas

Gazing out across the great expanse of
    mountains and trees,
An inner hush calms the sounds of the wilderness.
I stand here by the babbling stream, as its waves
    leap into space,
And crash noisily to their destiny beneath the falls.
The plight of many Souls, it seems.

This is your place, O Lord,
And my heart leaps to Thee in your presence.
And with the reassuring onement,
My yearning grows to return to Thee.
For here is Thy breath of freedom, as seized
    in rapture of this moment.
For to be of these heights and survey Thy lands
    is truly but a great blessing.
And yet to know is greater still.
Surrounded by many, yet here I stand alone,
And silent is the contemplation that is drawn
    from Thy omnipresence.
The driving winds rush upon the cliff face,
Sweeping spray from the falls, upward
    to fleck upon my face,
As refreshing now as the winds of heaven to Soul
    that sustained a special place.

All Giving

A quintessence; a placid moment of still time,
Captured not here nor there, but everywhere.
You share this moment, and in your giving I feel
    Love.
But what is the fine thing I have done
    to deserve this great gift?
The question rings, and Love is the only answer.

*What creations
unmanifest
must I bring
to life?*

The Answer

What creations unmanifest
    must I bring to life?
What breath today must I put
    to bring forth the Light?
The strangest thing then happened

as someone passed my way:
I smiled a smile of gladness,
    and saw it carried on its way.

I think this poem illustrates very well how we carry the Light of ECK into the world in ways that we often don't understand. The simplest and best way to express It is not through a long discourse on philosophy, but with a simple smile of gladness that we have found the Light and Sound of God.

Melbourne Regional Seminar, Melbourne, Australia,
November 6, 1983

We have become very intellectual, so the ECK Masters of today catch our attention by appealing to the intellect through books and talks.

7
THE
SECRET TEACHINGS
OF THE WORD

*T*he secret teachings of the Word are the teachings of the Holy Spirit. It is sometimes difficult to tie in the divine teachings with the everyday things that go on here on earth.

Today, when I opened the curtains in the hotel room, I saw a submarine surfacing in the harbor. Shortly after this, I heard a group of people demonstrating outside, singing to express their feelings about the nuclear issue. These political issues don't really concern me, but the submarine out there, the USS *Phoenix*, does represent a greater message.

A MESSAGE OF STRENGTH

It's interesting how the lower worlds work. Even Jesus, the individual most often described as the prince of peace, said that he had not come to bring peace but a sword. This is not the usual image that we carry of the prince of peace, or any savior; and yet the statement was made. He went on to say that he would turn son against father, daughter against mother. Maybe those words contain a message of

It's interesting how the lower worlds work.

87

strength. As we go about our spiritual quest, maybe there is something more important than being a meek, humble person who walks along with his eyes to the dirt. Maybe there is another way—a way of strength.

When my daughter was six years old, she had a problem at school. An eight-year-old girl constantly bullied her. Every time my daughter wanted to do something, the other girl would interfere, pushing her around and telling her she had to do this or that. Even though my daughter was the smaller one by far, the teachers on duty in the school yard wouldn't step in to protect her from this other child, who stood almost a head taller.

One day my daughter came home very unhappy. She didn't know what to do. I said to her, "If necessary, you may just have to fight. And in that case, if the teachers come to us and say, 'Your daughter is a troublemaker,' we're going to take your side. We'll ask them why they aren't doing their job so that a child doesn't have to be so afraid on the school grounds."

Soon after that, our daughter came home from school and told us what happened. The bigger kid had chosen the wrong day to pick on her. My daughter's favorite teacher had just left, it was her first day with the new teacher, and she was already upset about that. So when the other girl started to pick on her, she decided she'd had enough. In one quick move, she jumped on the bully and beat her up.

In this world, it sometimes takes strength.

In this world, it sometimes takes strength. It's easy enough to speak about peace when you're basking under the umbrella of strength, but without that umbrella, you would be like a six-year-old in the school yard.

In the spiritual worlds it's very much the same way. No matter how sweet and tender we try to be, if we are ignorant of the spiritual laws of God, we are at the mercy of life. Karma, in the way of hardships, comes from every side. It can make life so miserable that we often wonder why God let us be born into such a bleak and dreary existence that seems to have no purpose other than to be the first step to hell. And we say, Now, why would God allow something like this?

Man is looking for two things: peace and love. He wants happiness, and he looks for it everywhere. This desire stems from his dim memory of the Golden Age of man, long since past.

THE AGES OF MAN

The Lemurians lived on the continent of Lemuria, or Mu, out in the Pacific. New Zealand is likely a part of that original continent. Those days, so many centuries ago, were a time of perpetual strength. Plants would grow without anyone having to break the ground, fertilize the soil, or plant the seeds. When the first little sprouts came up, nobody had to water them and weed them. It was a garden paradise, a Garden of Eden.

HU was the sacred chant of the people in Lemuria. And in the simplicity of heart that characterized this Golden Age, they knew this was the direct link with the Holy Spirit, the Audible Life Stream or the Life Force.

HU was the sacred chant of the people in Lemuria. They knew this was the direct link with the Holy Spirit.

The Golden Age passed away, and as the Silver Age of man moved in, times became a little harder, the vibrations a little coarser. Perpetual spring was now replaced by four seasons, and this meant cooler weather. Man now had to forage for food. The ECK Masters at that time had to show him how to raise crops. The art of animal husbandry developed.

When the ECK Masters gave the teachings of Spirit to the people in those days, it was certainly not through books, as we do it today. They talked and worked with the people to accomplish very simple, practical things, almost too humble for us to consider today. When we need bread, we go to the store. For meat we go to the butcher shop. If we need medicine, we go to a drugstore. Life is very simple and easy in that respect.

In our evolution, we have become very intellectual, and so the ECK Masters of today catch our attention by appealing to the intellect—they write books and give talks. At the same time, they understand our emotional need for warmth and happiness.

The Silver Age of man was the age of the Atlanteans—the red race. They lived on the continent of Atlantis, which was located in the Atlantic Ocean. It was during this time that the people learned how to divert the pure spiritual force of ECK, the Holy Spirit, and twist It toward black magic. The leaders used different psychic powers, such as the evil eye, the all-seeing eye, to locate and spy on the people who objected to government policies. The persecutions were severe. At some point the power got out of hand, and the continent was destroyed. The Silver Age of man passed away.

RECORDS OF CIVILIZATIONS

Because there is no written record, many feel these two great civilizations never existed.

Almost all the records of these civilizations have been destroyed. Because there is no written record, many people feel it's very probable these two great civilizations never existed. Most of the records we know of today are from the Bronze Age, which followed the Silver Age. These records generally pick up right after the time of the Atlantean destruction. The earliest record of man's time on earth is in the Bronze Age. We have the Naacal records, which go back at least ten thousand years, and then we have the biblical records.

If it seems too farfetched that total civilizations could be destroyed two times without any record remaining today, just stop and think about what the submarine in the harbor represents. Imagine what would happen if the same nuclear power used in World War II was unleashed worldwide. The fountains of the deep would open, volcanoes would erupt, and the known land masses would shift beyond recognition. When all the factories had been destroyed, and the technicians were no longer in communication with each other, the man who knew how to write would have nothing to write with; he wouldn't know how to produce the pencil. The man who knew how to make a pencil wouldn't know how to produce the paper.

In two generations, all of the precious knowledge in which man takes such pride would be gone. The father could try to tell the son about the magnificence and wonder of a light that burned without fire, how a switch on the wall could suddenly illuminate an entire room. But the son would never understand. In time, legends would be born about strange vehicles that were propelled along broad city streets, but by then, no one would remember what a city street was.

And so the legends develop, and while they are based on a kernel of truth, the real truth is lost. This is also true of the spiritual works.

In time, legends develop, and while based on a kernel of truth, the real truth is lost. This is also true of the spiritual works.

How Religions Evolve

Historically, the leader or founder of any religious teaching comes forth and walks among men to bring the spiritual light and break the hold of materialism. But after he leaves, how many of his disciples have the ability to see the Light of God or hear Its Sound? Not very many. The next natural step, then, is to choose and accept leaders who henceforth rule by authority. Not divine authority, but man's authority, which is built upon fear.

We've come a long way in our evolution from the Golden Age of man down through the Silver, the Bronze, and to the Iron Age, which we are in now. Yet there is a yearning inside for happiness, peace, and love. The trick is where to find it. One may go to his religious teacher and say, "Show me the way to God." The teacher hands him a huge book and says, "This is the way." But after reading it, the follower concludes that he has to wait until he dies before he can find the way to God. And since he doesn't know any better, and his teacher doesn't know any better, it becomes an accepted, established fact.

You were taught that there are no miracles today, that miracles belong to the ancient past, to people who somehow were greater and grander than yourself; and the quality of Soul that they were able to reach is beyond anything you will ever be able to attain. This is one of the big spiritual fallacies that exists today.

THE SPIRITUAL EXERCISES OF ECK

My job is to point out there is a way for you to contact the divine essence of God. You can contact the Holy Spirit and guide yourself directly. You don't have to rely on the words and teachings of a person just because he speaks with authority from a pulpit. You don't have to believe me either.

We are looking for the Light and Sound. The teachings of ECK can give you, first of all, an understanding of the spiritual hierarchy and the construction of the other worlds—the different heavens, how they relate to each other, and what you could hope to find in each heaven. And how do you get this understanding? We have the Spiritual Exercises of ECK.

These are light, simple techniques that take only twenty minutes a day. Some of you will be successful with them, and others won't. Those of you who are successful will get experiences in certain directions, such as Soul Travel. Others will get experiences in the dream state; and others are

My job is to point out there is a way for you to contact the divine essence of God directly.

going to get experience directly with the Light and Sound of God.

Why Look for Both Light and Sound?

On the path of ECK, we look for more than the Light of God. The Light of God is something that the proponents of the cosmic-consciousness theory espouse very highly. In a passive state, through meditation, they open themselves to this Light. But it is not enough: You have to do more than this. To passively open yourself for this Light of God is still not acting in your divine capacity as a creator in your own worlds, in the worlds that begin right here.

Whatever path to God you follow ought to make you able to stand on your own feet here as well as in the inner worlds; here and now, in this lifetime, before you drop the body in death. If the path isn't able to do that, then you ought to keep looking until you find one that gives you this ability.

Whatever path to God you follow ought to make you able to stand on your own feet here as well as in the inner worlds, here and now.

In ECK we also look for the Sound. The Sound is the movement of the Holy Spirit, the movement of the atoms of God. The apostles at Pentecost in early Christian times were able to hear It as the sound of a rushing wind. As Jesus said, "The wind bloweth where it listeth," which means where It wants; and no man can tell where It came from or where It's going. This is the Sound of ECK.

The Sound of ECK may come as the beautiful music of a flute. At other times you may hear the buzzing of bees. I heard this buzzing sound for a long time. I wrote a letter to Paul Twitchell, the founder of Eckankar who brought out the writings in 1965, to ask what this meant. He pointed out that I could find it for myself in the ECK teachings. It's explained in *The Spiritual Notebook*. At the same time, I requested an ECK-Vidya reading, which was a look at the future through this ancient science of prophecy.

He said I had an aura of a certain color; it was silver and blue. But we change. At one point our aura may be predominantly pink, later it may be orange or blue.

This is the Light of God coming to cleanse Soul, to uplift and purify It in Its state of consciousness. And in the process, we learn the ways and means whereby our life may be made easier and more pleasant, so that we can find the first steps to peace and love.

No matter how difficult life in this world gets, even if the whole planet blows up, we know we are Soul and this is just one of the many bodies we have worn throughout all time. If we haven't finished our lessons, when the dust settles we can come back for another round. But if we learn the way to be raised in consciousness, we can get off this wheel of reincarnation so that we don't have to come back anymore. It's up to each of us. All I can do is put out the teachings and point this out.

It's up to you, each one of you, to decide first of all, What am I looking for when I join a church? What am I looking for in a spiritual path? In other words, what need are you looking to fulfill? You have to be really honest with yourself.

If you have any comments or questions, I'd be willing to answer a few.

THE SPIRITUAL HIERARCHY

Q: You mentioned a spiritual hierarchy. Can you expand a little on that?

HK: There are many different workers, as well as different orders, in the spiritual hierarchy. The Order of the Vairagi ECK Masters is a pure line unto itself, as are the Green-Robed Monks of South America or the Great White Brotherhood. They also have their own pure line through which they work. These are the workers in the spiritual hierarchy, but

No matter how difficult life in this world gets, we know we are Soul and this is just one of the many bodies we have worn throughout all time.

you also have the lords and rulers of each plane throughout the worlds of God.

THE PLANES OF GOD

Q: How many planes are there?

HK: We have named twelve planes, but actually there are many more. The most commonly known planes are in the worlds of matter, energy, space, and time—the material worlds. These planes are known as the Physical, Astral, Causal, Mental, and Etheric.

Certain aspects characterize each plane. The Astral Plane corresponds with your emotional body. When you cry or feel sympathy or compassion, these feelings come from here. It's also the plane where people can practice astral travel and see flying saucers.

Then comes the Causal Plane. The name itself indicates cause: the seed of every action you have ever done, and all the karma you have created in the past, can be found here. Here you can see what has occurred and figure out how to step around it so you are not fettered by it again in the future.

Next is the Mental Plane, the area from which all the intellectual and mental processes of man originate. Symbols, symbology, and all the different languages and alphabets spring from this realm. The Mental Plane is also the area where the heavens of some of the major orthodox religions are located. It upsets a lot of people to hear that the Christians, Buddhists, Hindus, Jains, and some of the others have their heavens in the same place. Not all in the same heaven, of course; they don't get together in heaven any more than they do down here. Each religious path has its own heaven, because each group has its own consciousness. They keep to themselves. The Mental Plane is still one of the heavens of separation.

In the Causal Plane, you can see all the karma you created in the past and figure out how to step around it so you are not fettered by it again in the future.

Then comes the Etheric Plane, which is kind of a subplane just before the Fifth, or Soul, Plane. These lower planes all have some degree of materiality. As you go higher, there is less materiality and more Spirit. The Etheric Plane corresponds to the subconscious, or the unconscious or primitive part of man, where one's basic attitudes come into play—the unknown and unconscious motivators that run us.

Right above the Etheric is the Soul Plane. This is the first of the true spiritual worlds. There is no element of materiality here; the worlds no longer depend on dichotomies for existence. But in the lower worlds, you need evil to counterbalance good. And whether it looks like it or not, they are always in perfect balance. They have to be, because if there were ever an imbalance, they would fall in on each other.

From the Soul Plane on, you find the higher worlds of God. Speech comes from the Mental Plane, so images, symbols, and words can't describe what happens above and beyond it. In each successive plane, the Light and the Sound become clearer, higher, and more beautiful.

In each successive plane, the Light and the Sound become clearer, higher, and more beautiful.

There are also the different gods, such as Sat Nam, on the Soul Plane, and Kal Niranjan and Jot Niranjan in the lower worlds. You can meet some of these lower lords. Most people who have an experience of any kind in the dream state, by trance, or through a vision will meet one of these beings, even the ones who stay very low on the spiritual ladder, such as Jot Niranjan.

Sometimes when a person is in a trance state and sees one of these beings, he'll believe God has spoken to him. God has appeared. God gave him a special directive to lead His following back to Him. Then this person will go out and start his own spiritual path, fully convinced that he has seen the highest God. You have to look very carefully at the actions of people who say the highest God has spoken to them. Often they do very erratic things, and their behavior and actions don't bespeak the God of kindness, goodness, and love that they claim to follow.

SPIRITUAL MASTERS IN HISTORY

Q: Were any of the saviors, such as Jesus Christ, ECK Masters?

HK: Some of them were, but some of them followed their own line. Zadok was the ECK Master at the time of Jesus, and they met.

Jesus traveled widely. The records in the Bible, for the most part, are incomplete. There are other records that mention his travels to the East through India and Tibet. The records of Western man are patchy at best, and this kind of revelation may come as a shock to some people. Records still exist today about the silent years of Jesus, from the time he was twelve until right after he was thirty. He didn't just sit around. Because of his family connections, he had the means to travel in those days. He had a mission, and he knew what it was.

There is a certain amount of time for each spiritual master who comes, and when his time is up, he leaves. The mission is then carried on again from another angle, for another time.

A STUDY OF TRUTH

If you are really interested, you can research some of this information for yourself. You can even ask for help. Just before you go to sleep at night, you can say, "God, I would like to know the truth about history." If you are interested in Jesus, just say, "Lead me to ways to learn the truth." It may come by way of books, or by the inner vision, or

Just before you go to sleep at night, you can say, "God, I would like to know the truth about history."

through a dream. It may take you weeks or months, but it will come.

Generally, a study of this kind first has to be undertaken outwardly. A study of the available records that existed before the manuscripts from which the present biblical writings were taken, such as the Nag Hammadi and the Dead Sea Scrolls, will reveal that certain passages were already spoken and written before Jesus used them. Whatever religious teaching you follow, it's an interesting thing to look into.

SELF-IMPORTANCE VERSUS TRUE SPIRITUALITY

We flatter ourselves that this earth theater is the center of divine creation. In the Middle Ages, man's vanity about his own importance was transferred to the earth—he felt sure the earth was the center of the universe. This was still the teaching at the time Columbus was planning to sail across the ocean. The church was still saying that if he went, he would fall off the edge of the world.

Columbus was traveling to what he thought were the Indies when he discovered America. The ECK Master of the times saw a need to tap into this new land and bring back food to restock and renourish Europe. The food supply in Europe had been almost completely depleted; each generation of people was becoming smaller and weaker, and the life span was very short. Something had to be done to bring vitality back into the stock of the physical race, so this new source was opened up.

When Columbus returned to Spain, he was wise enough to bring with him some Arawak Indians he found in the Bahamas. He even sent a letter from Portugal to Spain, and by the time he arrived in Spain, there was great curiosity about these strange red men that he was bringing. The feeling had been that no humans could exist outside the then-known

The ECK Master of the times saw a need to tap into this new land and bring back food to restock and renourish Europe.

world. The biblical scholars of the times had decided that the three sons of Noah had each started
a certain race of man: the white people were in
Northern Europe, the blacks settled in Africa, and
those with skin color halfway in between black and
white settled in the Mediterranean basin.

But they couldn't account for the red man, and
it threw the biblical teachings of the time into complete turmoil. The pope didn't even address this issue.
He was involved with wars and political infighting
just to keep things the way they were. About twenty
years later, during the reign of another pope, it was
announced that the church had made a full study of
this matter. By some manipulation of the Bible, they
determined that the red men were of the Lost Tribes
of Israel. Until that time, the biblical scholars had
ignored the Lost Tribes of Israel; but with the monks
in the monasteries losing faith in the church, the
pope eventually had to address the issue.

At this particular time in history, man had placed
so much importance on himself that he thought his
known world was the center of the universe. Today
we still think almost the same way: Our God is
greater and better than anyone else's. This attitude
exists not just in the Christian religion but among
many religious paths. There are even followers of
Eckankar who say the same thing: ours is greater,
ours is better. Sometimes I wonder about the mo-
tives. Isn't it just vanity?

You can see by their behavior that some people
are not getting any spiritual benefit from their path.
Some of them barely last through Sunday-morning
services before they go out and break most of the Ten
Commandments as fast as they can—stealing, covet-
ing, and so on. They can't even contain themselves
long enough to follow the Golden Rule—the Ten
Commandments condensed into one, with a splash
of love thrown in.

The biblical scholars of the times couldn't account for the red man, and it threw the biblical teachings of the time into complete turmoil.

ASKING WITH A SINCERE HEART

ECK is a teaching you can look into that works directly with the Light and Sound. You can test it and find out for yourself. There are spiritual exercises mentioned in some of the books you can try. *In My Soul I Am Free** has a technique called "The Easy Way." If you are of the Christian faith and you're looking, but maybe you're a little afraid, you can still test it very carefully. If you are more comfortable with prayer, you can pray to God: "Show me Thy ways, show me Thy truth." When you have asked with a sincere heart, this will be brought to you. But don't expect it to come in a wave, because it probably won't. It may come in the dream state or by way of a book. Ask to be shown in a way that is right for you.

ECK is a teaching that works directly with the Light and Sound. You can test it and find out for yourself.

PRAYING TO GOD

Q: When people pray to God, who are they praying to?

HK: That's a good question. Often people are praying to the lord of one of the lower planes. Sometimes they pray to Sat Nam, the Lord in charge of the Soul Plane, which is the first of the spiritual planes. To many of us, the light and power that come from these beings positioned by God on the other planes is blinding. It's overpowering. Sometimes people pray to Jot Niranjan on the Astral Plane. He is often known as Jehovah.

The God of the Old Testament is certainly different from the one in the New Testament. The one in the Old Testament was similar to a tribal god in that he required bloodshed and sacrifice, but the God in the New Testament was of an entirely different caliber and nature. People today try to somehow equate

---

* Now out of print, but the Easy Way technique can be found in *The Spiritual Exercises of ECK.* —Ed.

them and say they are the same God; but my question is, Which version of God are they praying to?

God has provided these different lords and different paths so that each Soul, in Its individual and unique state of consciousness, can find the divine truth according to the path that suits It best. This is why there is no reason for the people of one faith to become angry or intolerant of those who follow another faith.

As the Living ECK Master, I have still another duty—to prod people into gaining an understanding, beyond blind faith, of the religion they are following. I'd rather see you reading the Bible than sitting on it. You will probably learn something in your studies. So many people who claim to follow the Bible have never really read it. I'm not that interested in whether you follow the path of ECK, but I am interested in Soul becoming aware of Its true state, of Its divinity.

COLORS ON THE HIGHER PLANES

Q: Aside from the spectrum of seven colors that can be seen with the physical eyes, are there other colors that can be seen in the higher spheres?

HK: On the physical plane, no two people see any object in the same way. Different people have different abilities to see color—that's just how we are. If you worked in the printing field or with a camera in television, you would see how the different types of films can affect the reproduction of what looks like the same color.

The colors on the higher planes have a vibrancy that is totally indescribable. Sometimes they seem to glitter with life—like living light. So you are not just looking at yellow, for instance, but you are seeing a living essence which actually is one aspect of Divine Spirit. This is conscious contact with the high aspects of God.

The colors on the higher planes have a vibrancy that is totally indescribable. Sometimes they seem to glitter with life—like living light.

Q: Would you be inclined to think that there may be, in certain states of consciousness, perhaps twelve very distinct colors?

HK: They are infinite in number. Light is actually a lower vibration of the Sound. It may seem as if it would be the other way around, but it isn't.

There may be twelve colors, but only to the person who has expanded eyesight. There may be only two or three colors to the person who is partially color-blind. It's much the same way with the inner eyesight of Soul.

I can't say that you are going to have any one kind of experience, because as sure as I say this is how it's going to be, some of you will have it in a totally different way. Consciousness is so broad. The little chip of it that each one of us has is a fine and wonderful thing, and we must allow other people to experience any of the other possibilities that are provided.

I can't say you are going to have any one kind of experience, because some of you will have it in a totally different way. Consciousness is so broad.

Q: You mentioned the Green-Robed Monks earlier. Is there a color associated with the ECK Masters?

HK: Well, some of them are seen in maroon robes, but that doesn't mean they're stuck with maroon; they can change if they want to. Sometimes it's brown or white or green.

Q: Is Saint-Germain known among the ECK Masters, perhaps under another name?

HK: Yes, but he's from a different order. Whether legend or truth, what really counts is if you can somehow get inspiration because of the existence of a certain being, be it Jesus, Saint-Germain, St. John of the Cross, or others.

A MATTER OF PERSONAL UNDERSTANDING

Q: When Jesus said that he is the way, the truth, and the light, and that the way was only through him, what do you think he meant?

HK: At the time, he probably meant just what he said. But as you read the Bible, you have to ask whether he was a messenger only for his times or a messenger for all times. Jesus came two thousand years ago. Where does that leave the billions of people who existed long before that and followed other paths or religions, such as Hinduism and Zoroastrianism? Had God overlooked so many of his children for so long? The saviors of those religions were also valid for their times, because God has provided a way for everyone. But it's a matter of personal belief. Just because other people believe differently, it's certainly not an issue worth killing over. Mostly it's a matter of your personal understanding.

THE SEARCH FOR GOD

There is no way any lecture is going to get you to God instantly. Sometimes before starting a talk, I've been tempted to ask who is interested in the path to God. You would see a lot of hands. Then if I asked who wanted to get there the easy way, you would see some more hands. And it would be even more interesting to find out who wouldn't want to go if there were no easy way. The best way to say it is this: There is no easy way.

The search for God requires a deep yearning. Soul hears the Voice of God and wants to return to Its home in heaven. In the meantime, it's up to Soul, in one way or another, to find a path that gives the help It needs to take this step. When you graduate from one level of education in the spiritual works, God provides a step, then another and another.

No matter what path you are on or what faith you follow, be the best there is in it, be the cream of the crop. Because until you are that, you haven't learned

When you graduate from one level of education in the spiritual works, God provides a step, then another and another.

the lessons you need to learn; and until they are learned, you will not be able to graduate to the next step and learn the greater truth.

Through your efforts, you will have made the decision: I want to find this path to God and walk it for myself.

I will leave you with this. And if there is some little thing I've said tonight that makes you think maybe there is something to it—maybe you don't agree, but you've decided to look further on your own—then through this, you might find something for yourself that works. It may not be the path of ECK. But through your efforts, you will be doing something important for yourself. You will have gotten off the seat, stood up, looked around, and made the decision: I want to find this path to God and walk it for myself.

Auckland Regional Seminar, Auckland, New Zealand, November 9, 1983

The path of ECK is to teach us how to get to the kingdom of heaven. But, differently from the game of Monopoly, you don't bypass Jail or any of the problem areas and get to pass Go again. You have to go through every square.

8
I HAVE A PROBLEM

he talk this evening could well be titled "I Have a Problem." A couple of weeks ago, there was an item in the newspaper about an article that had appeared in *Izvestia*, the Soviet newspaper. It made a big thing about a new telephone counseling service. The article said there was a great need among the Russians for this counseling service because of the hard time they were having in coping with their daily life and their problems.

A Western correspondent decided to find out how the service really worked, so he dialed the number listed in the article. When the psychologist answered, the reporter said, "I have a problem" and began to describe it. The psychologist's solution was, "Take two sedatives, and call me in the morning." And then he hung up. That seems to be the standard type of service offered when one has a problem—but what are you supposed to do in the meantime?

When the psychologist answered, the reporter said, "I have a problem" and began to describe it.

FACING LIFE'S CHALLENGES

The path of ECK is to teach us how to get to the kingdom of heaven. But, differently from the game of Monopoly, you don't bypass Jail or any of the problem areas and get to pass Go again. You have

to go through every square. And when you get through
them and earn the right to buy Boardwalk or some
other expensive place, it's similar to reaching one of
the heavens.

We have to face this life. The fact is, we do have
problems. Most of us would be lost without them. Yet
our problems sometimes seem so heavy we cry for
help to God, to the angels, or to anyone else who gives
us at least a hope of lifting the burden, so we can face
life with some measure of happiness, contentment,
and peace. This is what many of us are looking for in
life. We search, but we never find.

THE CREATIVE IMAGINATION

In a recent trip to Australia, I learned a little
about the history of the Australian aborigines. The
aborigine was concerned with preserving nature
and living in harmony with it. For this reason, he
took meat only when it was needed for personal
nourishment. In order to survive, he had to combine
his skills with the creative imagination, which is
the Divine Self within us—the God-spark, or Soul.
He had to work with this divine faculty of imagination in order to find a way to win on the hunt.

Long ago, he did this by making a boomerang,
and on the boomerang he would draw a story picture
of the fowl or animal that he intended to reach on
the hunt. If it was a bird, he would draw not only
the wings but even a likeness of the insides of the
bird. He formed the object of his hunt so clearly
that when he went out, he was bound to get the
food he needed to bring back to the family. This was
a use of the creative imagination.

When the creative imagination is working in you, life is right; you wake up in the morning to rainbows and sunshine.

When the creative imagination is working in
you, life is right; you wake up in the morning to
rainbows and sunshine. This means you are operating under the hand of God, as if you are living in

the kingdom of heaven here and now. But unfortunately it doesn't last forever; it fades away.

BLOCKING SPIRIT

After the Australian seminar, we traveled to a
hilly region in a national park and met a wood-
carver. At one time this man had worked and oper-
ated out of the pure flow of Spirit. He made carvings
of the aboriginal tribesmen from the Australian
outback. On the path we took to his house, there
were all kinds of beautiful carvings on display. His
home was also his workplace, and for a small fee,
which we paid at the gate, we were able to visit
with him for a while.

*On the path
we took, there
were all kinds
of beautiful
carvings
on display.*

It was an interesting experience. We walked in
to find this eighty-three-year-old gentleman standing very quietly, just like one of his carvings. But
his face was very red, and we soon realized it was
the redness of anger.

One of the people in our party got into a conversation with him to see if perhaps this man had some
wisdom from all his years that we could take with
us. All around the garden and fountains below in
the state park, we had seen lovely carvings of little
people who seemed to be running through the foli-
age, so we thought surely there must be some truth
that this man could share with us. But instead, for
the next few minutes, all we heard was his anger
gushing forth. It was as if he couldn't stop himself.

Somewhere during the span of this old man's life,
he had lost the spark of the true creative Spirit. Due
to his own ideas of morality, he had put limitations
on the creations of Divine Spirit, and this caused a
block. Suddenly his artwork started to come out in a
lower form. At one time, he had made carvings of
living things—the aborigines and the animals; but
when he was no longer tuned in to Divine Spirit, he

eventually lost the contact. Ernest Hemingway, at one time, also lost his linkup with the creative flow.

When this happened, the wood-carver became frantic. He turned to religion, but he was so bitter and angry that his beliefs reflected a corrupted type of Christianity. He started to make carvings of dead things, such as the animal after the hunt. He even began to envision himself as the savior of the aborigine, carving an image of himself on a cross. It was an exercise in vanity of the most unimaginable kind.

His whole conversation led down the dark path. He turned out to be extremely bigoted about certain races which didn't fit into his pattern of life. Other people were there, too, and soon after he started speaking, they all left.

This old man had once touched the hem of the robe of the Lord. He had seen the face of God, and the creative flow came through. Spirit was trying to lift him higher, beyond his creations of the aborigines. But because he couldn't drop his opinions, he had put qualifications to what Spirit was trying to bring out in his artwork, and this kept him from going further. As a result, he eventually fell back into a base prejudice which certainly did not show in his early work.

It's wonderful to watch and listen to people who have learned how to tap into the flow of the Light and Sound of ECK, of Spirit. This creative flow is known under numerous other names, too, such as the Holy Spirit or the Audible Life Current.

It's wonderful to watch and listen to people who have learned how to tap into the flow of the Light and Sound of ECK.

WHAT IS HEAVEN?

There are many ways in which the ECK Masters begin working with people who wish to explore the heavenly regions. When you have a great creative ability, consciously or unconsciously, you have been lifted in your state of consciousness. In the dream state or in another manner, you have been taken into one of the heavens.

Some people are aware of being taken into the Astral heaven or to the Causal or Mental Plane, but the greater heavens lie beyond those material worlds. On the material planes we have the heavens of the Christians, Buddhists, Hindus, Jains, and most of the different segments that spill off from the major religions. These are the heavens where the orthodox seeker desires to go, where he can sit on the right hand of the deity and hopefully stay there forever in peace and quiet. He never stops to think that maybe this would be a dull heaven, with nothing positive or constructive to do.

We often have the naive notion that heaven is a place where one wears a halo and sits around at the right hand of God, playing a harp. In a heaven like this, one just lies around on spiritual welfare, having a good time while God pays the way. One would be eternally at rest. But I know when I go into the other worlds permanently, I'm going to be an active Coworker with God. This is the true mission of Soul: in some way agreeing to work as an agent for the Divine Being in the vast worlds that lie beyond the physical realm, to carry the message of the Light and Sound to all the different worlds.

I know when I go into the other worlds permanently, I'm going to be an active Coworker with God. This is the true mission of Soul.

LEARNING ABOUT PAST LIVES

A woman told me about a class she attended at a local college. The instructor was a psychiatrist who was teaching a course in psychology. One of the students asked for the teacher's opinion about the use of hypnotic regression as a way to go back and see what happened in a past life. The instructor's answer showed a good amount of common sense.

She told the story of a young woman who was taken back through hypnotic regression to a life she supposedly lived during World War II, where she found herself helping with the ovens in a concentration camp. This was a severe shock to her.

The instructor said that she strongly recommended against anyone looking at past lives through a method such as hypnotic regression. She remarked that we have enough problems to handle right here and now, without borrowing from the past.

Too often we want to live in the imagined splendor of days gone by. We picture a past life as a noble king or queen with servants waiting on us hand and foot, swirling fans to keep the flies away. That's the kind of life we would like to know about, because it makes us feel special.

People often want to know about their past lives because they feel they are a failure in their present life. They are not able to face the problems they have created for themselves here. Furthermore, they have absolutely no idea how to start the creative imagination working inside them. This can be done with the Spiritual Exercises of ECK; their purpose is simply to link up Soul and Divine Spirit.

HEARING THE TRUE VOICE OF GOD

By his presence, the Light Giver illuminates Soul.

The Living ECK Master is called the Light Giver. Some of you have actually seen the Inner Master as a being clothed in light. By his presence, this inner being illuminates Soul and makes a direct linkup with the Audible Life Stream, the Voice of God, which can be heard as Sound and seen as Light. This is the only way that the true Voice of God can be heard. It doesn't come in an audible manner, such as the way you are hearing me speak now, but in Light and Sound. These are two aspects of God which can lift Soul out of the material worlds, into the high states of consciousness here and now, in this lifetime.

But don't imagine that when you reach a state of illumination or enlightenment, people are going to look at you and say, "Yes, he is illuminated; this is a great man of God. I will sit at his feet in the dust and listen to the great words which come forth." You will find the saying of Jesus to be true: "A prophet is not without honor, save in his own country." This means simply that when you are touched by the hand of God, the people closest to you rarely recognize that something extraordinary has happened to you.

The teachings of ECK give direct methods, step-by-step, to reach the Light and Sound of God. There are ECK Masters who work to help us reach the divine state. But just because you hear a voice speaking from a burning bush, as Moses did, this does not mean it's the Voice of God. In the dream state, an individual may come to you and say, "I am the Lord; listen to me" and then make it more impressive by using words like *thee* and *thou* and saying, "I have spoken." Don't listen to the command given by this being just because he sounds authoritative. Check him out. Is he telling you to do something positive or something destructive? Or is this inner being, who seems greater than anything you have ever seen or heard before, merely a part of your first step into a phenomenal world?

THE PURPOSE OF THE SPIRITUAL EXERCISES

When we have problems, what we are trying to do in ECK is learn how to solve them. Not just in the other world but right here, because if we solve them here, the other world takes care of itself, after a manner.

Using the creative imagination means learning how to tap into the full powers of Soul in the awakened state, not the sleep state. How do we do it? Through the Spiritual Exercises of ECK, which are

Using the creative imagination means learning how to tap into the full powers of Soul. How do we do it?

given in the ECK books. One exercise is a simple technique called "The Easy Way." Try it, experiment with it. But if you are of an orthodox religion, there is another way.

PRAYER AS A FIRST STEP

First of all, ask yourself why you are here tonight. Some people want to criticize, some want to learn. The question is for yourself. What made you walk in the door? Was it because your life is exactly the way you want it to be? Are you happy where you are? You might discover the reason you are here is that you don't have all the answers in your life. No problem—that's what we're here for. God has created the lower worlds to give Soul a place to gain an education, in the spiritual sense, so that It can become a Coworker.

If you don't know anything about ECK, the main tool you have to work with at this point may be prayer—your communication with God. If you are sincerely interested in truth, in knowing who you are and why you belong here, ask God in your prayers: "Show me truth." If your heart is pure, the Lord will bring truth into your life. But don't expect it to come in a way that fits your expectations; it may come in a different way. It may come through the gift of a book or by way of a person telling you one small step that you need to take before you can go to the next step.

When you ask for truth with a pure heart, the Divine Spirit will take you one step closer to coming home to God.

When you ask for truth with a pure heart, the Divine Spirit will take you one step closer to coming home to God.

God is known as the Ocean of Love and Mercy. This is the nature of the true God—unlike Jehovah, the wrathful god of the Old Testament, who is a minor god, a tribal god interested in destruction, a petty god who liked to play with people such as Job. The Ocean of Love and Mercy is a descriptive term for the true

God, which is not a he or she but lies far beyond those regions of duality. The best we can say is It.

And so you can pray to God. Just say, "I want truth," or "Dear Lord, give me knowledge, wisdom, and understanding." But the greatest thing you could ask is, "Dear Lord, give me love." Knowledge, wisdom, and understanding are only the attributes of God, but when you have love, you have the whole thing. We seek first the highest, most divine, most sacred part of something, which is nothing other than our own inner being. And with this come the attributes of God and the spiritual liberation, which is something no baptism can ever bring.

How We Are Given Experiences

When people follow the path of ECK, they have experience with the Light of God. It may come in any number of different ways, but It always comes in a manner that you can handle at that time. The Light comes only after due preparations have been made, so that you will not be thrown into an emotional imbalance. You are given this preparation—a strengthening, a spiritual foundation—so that when the Light comes to you, It will come in a gentle manner which is right for you, which fits the vibrations at the level you have earned.

You are given preparation so when the Light comes to you, It will come in a gentle manner right for you.

And then comes the Sound. This is the pure Sound of God, which may be heard in various ways. It may come as the rushing wind, the twittering of birds, the song of a mockingbird late at night; or It may come as the sound of a flute heard so clearly that you think a radio is playing nearby—but the radio isn't on. It means the Sound and Light of God have come into your life, just a little bit, to uplift you in spiritual awareness.

As you go through the tests of life, there are times you will be given an abundance of the Light and Sound

of God. But at other times, when you have no awareness of any of these manifestations of the Voice of
God, it may seem as though the Inner Master has
pulled the curtain. It's at times like this that we cry,
"O God, why have you forsaken me?" God hasn't forsaken us. There are times we are given an abundance
of Light and Sound, and there are times the Lord will
withdraw these. Why? For the strengthening of Soul.
Saint John of the Cross called this the dark night of
the Soul.

CYCLES OF LIFE

Life runs in cycles, up and down, similar to the
waves that flow onto the beach and run out again.
When life gets at its lowest, if you retain your faith
in Spirit and in God and learn how to work with
these divine laws that govern all creation, you will
find that eventually the cycle of life has to go back
up. What we are aiming for on the path of ECK is
not to avoid the roller-coaster effect of life, but to
gain the middle path. This means the path of mod-
eration, the balanced outlook, the spiritual viewpoint
that no matter what happens, the sorrows of life
will not bury us forever. When our loved ones leave
in death, we cry—but not forever. We are able to
face life knowing that our friend or father or mother will still live on in full consciousness. We know
that the divine cause, the Divine Being, has put us
here to learn something. It is up to us to go out into
life and find out what it is.

Sometimes as we go along the path of ECK, we
feel we have been forsaken by the Inner Master. We
think we aren't having any of the great inner experiences. It's more important that after you have tried
everything and haven't gotten anywhere in solving a
problem, you have the experience of suddenly seeing
a mysterious straightening and smoothing of the path.

We aim to gain the balanced outlook that no matter what happens, the sorrows of life will not bury us forever.

And then you can say, "I had a problem, but I was touched by the hand of God, and here is the solution."

SOLVING LIFE'S PROBLEMS

No matter what problems are taken away from us, we must remember these are the worlds of time and space. Unless you have learned the detached state, how to take life as it comes without letting it crush you, it can crush you. We are looking for the preservation and survival of Soul, not the physical body. Although we have records of spiritually evolved beings who live for centuries, most of us won't have that mission. Most of us wouldn't be strong enough to watch our close ones grow old while we stayed at the age of thirty.

So we are not looking for life eternal in the physical body, or the resurrection of a body which has died, hoping that someday we will be put together by some miraculous means and live forever in a reconstructed heaven on earth. Salvation isn't for the physical body; it's for Soul. Here and now, while in the physical body, we are already learning how to move into the heavens in full consciousness and come back alive.

And why would you want to do this? To gain power over the fear of death. When you have gained this power, there is nothing that can hold you back in this life. Problems become stepping-stones, not obstacles that trip you. At this point you become a divine being; you become like the revered masters of the sacred writings. The stories of their lives have become distorted through time and glorified by legends. They, too, once walked this earth as people like you and me, but they learned the laws of Spirit and how to apply them to solve their own problems. This is all that I can offer you.

When you gain power over the fear of death, there is nothing that can hold you back in this life.

I'm not offering you a life of spiritual healings that last forever, because they won't. I'm not offering you a life where prosperity will last forever. It may not. All I am offering you is a glimpse of the face of God and personal experience in the Light and Sound of this Divine Being.

It's a rewarding opportunity.

Experiment freely with the spiritual techniques found in the ECK books. Make these exercises fit you. The path must fit you, not the other way around. It has to suit you. When it does, when you have tailored a technique for yourself which can put you in contact with the inner forces, then you truly are one of the divine beings. It's a rewarding opportunity.

*Hawaiian Regional Seminar, Honolulu, Hawaii,
November 12, 1983*

The architect couldn't shake the feeling that something was wrong. This is a good example of how the ECK, or Divine Spirit, works to help you in your daily life.

9

A SECRET AGENT
FOR GOD

 secret agent for God is not so
much a being as it is a force or
power, Divine Spirit, and learning
how to work with It.

HELP FROM SPIRIT

One of the ECKists gave a good example of how
the ECK, or Divine Spirit, works to help you in your
daily life. He was an architect in business for himself,
with a staff of four or five people. With the constant
flow of work that came through the office, it was
important to make sure everyone thoroughly checked
the details of each project. Checking the details en-
sured that the building would turn out to be structur-
ally safe and wouldn't collapse sometime in the future.
Since the architect had to delegate many different
parts of the architectural design to those who worked
with him, it was not always possible for him to personally check everyone's calculations point by point.

You might think that in very detailed and
mathematical work such as architecture, there
wouldn't be much room for Spirit to help. But in
this particular instance, after a part of the project
had been completed by one of his associates, the

*You might think
that in work
such as
architecture,
there wouldn't
be much
room for Spirit
to help.*

ECKist had a feeling that something was wrong. He looked over the man's drawings that showed where the beams would be joined together in the building. They seemed all right.

Yet he couldn't shake the feeling that something was wrong, so he began to go over all the numbers very carefully. And as it turned out, his associate had worked everything out correctly right up until he came to the last detail. Then he had missed something: The beams would be stressed more than they could handle—an oversight which would have caused a future tragedy.

Spirit often works as a secret agent to help you during those times when you may not even suspect you need help. I worked in a printing office at one time and routinely had to delegate some of the work to others. A mistake in laying out a job for the press wouldn't have caused the roof to collapse, but it could have been quite expensive for the company. Even though it was impossible for me to double-check the details of each job, I could always feel when something was wrong. It was then just a matter of uncovering it. So I would start digging through the different parts of the work until the error was revealed.

There were also times, long after the job had passed from my area of responsibility, when I would walk to the pressroom and see the stack of printed copies. Without knowing the reason, I would break the stack and find a poorly printed copy. Then someone would go through and make a spot check, and often they wouldn't find any more errors than just on that single piece of paper.

Spirit doesn't work like this all the time—only when you have put forth your best effort, and when you stay open to It. You don't constantly say, Spirit, please help, because then you are placing the force, Spirit, outside of yourself. You are putting too much attention on this force as something that will

Spirit often works as a secret agent to help you during those times when you may not even suspect you need help.

take care of your personal responsibilities for you. So what happens? You end up shirking your own responsibility—your own Godhood.

This is why you are on the path of ECK: to earn your own Godhood. To learn how to work with this divine law of Spirit, which will help you whenever you are in trouble.

A Manifestation of the Spiritual Power

In the Bible, the book of Daniel tells the story of the four men in the fiery furnace. It took place during the Babylonian captivity when Nebuchadnezzar was the king of Babylon. In those days the Jewish people, by their ingenuity and good business sense, had moved up in the government and become very powerful in the kingdom.

Daniel became a trusted adviser to King Nebuchadnezzar. He alone correctly interpreted one of the king's dreams after the Chaldean magicians and astrologers had failed to give the proper symbology to it. The king rewarded Daniel by elevating him to a powerful station in the country, and Daniel, in turn, named his friends, Shadrach, Meshach, and Abednego, to high positions in the government.

The Chaldeans were so jealous that they devised a plan to get the Jewish people out of power. They suggested to King Nebuchadnezzar that the way he could insure his sovereignty was to make a golden image before which everyone would be required to bow down. The Chaldeans knew the Jews would never bow down to such an image. But the king, not knowing it was a setup to get some of his best people out of action, decided it was a good idea. So he set a date and time for the dedication of this image.

On that day, the herald shouted the king's commandment to the people: As soon as they heard the cornet, flute, and all the different kinds of musical instruments, everybody was to fall flat to the ground

The king, not knowing it was a setup to get some of his best people out of action, decided a golden image was a good idea.

and worship the golden image. Well, everyone did—except for Shadrach, Meshach, and Abednego. The Chaldeans pointed out to the king that because these men had shown him no respect or honor, they surely must be put to death. And so they were sentenced to be cast into the fiery furnace.

The furnace was so hot that even the king's soldiers, who had been assigned the duty of throwing the three men into the fire, were burned to death. After the three men fell into the furnace, bound in several layers of garments, the king looked on in astonishment. He asked his advisers, "Didn't we cast three men bound into the fire?" What he saw instead were four men loose, walking around unharmed in the fiery furnace.

You could call this fourth being an angel; but the story is an example of the spiritual power manifesting Itself in one of Its agents, whether angel or Master, to bring protection to the chosen people at a time when it was greatly needed. This is a dramatic illustration of how the protection comes, but there are less dramatic ways we can receive it.

It would be great if each of you would have direct experience with the Light and Sound of ECK, where you would actually see this Light. Sometimes It comes as a blue light; other times you can see It as orange, white, or yellow. It depends upon the level, or the heaven, or the state of consciousness, you are working from at that moment. This Light of God is the upliftment which comes to purify Soul, to burn out the impurities, to burn off the karma so that Soul can fly free.

This Light of God comes to purify Soul, to burn out the impurities, to burn off the karma so Soul can fly free.

PROTECTION WHEN NEEDED

An ECKist in New Zealand told me that he has experience with the Light and Sound of God, but it's not necessarily a regular occurrence. What really means the most to him, he said, is the help he gets with daily problems. This kind of help has actually saved him from a lot of trouble, a lot of pain, and probably even death.

One rainy evening he and his family were driving down the highway. The road was packed with traffic in both directions. All of a sudden he saw something in his path. Because he was driving fast, he had to slam on the brakes. It caused the car to go into a spin, cross over the median strip, and end up facing the oncoming traffic.

A moment earlier, he had seen endless rows of white headlights coming toward him. Strangely enough, now he saw none at all. Nor was there any traffic on the other side of the road. As soon as the car stopped spinning, he put it into gear, turned it around, and drove across the median strip to his side of the highway. He got the car straightened out and heading the right way, when suddenly he noticed the most peculiar thing: The road was once again packed with traffic moving in both directions.

He doesn't know what happened, but he clearly recognized that Spirit came in to give him protection when it was needed.

Putting Aside the Fear of Death

This is the kind of protection which comes to an ECKist. It isn't limited to those who are in Eckankar; there are many others who experience not only protection but enlightenment. The difference is that the ECKist has an idea of where it comes from and how to get it again.

An ECKist told me a story about how his parents viewed Eckankar; at one time they felt there was nothing to it. Both his mother and father believed it wasn't possible for Soul to be able to leave the body while one is still here in the flesh, or to gain a certainty that Soul survives beyond the physical body.

Many others experience not only protection but enlightenment. The difference is the ECKist has an idea of where it comes from and how to get it again.

Then, while she was hospitalized for a very serious illness, his mother had the experience of consciously being out of the body. She could see what was happening. She was taken through a tunnel of light and given the choice of whether to stay or go back. But her time hadn't come, so she returned to the body.

Her husband continued to express his disdain for the ECK teachings. He still would not accept the fact that some people had the ability to go beyond the physical body, to actually see what happens in the heavens and experience the joy, peace, and happiness that is lacking here on earth. But after this woman had experienced this for herself, she no longer disbelieved. One day while her husband was making fun of ECK, she said, "Be quiet. You don't know what you're talking about."

When she told her son about her hospital experience, it served another purpose too: It gave the son, who was an ECKist, the reassurance and comfort of knowing that the ECK Masters also work with people dear to him, even if these people are not on this spiritual path.

If we can learn to put aside the fear of death, we find a joyousness in this life which then helps us make a very natural step into our next life.

A nine-year-old girl said to her father, "There's something wrong with the story of God, the devil, and hell."

THE PURPOSE OF THE NEGATIVE POWER

Someone gave me an article which told the story of a nine-year-old girl who said to her father, "There's something wrong with the story of God, the devil, and hell."

"What do you mean?"

She said, "God loves good people, isn't that so?" Her father said yes. "And the devil favors the bad people, right?"

"That's right," said her father.

"And the good people that God loves go to heaven

and have all kinds of good things?"

"That's true," said her father.

"But the people who like the devil go to hell, and for their reward, the devil then punishes them by putting them in fire and eternal damnation."

"Yes, that's right."

She said, "That doesn't make any sense. If the devil wanted more followers, it would make more sense for him to treat those people who had served his purpose very nicely."

In her own way, the little girl had figured out that perhaps the devil was actually a secret agent for God, whose job is to test people in the principles of God and to find out if they understand them. She had more insight than a lot of the clergy who preach that Satan is a totally negative being who is somehow able to continue working in this world. If that were the case, you'd have to ask why God didn't just squash him like a bug. It's because Satan has a very useful purpose here, which is to put Soul through the tests and trials necessary for It to come into a realization of Its Godhood.

In her own way, the little girl had figured out that perhaps the devil was actually a secret agent for God.

The purpose of the negative power is to work as a part of the divine plan. The devil is of a negative nature but still working the purpose of God. When we have troubles, we like to put the blame on the devil or somebody else because it's an easy way out. Then we don't have to say, My words and actions have caused my own troubles.

Lai Tsi's Mission

Lai Tsi was an ECK Master who had studied religion in the schools of ancient China. He was one of the many monks who became a doctor of divinity. But at one point he came to understand that the realization of God could never be found in books. Instead, he found it in the solitude and stillness of nature.

Lai Tsi went off to a cave in the mountains up above the Yellow River in north central China. Up in the mountains he was visited by the ECK Master Tomo Geshig, one of the secret agents of a pure positive nature, who came to Lai Tsi in the Soul body for seven years before he saw him in the flesh. Lai Tsi's own Master was Yaubl Sacabi. These two ECK Masters, Yaubl Sacabi and Tomo Geshig, had been trained by Gopal Das in ancient Egypt several thousand years ago.

As Lai Tsi was readied, these ECK Masters led him into the God Worlds, heaven by heaven. There are many different levels of heaven. The Christian Bible refers to this when Jesus says, "In my father's house are many mansions" and where Saint Paul says he knew a man who had been caught up to the third heaven. And so the ECK Masters took Lai Tsi to these heavens and more.

Lai Tsi experienced the bliss and happiness which is the birthright of every Soul—of you and me.

One day, because Lai Tsi's love for God was so great, all the barriers of fear were removed, and he was taken into the Light of God. He was taken to the Anami Lok, where he saw the face of God. Here he experienced the bliss and happiness which is the birthright of every Soul—of you and me. There is nothing that prevents us from having this experience except ignorance. The Light of God eventually dispels the ignorance, and the Sound of God carries us home.

When Lai Tsi awoke on the cold floor back in the cave, he found that a lion had cooled his fevered brow and that the wild deer had snuggled up against his body to give him warmth. It now seemed as if all life, all nature, had the single-minded purpose of insuring his survival. And when he opened his eyes, he saw Tomo Geshig working in front of a roaring blaze, preparing food to nourish his body.

At this point, Lai Tsi had become the Living ECK Master. It's something one cannot talk about to anyone else. It's something no one else may recognize, except for the chosen few.

A sheepherder passing near the cave one day heard a sound like a lute. At first he thought it was one of the demons of the hills. He started to run away, but the beautiful music of the lute drew him closer. There he saw Lai Tsi sitting outside his cave. Seeing the Light of God shining from his face, the shepherd knew this was the Master who had been promised. He came nearer still; and when he had been touched, when he received the bliss of God, he went home and told the people, "The Master who has the secret of the true knowledge of God, the Light and Sound, is here among us." This is how the mission of Lai Tsi began so many years ago.

THE LIGHT OF GOD

Of the creative techniques we use today, we are most familiar with the Blue Light. This Blue Light of the MAHANTA, the highest state of consciousness known to man, usually comes during contemplation. It signifies the presence of the MAHANTA. It is not limited to the path of ECK; many people in other religions see It too, but they have no idea or understanding of the state of consciousness which has come to give them comfort of the heart, comfort of Soul, and healing of the body.

This Blue Light of the MAHANTA has come to give comfort of the heart, comfort of Soul, and healing of the body.

I have to explain that the white Light of God comes forth and carries the spectrum of all the different colors, including the blue light. Each color has its place and purpose. One of the sublights is the orange light, which is usually used for healing the physical body. The healing is for yourself, not for other people, because to direct or divert the stream of God in any way except to heal yourself is the misuse of a divine power. We never use these lights or this healing power on another individual without permission. And even with permission, we risk taking on the karma of that person.

Anyone who has reached a high state of unfoldment will never take on another person's karma,
but it is possible to perform karmaless action. One
way is to do everything in the name of God. Another way is to turn it over to an ECK Master who
has the ability to throw the problem into the ECK
Life Stream or, to put it another way, hand it over
to Divine Spirit in such a way that the karma has
no lasting effect on him. When the load is taken
on, there is a momentary dip in his health as he
passes it off. But he has learned the knack of passing it off as quickly as possible. Failure to do so
could destroy him and his physical body.

A TECHNIQUE FOR SELF-HEALING

*Visualize this
orange light
coming off
from the white
light and
flowing through
to the damaged
part or the
point of illness.*

Here is a spiritual exercise for self-healing: When
you have a physical ailment—the flu or something
of this nature—shut your eyes and chant *HU*, the
secret name of God. Visualize this orange light coming off from the white light and flowing through to
the damaged part or the point of illness. Just let it
flow through for twenty minutes. This is the regular length of time for contemplation in ECK. The
orange light is usually used for physical ailments
and any kind of physical problem.

The blue light is also a light of healing, but it
is usually used for the inner bodies—the Astral,
Causal, Mental, and Etheric. The Blue Light is also
how the MAHANTA, the highest consciousness, makes
Itself known in the lower worlds. Then as you go
further, you see the Light change to yellow and then
into the white light.

The blue light is used in a similar way for a
healing of the heart, healing of Soul, or the upliftment of consciousness. You shut your eyes and chant
HU. Put your attention at the Spiritual Eye, and

visualize this blue light flowing through you as a great wave. Not as a river, but as a great wave that flows through, purifying and uplifting you. Trust in Spirit to bring you whatever you need for your unfoldment.

I would like to thank you for your hospitality, your goodness, and for your love.

May the blessings be.

Visualize this blue light as a great wave purifying and uplifting you.

Hawaiian Regional Seminar, Honolulu, Hawaii, November 13, 1983

It is your parents' job to say, "You're going to a new school today, but remember the MAHANTA will always be with you."

10

A Special Message to the Youth in ECK

*I*t's late at night. Most of you in the Western hemisphere—North America and South America—are asleep. Those of you on the other side of the world are wide-awake. The Dream Master is working with some of you, and the Inner Master is working with all of you.

The Importance of the Spiritual Exercises

I would like to encourage you to do your spiritual exercises every evening before you go to sleep. You may have different ways of doing them. One way is to shut your eyes and chant *HU* or your secret word for about five minutes. Then just before you go to sleep, say to the MAHANTA, "It's OK to take me to the place where I can learn whatever is important for my spiritual unfoldment. Take me to a Temple of Golden Wisdom." Or say, "Let me see what it's like to Soul Travel; you have my permission."

Just before you go to sleep, say to the MAHANTA, "Let me see what it's like to Soul Travel; you have my permission."

Steps That Prepare Us for Life

When I was in the seventh grade, I made up my mind to leave the farm and go off to a boarding school in the city. I convinced my parents that there I would learn all the knowledge that could be given to me.

The real reason I wanted to go was that the school's information brochure included a picture of a brand-new swimming pool. As soon as I saw it, I thought, *Boy, would I like to go swimming in that pool!* So while my brothers stayed home and attended the local high school, I went off to learn all this great knowledge—and to go swimming in the pool.

I would pay dearly for this decision. But the ECK Masters were already working with me.

I would pay dearly for this decision. Once I got to the school, no matter how homesick and lonely I got, my parents made me stay there and follow through on my decision. If I'd had the choice to make over again, I would have stayed home and gone to school with the others. But the ECK Masters were already working with me. They knew just what it would take to get me to this particular school, which had a very high educational standard. There I could learn some of the things I would need to know for my future position as the Living ECK Master.

I didn't know this at the time, of course. I was just a kid going off to school, thinking I was going to have a great time in the swimming pool. As it turned out, I got to spend no more than three hours a week in the pool. The rest of the time I was in the classroom or the gym, studying in the dormitory, or performing duties that we were given to keep the campus clean.

WHY PERSONAL CLEANLINESS IS IMPORTANT

Very early on I learned that if I didn't bathe regularly and keep my clothes clean, other people wouldn't like me. I didn't know the word *karma* at the time, but I was still learning the lesson. Many times we make our own karma simply because we don't know how to take care of ourselves. This is true whether we're talking about our spiritual life or our physical life.

It is your parents' job to provide you with education that covers both the spiritual and physical areas. They're the ones who have to remind you to pick up your shirt or your blouse, put away your shoes, and pack your lunch for school tomorrow. They're also the ones who say, "Have you done your spiritual exercises? You're going to a new school today, but remember the Mahanta will always be with you. When you're afraid, put your attention on the Mahanta."

The school I attended didn't have washers and dryers where the students could just wash their clothes for a couple of quarters. There was a laundry service in the basement of one of the buildings, but very few students could afford it. The usual routine was to accumulate your dirty clothes, pack them in a box, and send them home to Mom every couple of weeks. Then you'd hope she would get the stuff back to you quickly, because you were soon out of clean clothes.

At the age of fourteen, I didn't have enough sense to just go to the sink and wash a few things by hand, even if I had to use bar soap instead of laundry detergent. It was embarrassing to admit that I didn't have as many clothes as the others. Our family didn't have much money, and my parents had sent me to the school on a shoestring. But I learned quickly that after wearing the same pair of socks for a week and a half, my five roommates didn't like me very much. And this caused trouble for me. I made a lot of bad karma for myself simply because I wasn't clean.

I learned quickly that after wearing the same pair of socks for a week and a half, my five roommates didn't like me much.

These are the kinds of things Soul learns while here in the lower worlds. You must do things in a certain way; otherwise you have to pay the price, you pay the karma. And if you walk around with dirty socks, no matter how much you do in the name of the Master, it still isn't going to make other people like you.

LIFE'S GOALS

You can fit into society while living the spiritual life of an ECKist.

I would like to encourage you to enjoy your youth. Sometimes you have to listen to your parents. It's their job to make sure that when you go out into the world, you can stand on your own feet and earn your own living. In this way, you can fit into society while living the spiritual life of an ECKist. You learn the lessons you need so that one day you, too, can become a Coworker with God and a member of the Order of Vairagi Adepts, the great ECK Masters.

Special Recording, January 9, 1984

Paul Twitchell continually tried, in a way that very few people ever do, to find spiritual enlightenment in all facets of his life.

11

THE STORY OF
PAUL TWITCHELL

aul Twitchell was a person who had
to go through experiences of all kinds
so that he would be fit to become the
MAHANTA, the Living ECK Master. To say
he had a checkered life is an understatement. In
many ways he was quite a rascal.

A CORRESPONDENCE TRAIL

In January I got to look at copies of some of the
letters Paul had written over the years. He was an
avid letter writer, and he always kept a carbon copy.
His correspondence was so diverse that there were
times I couldn't quite figure out if this was the real
Paul Twitchell or if it was one of his masks.

At one time Paul made his living by writing for
pulp magazines. He also wrote public-relations copy
during his stint in the US Navy. He was always
thinking, always writing.

Tracking Paul through his letters revealed a
unique, highly talented being. He sincerely cared
about spiritual unfoldment and growth. He went
through volumes of books on consciousness, a subject which was not in vogue in those days. In fact,

*Tracking Paul
through his
letters revealed
a unique, highly
talented being.*

it's barely in vogue today. But he loved it, and he thrived on the study of the different philosophies.

EARTHSHAKING EVENT

At the moment of Paul's past-life birth, a huge earth-quake rocked parts of the United States.

A couple of years ago I decided to research Paul's past life which he writes about in *The Drums of ECK*. In that life he was born on the Mississippi in 1811. At the moment of his birth, a huge earthquake rocked parts of the United States and formed Reel-foot Lake in northern Tennessee. The earthquake of 1811 came at a time when the world was in turmoil. Napoleon was marching across Europe to invade Russia, probably in much the same way that Hitler, in more recent history, marched across Europe. The world was turned upside down.

It was at this time in 1811 that a series of earthquakes hit the Midwest. But this one that formed Reelfoot Lake was actually the worst that ever occurred in the United States, far more severe than the San Francisco earthquake of 1906. It started in November, with tremors lasting through-out the month. More were felt in January and some even as late as March. They came in three main groups. The only reason there wasn't more loss of life or destruction of property was because it didn't happen in a heavily populated region.

It was during this time that Paul was born into his previous life. In *The Drums of ECK*, he tries to tell the story about his service in that lifetime. Even in his most recent life, he still had a great fascina-tion for the Civil War. He and his father used to have contests to challenge each other's knowledge about some bit of trivia—which regiment did this or that—and they would try to match names and dates and events.

There are several different versions of the date Paul was born into this life. One person I talked to said the Twitchell family Bible recorded the year as 1910; another person, who also told me he'd seen the family Bible, said Paul's birthdate was shown as 1908. It's amazing how certain each person was that he knew the truth. Each one claimed to have seen it with his own eyes. So by some accounts, he was born on October 23, 1908 or 1910, while other accounts give the date as October 22.

UNSCRAMBLING THE PIECES

Paul loved his privacy. Early in his youth he was involved in a variety of activities, but he made it a point to obscure any facts associated with his life. In so doing, he left a trail so clouded that it's going to take our historians years to piece it together.

It reminds me of the philosophy of the tax protesters. With taxes being so high today, they go to great lengths to conceal their income. They won't use credit cards and rarely open any bank accounts. In a way, they feel they can protest against the tax system by not participating in it. But, of course, they began to participate in it even before they had a voice in the matter—by way of a social security number.

A tax protester might reason that one way to obscure your record is to provide the computers with such a mishmash or volume of information that no one could keep up with it. You open a few bank accounts here and there, close one or transfer a little bit of the money to another, buy up stocks or property, take a loss on one, and reinvest in another. In a sense, this may have been Paul's philosophy in covering the trail of his life. He kept adding and changing so many things that it's taking a while to unscramble it and figure out who he really was.

And I was very curious about the man behind the MAHANTA, the Living ECK Master who came out in 1965.

Paul loved his privacy. He made it a point to obscure any facts associated with his life.

BASIC FACTS

Paul was quite athletic. He was short, of course—five-and-a-half-feet tall—with a very powerful upper physique. He was also rather bowlegged. Some people who didn't think so kindly of him joked that when he was walking down the street, you could almost run a billy goat between his legs.

It's hard to tell exactly when he graduated from high school. Back in the early 1930s, the record-keeping wasn't as accurate as it is today. Nowadays, if you follow the usual course of education, generally you will graduate from high school at the age of eighteen. But in those days high school was the way college is today—you could quit for a while and then go back. So Paul probably graduated from high school between age eighteen and age twenty-three.

His first jobs after he came out of high school were as a physical-education instructor. He started with positions in a couple of different towns through the YMCA. Around the same time, he was the director of municipal recreation in Paducah, Kentucky, which in the book *In My Soul I Am Free* is called China Point. There is no such town as China Point in Kentucky. He constructed the story to protect his family, so that later on, when people sought him out to learn about Eckankar, his family wouldn't be pestered by well-meaning people intruding in their lives.

HIS OWN DRUMBEATER

At the tender age of twenty-seven, he decided it was about time that he got his name in Kentucky's *Who's Who*. This is a publication which lists the accomplishments of all the renowned people in the state—lawyers, doctors, geologists, politicians, and people of this caliber. At twenty-seven years of age, the most Paul had ever done was teach physical education. But by the time he wrote it all up, exag-

At the tender age of twenty-seven, Paul decided it was about time that he got his name in Kentucky's Who's Who.

gerating and twisting the facts, he had worked up a nice little paragraph about all the grand achievements of one Paul Twitchell. He made it sound quite impressive. You can see why, after hours of reading so many dull entries, the editor of *Who's Who in Kentucky* thought Paul sounded pretty interesting. Without bothering to check out the dates or details, he probably said, Oh, why not—and Paul gets into *Who's Who in Kentucky* right along with the most distinguished leaders in the state.

This was followed by a lot of dark years for Paul. It is important to recognize that one who is in training for Mastership is a prototype for the initiates in ECK. When you say, "I have problems, I am crying, I am weary"—realize that Paul cried and grew weary too. In fact, there were times when his burdens seemed so heavy that he didn't know how he could get up and face another day.

When you say, "I have problems, I am crying, I am weary"—realize that Paul cried and grew weary too.

Starting as early as the 1930s, Paul was his own best drumbeater. Anytime he did something, he would write an avalanche of press releases about it. He promoted himself all the time. When he was ready to go into the Navy, he wrote up a blurb about how Paul Twitchell has just finished basic training, and now he's ready to go off to war. He sent it to the newspapers in Kentucky, to the local librarian, here and there. As if anybody cared at the time. But without realizing it, he was just practicing. Someday he would have a chance to take this teaching called Eckankar—maybe he didn't even know the name then—and put it in front of people.

I saw an article in the obituary column in one of the West Coast newspapers a few weeks ago about a seventy-seven-year-old lady who had founded a certain church many years ago. But who ever heard of it? This talent of self-promotion was necessary for Paul's mission.

Paul was preparing for when he would use his talents to promote his books and articles on Eckankar.

The ECK teachings have been here from the earliest times, but they haven't carried the name of Eckankar. They have been brought out under different names at different times because they could not be presented openly, but at this point in history they can. So Paul was advertising himself in any way he could and, in general, preparing for the future when he would use his talents to promote his books and articles on Eckankar.

EARLY COMMITMENTS

In about 1942, during World War II, two major events took place in Paul's life. He got married to a woman named Camille Ballowe, and he enlisted in the Navy. For some reason he never got assigned to combat duty. When his Navy bosses discovered his gift with words, they put him into public relations.

There are several photographs of Paul with prominent people. In one he's with Pat O'Brien, who was a famous actor; and in others he's posing with Franklin Delano Roosevelt and General Eisenhower. There was more substance to Paul than appears in the current superficial writings about him by people who don't quite understand that he had something special.

He and Camille were married in Providence, Rhode Island, in 1942. When he got out of the Navy in 1945, they moved to New York. Paul wandered around a bit and eventually took a job with the Navy as the Washington, DC, correspondent for *Our Navy* magazine. He kept copies of a lot of letters written from Washington, DC, or the Washington Press Club, so we know he worked there for quite a while.

Paul became interested in occult teachings around 1950. About this time he hooked up with Swami Premananda, who headed the Self-Revelation Church of Absolute Monism in Washington, DC. Paul and his wife lived in the ashram on church property for quite some time.

THE CLIFF HANGER

In 1955, two more striking events happened in his life. He was kicked out of the ashram for some kind of misbehavior, and he separated from his wife. On July 4, while Paul was in the kitchen of the swami's church, he got into a fistfight with one of the other church members. Paul used to work out with weights and was a very strong person, but the other guy was just too big for him.

The fistfight started in the kitchen of the church, moved through the screen door, and ended up out in the backyard. Being the smaller of the two, Paul could only try to defend himself. He attempted to run for the back porch of the parsonage, where he hoped to find some help, but the other fellow caught up with him. The fight resulted in a permanent injury to Paul's right eye, as well as a broken rib and general bodily damage. He was in such bad shape that some friends put him in a car and drove him down to Florida, where it took him several weeks to heal. It was during this time that he got kicked out of the swami's church.

Paul was a feisty person. He called himself a Cliff Hanger. This evokes an image of a man hanging on to the side of a cliff, high above the swarming masses who are lost in the drudgery of day-to-day living. The Cliff Hanger could feel the wind and be close to the eagles—but he'd better not let go. This was Paul.

At that time he ran into Kirpal Singh, who was in charge of the Ruhani Satsang. Paul said there were many Masters who taught him. We sometimes like to think that truth is isolated, that it comes all by itself, that it has never appeared anywhere else in the world, and that it has never touched shoulders

High above the swarming masses, the Cliff Hanger could feel the wind and be close to the eagles—but he'd better not let go. This was Paul.

with anything else at any time. But truth builds
upon itself; it always has. In the old days, the scribes
in the monasteries would say, This is wisdom, this
is truth. And they would take the truth they found
and use it as a springboard to go even further.

TOUCHING THE FACE OF GOD

If he touched the face of God in 1956, some people may wonder why it took him until 1965 to become the MAHANTA, the Living ECK Master.

In late 1956 or early 1957, Paul had the experience that is recorded in *The Tiger's Fang.* If he
touched the face of God in 1956, some people may
wonder why it took him until 1965 to become the
MAHANTA, the Living ECK Master. It's really quite
simple. Your habits and emotions have been built
up over the years, and although your consciousness
has gone far ahead, the emotions feel lonely. You
feel truly left out. If Paul ever felt left out before,
he must have really felt it after this experience.
Even at the point when he had experienced God-
Realization, as he returned from the inner planes,
one of the ECK Masters said to Rebazar Tarzs,
Paul's teacher, "I see he still has much to learn."

Paul cared deeply about spiritual enlightenment.
He continually tried, in a way that very few people
ever do, to find spiritual enlightenment in all facets
of his life. And finally it came to him. But when
you touch the hem of God's garment, you are never
the same again. One of the biggest changes you find
when you come back to the physical consciousness
is that you are the only awakened individual in a
world of sleeping people.

During these years, Paul Twitchell came in
contact with Scientology and L. Ron Hubbard. They
knew each other, and Paul learned a lot from him.
Strange as it may seem, even as late as 1961 Paul
was still trying to find a shelter and a haven here
on earth. On the one hand, he had had the great
experience of God-Realization; on the other hand,
he was still trying to get baptized into the Catholic

Church—but the priest wouldn't allow it because of his separation from his wife. Paul got outraged and wrote him a blistering letter. Later he concluded that although the priests of the church are knowledgeable and intellectual, they certainly aren't enlightened. Paul had his own view of enlightenment, and it was broader than that of the church.

It's important that you know who Paul Twitchell was. There are things we have to look at. We are initiates on the path of ECK, and as it says in *The Shariyat-Ki-Sugmad*, it's never the written works which are important. It's always the Light and Sound.

THE LIVING SHARIYAT

Anything in the material worlds is fallible and subject to error. *The Shariyat* is merely a translation. Paul even explained that the Shariyat-Ki-Sugmad comes out in many different ways. With a certain person as the vehicle or instrument, it comes out as poetry; with someone else, it comes out as parables and stories; and for another person it comes out largely as prose.

The Shariyat-Ki-Sugmad is gathered by the Nine Silent Ones. It is drawn from the experiences of the initiates as they go through the lower worlds and meet the hardships in life—as Paul did and as we do. As we meet these experiences, there is always something to be learned.

The Shariyat-Ki-Sugmad is drawn from the experiences of the initiates as they go through the lower worlds and meet the hardships in life—as Paul did and as we do.

It reminds me of a story about El Paso, which is in West Texas. One day a young man moved to town during a dry spell. It's nearly always dry, but when it does rain, it's constant. For weeks there isn't any rain, but when the rain finally starts falling, it won't stop. It just floods everything.

The newcomer commented on this to an old man who had lived there for many years. The old man, who usually couldn't put two and two together, came up with an interesting statement which may have reflected the sum total of his observations in life. He said, "I spend 75 percent of my life praying for rain and the other 25 percent praying for it to stop." This old man's viewpoint displays a certain degree of wisdom.

The ECK Masters and the Nine Silent Ones gather a statement such as this out of each person's life. Some people have more than one statement; some people have chapters of statements. These are distilled and put together, and they become the teachings in the books of the Shariyat-Ki-Sugmad, which are always being written. They are not yet finished.

I would like to leave you with this: As you do your contemplative exercises tonight, look to the Inner Master. Chant your secret word, or chant *HU*, and in the spirit of love and a desire to know truth and to know the SUGMAD, say, "Teach me Thy ways, O SUGMAD."

May the blessings be.

Chant HU, and in the spirit of love and a desire to know truth and to know the SUGMAD, say, "Teach me Thy ways, O SUGMAD."

ECKANKAR International Youth Conference, Las Vegas, Nevada, Friday, April 20, 1984

I was looking at source manuscripts in a library in the inner planes, when I saw Paul, busy as usual, researching and writing.

12

THE WRITING OF
PAUL TWITCHELL

*A*t one time there were three little boys named Matt in our neighborhood. To make it easier to tell which one you were talking about, they were given nicknames: Little Matt, Middle Matt, and Big Matt. When Middle Matt's friend Little Matt moved away, Middle Matt didn't have anyone to pal around with.

REAL COMMUNICATION

One afternoon I was at home, working in my office upstairs, when the doorbell rang. The day had gone by so fast that I was wondering how I'd ever get my work finished. I wasn't thrilled at having to go downstairs and answer the door. When I opened it, there stood Middle Matt.

He asked if my daughter could come out and play, and I said no, that she was still at school. He said, "When will she be home?"

I looked at him and tried to put myself in his shoes. What does time mean to him? I gave it a try: "She'll be home in two hours."

He just stared at me for a moment. Then he said, "I'm only four and a half years old."

I looked at Middle Matt and tried to put myself in his shoes. What does time mean to him?

151

In that simple way he was saying, Why don't you tell it to me in a way I can understand?

I still didn't know what to say, but he gave me a clue. "Is it before I eat?" It was the middle of the afternoon, and I wondered if he normally got an afternoon snack. But then I figured he probably wouldn't get fed until dinnertime. Finally I said, "She'll be home right before you eat dinner." He looked so disappointed. "That's a long time," he said.

The way my day had been going, two hours had passed in what seemed like ten minutes. Yet for him it would seem to take all day. "Yes," I said, "I guess it is." He turned and headed slowly back to his house, probably wondering how he was going to get through that long desert of an afternoon.

This is how it is when we speak with each other. Although we know what we mean, we don't know how other people think or what's important to them. Often we look for ways to communicate with and understand each other. The point to this story ties in with the writing of Paul Twitchell.

A LIVING HISTORY

We've been busy interviewing some of the people who knew Paul personally. The purpose is to compile a living history which will provide valuable information to historians of the future. In a hundred years, people are going to be able to say, "This was the foundation of Eckankar." It will answer a lot of questions about how the ECKists of our time thought and felt, how they got through all the different changes which shook the very foundations of ECK— and who got through it and who didn't.

The one thing every single person remembered the most was the great love Paul had for others.

The one thing every single person remembered the most was the great love Paul had for others. It was described as an overwhelming love, and it touched other people. He showed kindness and consideration for even the smallest concerns of others.

One person told of an instance that took place at a seminar in Chicago in the late sixties. Large groups of youths had come to the seminar by hitch-hiking or whatever means they could. When Paul heard about this, he very privately told one of the initiates, "Whatever it takes, just don't let them sleep outside." It was cold outside, and he said, "Make sure they don't have to sleep in the cars." Paul had slept in cars himself when he didn't have enough money, and he knew how uncomfortable it was.

He was such an individualist that when he tried to make a living working for someone else, he generally aggravated his bosses and got himself fired. He found it difficult to make himself fit into this society and to the state of consciousness that was prevalent at the time. Often he barely had enough money to live on.

STRUGGLE FOR MASTERSHIP

It's important for us to know that someone like Paul, who reaches the heights of spiritual attainment in this lifetime, doesn't get there the easy way. We somehow knew and felt the great compassion he showed as the MAHANTA, but so little has been said about him that we never knew what trials he had to go through before this could develop. I've read letters in which he openly admitted, over and over again, his selfishness and how he had hurt people.

About two years after he separated from his wife, Camille, he had the experience that he later wrote down in *The Tiger's Fang*. This experience came in late 1956 or early 1957. From the time he and his wife actually separated until about 1963, when he met Gail, Paul tried to find another person with whom he could share his life. He knew he had a mission, and he knew he needed someone to help

Someone like Paul, who reaches the heights of spiritual attainment in this lifetime, doesn't get there the easy way.

him with it. He dated a number of different women, but it was a rocky road he traveled.

As late as 1961, the breakup of one of his relationships so distressed him that he spent every night for the better part of a week in church, praying for forgiveness. And this was after he'd had the experience recorded in *The Tiger's Fang*.

One might think that the instant he had experienced God Consciousness, he could have risen above the human emotions. This is one of the popular myths that has been put upon people by those who don't know any better. When the God Consciousness comes in, it does not immediately dissolve all the habits that have developed over a number of years. Instead, the ECK gradually begins to move the person into circumstances which are best to allow him to grow. It's usually done under great protest. We don't like it. I called my first book *The Wind of Change*, which refers to the ECK; and when the change comes, we resist. We fight it. This is true whether one has the God Consciousness or whether he has the initiation of the First Circle, which comes in the dream state.

For a few years Paul was a member of Swami Premananda's church in Washington, DC. When that association ended, he came in contact with the works of Kirpal Singh, who was based in India at the time. Paul had some experiences in which Kirpal Singh came to him in his room. They began to correspond. When Paul wrote to tell Kirpal Singh about the series of discourses he was working on, Kirpal Singh replied: "Let's see what you have. Perhaps we can use them."

Paul was a prolific writer. Kirpal Singh was very interested in Paul's account of his experience in *The Tiger's Fang*, and he even offered suggestions. He said, "When you talk with these Masters, ask them questions like, 'What is the process of death? How did the creation of the worlds come about'" It was interesting that Kirpal Singh knew Paul had the ability to go into the other worlds, come back, and report on certain things.

Kirpal Singh told several of his close followers that his line of mastership would end with him, and that the mastership would then be picked up in one of the Western countries. But I sincerely wonder if he recognized Paul, a former chela, as being the carrier of this Light and Sound of ECK.

Paul sent his manuscript of *The Tiger's Fang* to Kirpal Singh in India, which triggered a series of letters back and forth. It caused a very disagreeable situation when Paul wanted the manuscript back later. Paul had admired Kirpal Singh for a long time, but then they had this little falling out. Perhaps they worked it out later.

In about 1961, Paul's father translated. Paul had just moved from Washington, DC, to the West Coast. At the time of his father's passing in Kentucky, he was not able to be there. He later wrote a letter to the person who had been taking care of his father. He said, "I was in the hospital for some tests, and I simply wasn't able to get there. But I wanted you to know that at the moment it happened, I was lying on my couch when all of a sudden my father appeared in the room. It looked as if he was standing there in the flesh."

When Paul got up to go over and greet him, his father just faded away. This was his way of letting his son know that he had left the physical body. Paul looked at the clock on the mantle and noted the time.

It was an indication of Paul's closeness with his father and of his ability to move out of the body and see and know things beyond the perceptions of the physical senses. It was something his relatives never recognized in him.

Paul sent his manuscript of The Tiger's Fang to Kirpal Singh in India, which triggered a series of letters back and forth.

BEGINNINGS OF ECKANKAR

Paul got into his early efforts to present the teachings of ECK even before he called them *ECK* and *Eckankar*. He started with weekly lectures to small groups of fifteen to thirty people at the California Parapsychology Foundation in Southern California. In those days he referred to Soul Travel as bilocation, and it was explained as a way to reach the Supreme Oneness. He was trying to express the SUGMAD, the Supreme Being, and that the way to It was through the Voice of God, which we know as ECK.

The people were very enthusiastic. They liked his lectures, and as he worked with them, some had success in going out of the body. But Paul ran into problems. Just when everything was going very well, two things happened.

First of all, the people in his audience noticed that Paul would try to put them to work, and they felt uncomfortable about it. He had a message, and it worked. It was to show people how to make contact with this mysterious force—which many could observe but very few could really tap into—and learn how to become clear vehicles for this ECK power. So after he showed them how to go out of the body, he would then ask them to set up other meetings for him. Paul had very little money at the time, so if they could meet the expenses, he would go and conduct a workshop. But he found that the people were reluctant to help in this way.

Secondly, when Kirpal Singh found out about Paul doing these Soul Travel workshops, he wrote a letter to the Parapsychology Foundation and informed them that Paul's works were a lot like his own. But Kirpal Singh never mentioned that he, too, had picked them up from someone before him. In a way, he was trying to possess truth. But truth

People were very enthusiastic. But just when everything was going very well, two things happened.

builds upon itself. Kirpal Singh had gathered it from other groups, Paul had taken it and built upon it from many different areas, and he then moved it more than a step further. More than just identifying the mysterious force—which he later called the ECK—that works through all the God Worlds, Paul said, "I also know how to begin working with It."

Paul had figured out the key—how to teach others to become Coworkers with God.

He had figured out the key—how to teach others to become Coworkers with God. This was the major difference between Paul and many of the other teachers. Paul had the ability to work as the Inner Master. Kirpal Singh also did to his chelas, and there are many other teachers who can do the same thing. Each teacher can take his chelas to the level at which he has established himself. Paul began here and went much further.

EARLY BOOKS AND DISCOURSES

In the early years of Eckankar, Paul didn't have enough up-front money to get the new books printed. He couldn't afford to go to the printer and say, Here's the manuscript; go ahead and get it ready for press. Print it, and we'll pay for it upon delivery. To earn the money to pay the printer, he decided to make some of the early books available by subscription. He would write chapter 1 of *The Spiritual Notebook*, and then he'd send out a notice to the ECK chelas. Those who placed an order would receive the book in serialized form, run off on the copier right from the manuscript. He did the same thing with *The Shariyat-Ki-Sugmad*, Book One and, later, Book Two.

A very curious comment was included toward the back of the original version of *The Shariyat-Ki-Sugmad*, Book Two. It said the MAHANTA reappears to renew and wage battle against the Kal and to lead Soul out of the lower worlds, and this occurs every five to a thousand years. This was very heartening to me because it meant that in my lifetime,

I, too, would have the opportunity to reach this step of Mastership.

Later, as these serialized chapters were put into books and reprinted, a proofreader or someone else changed the "five to a thousand years" to the impossibly high range of "five hundred to a thousand years." The incorrect version of the sentence was printed in *The Shariyat-Ki-Sugmad*, Book Two, for a number of years.

Earlier this year, for the first time, I was able to read some of the letters that Paul had written, and also see carbon copies of the manuscripts that he had typed. That's when it occurred to me that I could check this sentence on the carbon copy of the original manuscript.

In those days you used nothing but a typewriter. There were no IBM Selectrics with the correcting feature, nor were there yet any word processors where you could correct words right on the screen. Paul would type along as accurately as he could, then all of a sudden there would be xxxxx. Or sometimes there would be a slash mark between words where he would insert something in the space above.

In the manuscript for *The Shariyat-Ki-Sugmad*, Book Two, he had typed, "reappears every thousand years" and then, with a little slash mark, he careted in "five to a" thousand years. This copy conforms to the serialized version that he sent out. Some Higher Initiates might still have a copy at home. This is an important point for those who are studying on the path of ECK.

A very significant event in Paul's spiritual evolution took place in the summer of 1970.

PAUL'S LAST YEAR

A very significant event in Paul's spiritual evolution took place in the summer of 1970. During a trip to Spain, he was poisoned. A young man, under the influence of the Kal Niranjan, slipped an extremely potent poison into Paul's citrus drink. Paul

had walked into this individual's home with complete
openness and an abounding love, and when he was
handed the juice, he drank it. But he knew it would
harm him, in the same way that Buddha did when
he ate the tainted rice.

The damage to Paul's body was severe. The doctor who treated him said he consumed enough of
this poison to kill three horses. But Paul went on
for another year before he dropped the body. Some
of the initiates who knew Paul very well said that
while the MAHANTA, the Living ECK Master went
to Spain, only the MAHANTA came home. Though this
was not accurate, it expressed the spirit of what
they were trying to say.

*Paul continued
to push
himself so he
could write the
things that had
to be said.*

Paul's body had taken such a beating that he
was barely able to keep it going, yet he continued
to push himself so that he could write the things
that had to be said. There were days his body actually looked black, and other days when it would
suddenly glow with a pink countenance, just like a
child's. Some days he was able to restore the body's
vitality, while other days he was close to death. He
would periodically drink a special concoction, probably made of extra vitamins and herbs, so that he
could carry on. He sought no personal gain from
this struggle; he had no personal motive.

MASTER COMPILER

The high teachings of ECK had been scattered
to the four corners of the world. The different masters each had parts and pieces of it, but they attached little requirements, or strings, to it: You must
be a vegetarian, or you have to meditate so many
hours a day if you want to really be a true follower on the path to God. And this was wrong for
our day and age. It was geared for another culture.

Paul gathered up the whole teaching and took
the best. Though it may be a strange thing to say,

in this sense I see him as a master compiler. He gathered the golden teachings that were scattered around the world and made them readily available to us. So now we don't have to feel that we must spend ten or fifteen years in an ashram in India, sitting around in the dust with the flies, or locked in a walled-up little cell to keep our attention from the outside world, in order to live the spiritual life.

The consciousness here in this century is a valid one. We have a family, we go to work, we have recreational activities, we meet with friends after work, and we take the kids to Little League practice. This is the way of our society, and it's a valid consciousness for Soul to gain the experience It needs on Its way back home to God.

The way of our society is a valid consciousness for Soul to gain the experience It needs on Its way back home to God.

All It needs is the linkup with the Light and Sound; and this, of course, always comes through the ECK teachings, through the MAHANTA, the Living ECK Master. It always comes in this way.

As I was trying to write something about the earthquake of 1811, I read a book about life on the Mississippi. It was a compilation of a series of essays written by a number of people and edited by one man. But I wasn't able to find out who owned the rights to it. No one knew, because as a book gets older, publishing houses are sold, management changes, and records are lost or thrown out. This is only one of many problems encountered in doing research.

It should have taken more than a lifetime for Paul to gather the ECK teachings, and yet he put it all together. This is what Paul did.

THE REAL FOUNDATION

Paradoxical as it may seem, my point in bringing out all of this has been to strengthen your faith in the MAHANTA—but not at the expense of making a god out of the MAHANTA's vehicle, which is the Living ECK Master. It's a price we cannot afford to pay. As soon as we set someone above us, in potential or in fact, we have committed a crime against ourselves: We have limited the opportunity for our own unfoldment.

We recognize that there are some people who have unfolded more; but Soul, in quality, is Soul. The difference in consciousness is the difference in unfoldment. It doesn't make one person bigger or another person smaller—as Soul.

Sometimes we've wondered, *Where really is the foundation of ECK for me?* And I'm telling you, it's not in the physical writings. It's always within, with the Light and Sound.

The writings inspire us. They give us words we can understand, but they never replace living the life of ECK. It doesn't work that way. The books are good, the discourses are good; they inspire, they give us enthusiasm, they show us how to meet the Inner Master as the Blue Light of the MAHANTA. But by themselves, they are imperfect translations written in an imperfect world.

Paul encouraged people to read *The Shariyat-Ki-Sugmad* and make their own study. He never said to take the words as holy, as the last word. You take the words and check out the teachings from within: Does this work for me or doesn't it? You have to know. And based upon what you know is how you conduct your life out here. This is what governs your relationship with your friends and your family. It governs every aspect of you in the lower worlds, including your ethics and morality.

You take the words and check out the teachings from within: Does this work for me or doesn't it? You have to know.

Ethics and morality will be different for each one of you. But I do expect more from the leaders of ECK when they're out in public. Whatever you do in private, it's your life. But when you go out in public as an ECK leader, you should epitomize the highest points of these golden teachings of ECK.

DEATH OF AN IDEAL

And so we have, perhaps, the death of an ideal. This means that no longer can we make a god out of a man. It was never intended. Many of us haven't done this, but some of us have.

Elisabeth Kübler-Ross made a study of the cycles or stages a person goes through when he finds he has a terminal illness. These are the same five stages one goes through at the breakup of a relationship or the loss of a job. They affect some people very strongly, while for others, the same five steps come as just a very soft, gentle touch.

The first feeling that comes at the death of an ideal is denial: Tell me it ain't so. The second stage is anger. In the third stage, a person wants to bargain: Maybe we can mediate this—isn't there a way it can be worked out? Next comes depression, and finally, acceptance.

These phases can take place over a period of months; you may go back and forth between the different stages. You may fluctuate between the second and third for a while, and then go into the fourth and come back to the first. The second time you'll get out of the first stage more quickly than you did the first time. And the way you get out is by chanting your word and doing the spiritual exercises.

The planes of God are not stacked up like pancakes on a plate at breakfast.

This is similar to the way it works in the planes of God. The planes of God are not stacked up like pancakes on a plate at breakfast. This is how we illustrate them graphically in the God Worlds chart, but only because it's a convenient way to establish them in our mind.

ANOTHER WAY TO USE YOUR WORD

The Astral Plane has over 150 regions. There are many different words for the Astral Plane that can be used in conjunction with the word you get at the

Second Initiation. You can start working with these words in your spiritual exercises. Using your word for the Second Initiation to bring you to the Astral Plane, you just accept that you are here—even though you may not see or know anything at the time. From here, start chanting another word of God. It can be a word such as *Mearp*, which is found in *The ECK-Vidya, Ancient Science of Prophecy*, or some other word.

Start by chanting your secret word or the ECK word of a plane, and then add another word in conjunction with it. If you want to look at a past life, for instance, start chanting the word for the Causal Plane. Work at this: Try it out for a week or two. If it doesn't work, then try some other word. Keep trying, but in a gentle way. Don't force it. Assume the attitude that someday you know this is going to work—and you just keep trying.

This is another way to use your word. For some initiates, using your word when you first have an initiation will bring many grand and glorious experiences. For others it won't. This word opens you only to a room, such as the one we're in. But as you get established on the plane of your initiation, you begin chanting another word, perhaps for the Mental Plane, or one of the words that you find in *The ECK-Vidya, Ancient Science of Prophecy* or an Eckankar dictionary. It's a password that will get you through one of the doors. When you get there, the guardian of the door says, "Yes?" Then you chant or say this word to him, and he lets you into the hallway. From there you enter into another room—a whole new dimension.

FINDING TRUTH

Begin by working with the creative element that you, yourself, are; because Soul, the creative spark, is the divine aspect that reflects the SUGMAD. It's that simple. Begin working with this God power

The guardian of the door says, "Yes?" Then you chant or say this word, and he lets you enter another room—a whole new dimension.

within you. I can only show you how to do it; you are the one who has to develop it and work with it.

This is how you find out for yourself what is truth. You're going to hear so many different versions of what is truth and what is not that finally you can't believe anyone. This is good, because it puts the responsibility back upon you to learn how to get the answer for yourself. Otherwise, you're just going to have to take someone else's word for it—and this is not a position you want to be in as a person who's looking for spiritual freedom.

You're looking for God-Realization, and with this come the attributes of God: wisdom, power, and freedom. But you don't look for the attributes, because when you have the state of God Consciousness, these attributes come with it, as part of the package.

THE INNER-PLANE LIBRARY SYSTEM

I'd like to conclude by mentioning how the libraries on the inner planes work. On these planes there are main libraries connected to the Wisdom Temples. But there are also many branch libraries. The main library of each Wisdom Temple is like the Library of Congress, providing the greatest source of all the books and materials. One particular library I was visiting on the Astral Plane is adjacent to the Temple of Askleposis. In this place, some of the writings of the Shariyat, which then are brought here to the physical and translated, are stored in an archival warehouse. The Astral Plane is an immense world, so the writings are stored in huge rooms.

The Astral Plane is an immense world, so the writings are stored in huge rooms.

Back in this archival storeroom are the library staff. These are people who work quickly and efficiently and know exactly what they're doing. They're quite cheerful as they move here and there, going about their business, compiling things, doing this and that.

In the back room is a metal contraption that has huge sheets laid on it. The stacks of paper look like computer printouts, but these sheets are many times larger than we are used to seeing on earth. These are unprocessed manuscripts—source manuscripts from which writers of the earth world and other places come and take material. The sheets feed up on a sprocket, then run off onto racks that go down the long aisles of the warehouse, carried along on little tracks. If you want to see a certain section, you press a button, and the sheets slowly run forward so you can read them.

There are very few writers who can come to this library. Most of the writers from earth go to the branch libraries, so they don't get to use the best sources. But the good researchers—such as Paul, Julian Johnson, Paul Brunton, and others—can come in here and select the paragraphs that suit their audience. A certain key concept will be expressed, such as a certain aspect of spiritual liberation. Then this one idea is written in eight different paragraphs, reflecting eight different levels of consciousness.

A key concept, such as spiritual liberation, is written in eight different paragraphs, reflecting eight different levels of consciousness.

In the margin next to the different paragraphs on the manuscript I was reading were notes written in Paul's hand: "Far Country," "Shariyat-Ki-Sugmad, Book One," "Shariyat, Book Two," "Spiritual Notebook," and again "Far Country," and so on. Under his notes a librarian researcher had placed the specific page reference where these ideas could be found in the current manuscripts.

For some reason, these sheets had carbons—they were in sets of four copies. In order to study it further, I loaded this manuscript stack on a handy little cart and took it to another area. Here it was again placed on a sprocket and stretched out in different directions so that you could separate the four copies and walk between them. Then you'd take one off and load it on another sprocket, where it would wind itself up. The manuscript was just in rough form. Later the researchers would compile it into a form that was easier to work with. This may sound complicated, but they really do have a sophisticated system. They're quite a bit ahead of us.

I'm doing all this research in a soundproof booth so it doesn't disturb the other people who are doing research. As I look over at a table, I see Paul—busy as usual, researching and writing. He looks at me and says, kind of gruffly, "What's that?"

"Source manuscripts," I say.

"For what?" he asks.

"For a lot of the ECK writings to be done on earth," I reply.

"Oh," he says. "Well, we'll have to do something about that someday." Then he picks up his notebook and leaves, heading out into the stacks.

Yeah, I thought to myself, *and I know who is going to have to do something about that someday!*

ECKANKAR International Youth Conference, Las Vegas, Nevada, Saturday, April 21, 1984

I thought to myself, I know who is going to have to do something about that someday!

It's like rising in a hot-air balloon: The higher you go, the more you can see. And the more you can see, the better you are able to arrange your life.

13

THE INITIATIONS
IN ECK

few weeks ago, someone happened to ask, "If the ECK initiations started in 1965, where does that leave the people before 1965? How important are the initiations in that respect?"

This is the kind of question that takes more than two or three minutes to answer. It's similar to the question the Christian church ran into when they decreed that you must be baptized to go to heaven. This sounds like a very simple statement until someone asks, "What about those who were born in the centuries before baptisms were given? What about all the people in India and China who don't practice Christianity?" Well, what about them?

The church had to come up with a way to explain this, so they said things like, "God's grace is sufficient unto them." That's fine, but the teachings state that if you are not baptized, you go to hell. And yet for many years there were very few people who got baptized. It's a sticky problem for the church. They don't quite know what to do with it, especially since they teach that you live only one lifetime. It's all or nothing: You either make it this time, or you don't. Feathers or fire.

Baptism is a sticky problem for the church, especially since they teach that you live only one lifetime.

169

ARE INITIATIONS IMPORTANT?

How important are the ECK initiations? They are very important. The initiations take Soul step-by-step through different grades of enlightenment into the higher levels of consciousness where It can have God-Realization. It can touch the face of God. This is the function of the initiations in ECK.

Even before 1965, Rebazar Tarzs was initiating one or two or three or four people here and there. Maybe a hundred or five hundred as he moved around.

Without the initiations that take you beyond the Astral world, what happens when Soul leaves the physical body? It does a round-trip shuttle run between the Physical Plane and the Astral Plane. Every so often It may go to the Mental Plane or the Causal, but mostly it's between the Physical and Astral. Sometimes Soul will eventually start working Its way up just a little bit, and then it's Astral, Causal; Astral, Causal.

The ECK initiations are important because they take people farther than they've ever been before.

The ECK initiations are important because they take people farther than they've ever been before. Unless you have the ECK initiations, you rarely have experience beyond the worlds you already know. You travel along the Wheel of the Eighty-Four, reincarnating from the Astral Plane, again and again.

The initiations help you expand the loop and take in another plane and then another, until you come to the Fifth Initiation, at which point you no longer have to run the loop.

Now you have a choice. If you want to take a one-way trip to the Soul Plane and stay, you can. Or if you want to serve the SUGMAD by coming back to the lower worlds, you may take a round-trip from up there. Once you reach the Fifth Plane, you come back if you choose to, but you're not stuck in the lower worlds. And you're going to be an unusual person. Others are going to know it, and they may resent you for it, because they can tell there's a difference.

WHAT HAPPENS DURING AN INITIATION

Interesting things happen during an ECK initiation. The Second Initiation which Paul gave me was sort of a combination initiation-consultation. I nervously entered the room, and after we talked for a while, he started the initiation. I shut my eyes, tried to relax, and chanted the word he had given me. But for some reason, it seemed as though Paul couldn't sit still. I heard him get up and walk toward the door to the next suite. I was having enough of a problem controlling my thoughts as it was, and there's Paul running around the room. To make it even worse, when he opened the door, I could hear a bunch of people laughing in the other room.

But I just kept sitting there with my eyes closed. After a while he came back and said, "Well, that's enough. Did you see anything?" I had, but because I didn't know what to expect from Paul at an initiation, I was cautious, still playing my cards close. "No," I said. "I didn't see anything." And then I went home.

Later the ECK started working on me; my slow lower mind began to catch up with the enlightenment that comes through this linkup with Spirit. I suddenly thought to myself, *Did you open your eyes to see if Paul actually got up and walked to the door? Do you realize that what you heard was the MAHANTA at your initiation, opening the door to another room?*

Paul opened the door to a world of more light and happiness than I knew.

Through the open door was happiness and laughter. It occurred to me that he opened the door to a world of more light and happiness than I knew in that room where I sat so tensely, concentrating so hard, trying to ignore all those distractions.

One of the High Initiates mentioned a similar experience with one of her initiations. Paul got her started chanting her new word, and she sat there trying to get her attention focused. All of a sudden he got up, went into the bathroom, and began to brush his teeth.

Then he flushed the toilet.

So maybe an opened door and laughter isn't so bad.

This High Initiate is making a personal study of the waking dream. In the waking dream, you see a tie-in between everything that happens around you and what is happening within you, and vice versa. As above, so below. They always go together.

Working with the waking-dream concept, a greater picture came to her. What was Paul doing in there? Brushing his teeth and flushing—which represented a cleansing. And this is what happens during an initiation. The dross of a certain level is cleaned and flushed away.

During an initiation the dross of a certain level is cleaned and flushed away.

Anything that happens here in the physical is reality; illusion is only our imperfect way of looking at reality. This is reality, and we are getting spiritual experience here. If this were all merely an illusion, there would be no purpose for being here. But we are here, and there must be a reason for it.

WHAT IS THE DIFFERENCE IN INITIATION LEVELS?

A First Initiate can see a small circle, a small part of the interrelationship between what is happening out here and how it connects with the inner worlds. An initiate of the Second Circle sees more, his scope is greater, and so on up. It's like rising in a hot-air balloon: The higher you go, the more you can see. And the more you can see, the better you are able to arrange your life. Notice I said *you* are better able to arrange your life; it's not me arranging your life.

Because really, if you don't care about your life, who else would?

When we have problems, they're self-made problems. I try to work with you and help you at first to work out of them yourself. But eventually, as you become stronger and more able, I give more and more back to you. As you become able to do more, I let you do more. The more ready you are for responsibility, the more you get. And this means you have more freedom.

This is what happens each time you come to a greater circle of initiation. You become more responsible and better able to handle your own life. The problems get bigger, but so does your ability to solve them.

Each time you come to a greater circle of initiation, the problems get bigger, but so does your ability to solve them.

THE SECRET WORD

Amusing situations sometimes come up at initiations. An ECK Initiator was giving an initiation of the Second Circle to a family. They were all very close and liked to do everything together, so she gave them a secret word to be used for the family. But it happened to be a bilingual family, and since they liked to do their spiritual exercises together, this presented a problem. The husband wanted to chant the word in Spanish, while the wife preferred English.

They eventually started to argue about their word. In which language did it have the most power? In which language were they going to chant it during their family contemplations? At first they bargained: Trying the English version of it first, the wife had great results. But the husband said, "It's not working." So they tried it in Spanish. Then the wife couldn't get it to work. Soon they were squabbling about it.

After a few weeks of this, they called up the Initiator. "Which word is right—English or Spanish?" The Initiator tried to give them some ideas, and they went through an experimental stage for a few more weeks to see how the ideas worked. After six months, they went back to the Initiator and said, "We've decided that we would each like to have our own word."

They realized that as individuals, they needed their own secret word. From this time on, they each did their own contemplative exercises in their own language, and all of a sudden things worked.

THE ECK INITIATOR

The Initiator is not the one who gives you the initiation. The Initiator, man or woman, is just the instrument for the MAHANTA. It is always the MAHANTA that gives the initiation.

The ECK Initiator Book is arranged so that everything needed for each initiation is in one place. The Initiator can open the book to the particular initiation and find a clear set of guidelines to follow. The book gives the Initiators guidance on such things as how to open themselves for Spirit and how to go about the procedures, so that it's a clean, clear initiation.

TWELVE POINTS ON THE ECK INITIATIONS

These points will give you an understanding about the commonsense facets of the ECK initiations.

There are twelve points that concern the initiations in ECK. These twelve points will give you an understanding about the commonsense facets of the ECK initiations.

1. *An Initiator appointed by the Living ECK Master may give any initiation below his own circle of initiation.*

I appoint the Initiators, who are drawn from among those of at least the Fifth Circle of initiation. They have to be out of the lower worlds of matter, energy, space, and time. Of those specifically designated as Initiators, an Eighth Initiate can give a Seventh Initiation and below, a Seventh Initiate can give a Sixth and below, a Sixth can give a Fifth and below, and a Fifth can give it from there on below.

2. *ECK initiations are given only to people who have a pink initiation slip from the Living ECK Master.*

The question came up: Should we change the color of the initiation slip? Is it a better idea to have a different color for each initiation? We thought about having a green slip for anyone who was going to be in the First, or Dream Initiation, a pink one for the Astral (Second), an orange slip for the Causal (Third), and so on.

But eventually you get to the Fifth Plane, where the color starts to be a certain shade of yellow, and then it becomes a lighter yellow in the Sixth. Pretty soon we'd have to work with several paper companies to get the right color. As we get into the fine shades of yellow, we might find out there are some who feel that if it isn't a particular shade for the Sixth Initiation, it's no good. And in paper shortages, the first thing they usually run out of is the colored paper stock.

Finally I said, "Why don't we just keep it pink?" This has had special meaning for me all through the years. Whenever I got a pink slip, I said, "Good!"

3. *In a home where the spouse is not an ECKist, the chela who wants the Second Initiation is to talk this over first with his mate. If there is a disagreement between them about ECK, it is better that the matter be resolved before the initiation is given, or the couple should follow another teaching that is acceptable to both of them.*

Through the years, whenever I got a pink slip, I said, "Good!"

I have found that many times the first two years of study are done by either the husband or the wife. You have one partner who seems not as interested, who stands back and looks with a critical eye. This is the balance in a marriage. One mate goes wild for ECK, and the other one is more cautious.

After two years the cautious mate might say, "I like this ECK, and I'd like to take the Second Initiation with you." We have provisions for that.

Keeping Harmony at Home

But what happens if the wife now wants to request her Second Initiation, and the husband says no? It could mean there is a basic problem in the family about spiritual freedom. Maybe the wife needs an issue that gives her the opportunity to say, "Hey, I've got to have the freedom to follow my own inner guidance and my own mind."

If the family can't agree on ECK, it would be better if they can find something they can agree on, even if it's another church.

If the husband says, "No, absolutely not," I won't get involved. If the family can't agree on ECK, it would be better for them if they can find something they can agree on, even if it's another church. Many times if they can't allow each other the freedom for one to go to a traditional church and the other to study ECK, they've got deeper problems than show on the surface, and that marriage is in for a rough time over the years.

The individual who has an initiation slip for the Second Initiation, or has put in enough study time to request it, can do absolutely anything he wants to do—request it or not. He may want approval or permission from the spouse, and the spouse may say either yes or no. What the person does at that point is totally up to him. The relationship between Spirit and Soul is already working, and you should do whatever is right for you.

I do recommend keeping harmony and balance at home. Whatever you can do to preserve the family, do it. You can be in ECK, follow the spiritual principles, and get unfoldment, even though outwardly you may not be able to do the things you feel you ought to do.

4. *A spouse who has not yet studied the ECK discourses for two years may, upon request, take the Second Initiation with their mate.*

Maybe one mate was holding back while the other one went ahead as a scout, studied two years, and said, "It's good; I like it." Now the other person can say, "You know, I like it too." And actually, they have been studying the principles of ECK together, and they can share the discourses which have already come into the home.

Maybe one mate was holding back while the other went ahead as a scout, studied two years, and said, "It's good; I like it."

Children in ECK

5. *Children of any age may take the Second Initiation with their parents, who will explain the rite to them when they are old enough to understand the use of the secret word.*

The children can take the Second Initiation with the parents. If you have a baby, the baby can also be initiated.

When a young child takes the initiation with the family, the parents must decide when the child is old enough to tell him the word and explain the importance of the word and how to keep it to himself. This is done in accordance with the family's judgment, not an Initiator's and not that of someone outside the family circle. The decision is made at home.

The parents have to be the teachers of their children. We can have children's Satsang classes, but the principal duty of teaching the path of ECK to the children begins in the home. The timing depends upon the insights the parents get, coupled with the kind of material we can provide to them which they feel will help them teach their children.

> 6. *A child born after the parent's Second Initiation may begin a study of the youth discourses at age four. Any children included in the ECK enrollment of a parent who is a Second Initiate or higher are also Second Initiates. They may share the parent's Second Initiation secret word. It is also allowed for them to have their own initiation ceremony.*

The protection of the MAHANTA is with all in the family who love and put their faith in him, even before they have gotten the Second Initiation.

The protection of the MAHANTA is with all in the family who love and put their faith in him.

Discourse Study toward Initiations

> 7. *People who have passed their sixtieth birthday may request the Second Initiation after only one year of discourse study.*

This is something Paul used to do. [Update: Life expectancy has increased significantly, and therefore this point no longer applies. —Ed.]

> 8. *Study of the adult discourses gives credit toward the ECK initiations. After the Second, a period of four to six years or more is established between each initiation, and no one is to ask for an initiation beyond the Second. To do so stops one's spiritual growth, and it will not start again until the Master steps in.*

I want to make sure that a study program of at least twenty-five years is set in motion. There is such a thing as being spiritually illumined, but down here on the Physical Plane, you have to have enough experience, enough gray hair, before you can be a Fifth Initiate. You have to be able to stand on your own two feet.

Putting In Your Time

You can be really smart in head knowledge, but you still have to put in your time. It has to be done, because there are some things a book just can't teach you about living. It can't tell you about a broken heart. It can't tell you about how to cope with seeing a family member sick, or give you the experience of coming through it. You can't get that from a book. Until you have this seasoning, you really don't have the understanding and compassion that one needs as he goes higher and higher in the ECK circles of initiation.

The word of your initiation level is the starting point to get you into your plane; then you begin to experiment with other words in conjunction with your own. In the Second Initiation you are going to be able to explore more than just the Astral Plane, although there are at least 150 different regions on the Astral Plane, and many of them are highly interesting and enlightening.

I think we have limited ourselves up until now. There should be more for a person to do in an initiation level than would fill a lifetime. It's an enjoyable thing. I spend a lot of time in the Astral Plane, the Causal Plane, and the other planes. There's a lot to see. I also spend a lot of time here on the Physical Plane, and so do you. Being on the Physical or Astral Plane is not an invalid experience. There are a lot of good things to learn and see.

There should be more for a person to do in an initiation level than would fill a lifetime. It's an enjoyable thing.

The Family and the Individual

9. *A couple or a family may take the Third or Fourth Initiation together, but each person must have a pink initiation slip from the Living ECK Master.*

The family, if they want to, can definitely take the Second Initiation together. In the Third or Fourth Initiation, you may or may not want to take it with your spouse—that's up to you. But eventually you are going to have the Fifth Initiation, and that one is given just for you. Already some of you at the Third and Fourth are saying, I'd like to do it myself.

> 10. *Initiations from the Fifth through the Eighth are given singly, to only one person at a time.*

The primary relationship we have in this world, and in any of the worlds, is Soul to SUGMAD.

At the Fifth Initiation each person has his own initiation. The family is near and dear, but the primary relationship that we have in this world, and in any of the worlds, is Soul to SUGMAD. No matter what else happens, it works like this: I was born myself, and I must die myself. No one else can do it for me. It starts and ends with Soul and Its relationship with the SUGMAD.

We can love each other, hold each other dear, and devote our entire lives to each other if we choose. But we also know that we are unique, spiritual beings—individual drops in the Ocean of Love and Mercy. We are surrounded on all sides by other drops, the ones we want to be around. But we are still Soul—individual and unique. In the ECK initiations, I am working toward emphasizing the spiritual principle of the Atom of God, which is Soul.

Taking a Rest

> 11. *If a person is inactive from the ECK study program for five years, his initiations will be withdrawn, and he must start the study program over again if he returns to the path of ECK.*

At the office we send out a notice to the person

who has finished two years of study that he is now
qualified to request his pink slip for the Second
Initiation. This request from the student, then, is
his signal that he is ready to make a commitment
to ECK.

The person may also say, "No, not yet," and hold
on to his invitation for a while. It may take him
two or three years after finishing the first two years
of study before he feels ready to say, "Now I've
absorbed it, and I'm ready to ask for my Second
Initiation." In that case, as long as he requests it
before five years are up, nobody cares whether he
has been studying in the last year or two, or not.

I'm interested in your spiritual growth. It's you
and the Inner Master who have to be the ones to say
when to push the throttle forward and when to put
on the brakes. I've had to establish a cutoff period of
five years because there is the matter of managing
Physical Plane records—and this counts too. These
are also the worlds of ECK, and while we're here, we
need to work with the things that are around us.
They, too, are part of the spiritual experience.

It's you and the Inner Master who have to be the ones to say when to push the throttle forward and when to put on the brakes.

> 12. *The Master may make exceptions to this
> initiation policy when there is evidence of
> unusual service or spiritual unfoldment in
> a person of any age.*

It's helpful to have rules and guidelines, but it's
nice to have a way out too. This information on the
initiations in ECK may give you some insight about
their importance both in your outer life and in the
inner planes.

MAINTAINING BALANCE

As you leave to go home, I'd like to caution you
that after a seminar, some of you can get a kind of
spiritual high. This is sometimes the reaction when

Spirit starts coming in. Just be aware of it. Throw yourself into your activities at home. Get right back into work. The glow from a seminar may continue for two or three days, or even two or three weeks. You'll be flying high for a while, and then you have to balance it out. If you're not careful, you could go into a depression where you'll have this sick feeling inside. It's a reaction to having felt so good.

Back home, the physical senses suddenly become aware of the changes that have been made in you—you're not the same person you were when you came to the seminar. You're different, and now you have to come to grips with it and with the people around you. The initial golden glow will help you over the hump, but don't let it trip you. Because like being on a slide, what goes up must come down.

You want your viewpoint to go right through the middle. This is the state of vairag, or detachment. Enjoy what happened, but when you see yourself heading into a dip, go out and do something. Go bowling, have a picnic, try something different at work—just do something.

When you see yourself heading into a dip, go out and do something. Go bowling, have a picnic, try something different at work—just do something.

This is a caution to help you through the letdown that you can experience after something of spiritual importance occurs in your life. Even though you may feel a little low for a while, as long as you are aware of what is causing it, you'll at least know what's happening.

I would like to thank all of you for coming. On your journey home, know that the Light and Sound of ECK are always with you, and that as the Inner Master I am always with you.

May the blessings be.

ECKANKAR International Youth Conference, Las Vegas, Nevada, Sunday, April 22, 1984

The potential of the rose is in the bud, but before you can see its beauty, the bud has to unfold.

14

SO YOU THINK I
KNOW EVERYTHING . . .

*T*he Eckankar staff members are learning how to work with me, and it's awkward for many of them. They think to themselves, *Maybe this guy knows everything.* They think that all they really have to say is, "OK, whatever you want; sure, we'll do it." But what I'm trying to show the people who work with me is how to face problems as they come up.

HOW A MASTER WORKS
WITH THE CREATIVE PROCESS

On the other planes, sometimes the spiritual leader—the MAHANTA, the Living ECK Master—sits at a table with the rest of the ECK Masters, and they talk things out. According to the way we regard ECK Masters, any one of them ought to be smart enough to handle anything that goes on. So why do they talk things out?

This is simply an educational process. We learn what a Master does and how he works with the ECK, or Divine Spirit. How do you work with the ECK? Sometimes it's easy to say, Just let the ECK do it. Then you sit back and wait. That is not going to work.

Any one of the ECK Masters ought to be smart enough to handle anything that goes on. So why do they talk things out?

185

A better way is to contemplate on the problem and look at it from every angle. You may talk it over with everybody who's got the least bit of knowledge about it. Eventually, if you ask a good question, the answer is going to suggest itself. At some point, it's going to become very clear what to do.

The creative process is actually a misnomer, because creation is finished, and all we do is manifest what is already there. So you're not really creating a solution to the problem; you are manifesting something that is already there. The potential of the rose is in the bud, but before you can see its beauty, the bud has to unfold.

Sometimes we like to imagine that an individual with a high state of consciousness (which is something you can't prove) has a smooth and easy life. You watch him for a while; by his actions, you think you're going to know if he's a Master. But when you finish studying him, you realize that you can't see too much difference between him and the next guy.

Last night, about one thirty, I happened to notice that one of the sliding glass doors to my room wasn't locked. It didn't have the safety latch that is needed to secure it. Because I had the air conditioning on and wanted to keep the cool air inside and any uninvited visitors outside, I decided to secure my door. So I started fiddling with it. But it's dark, and this is about the last thing I wanted to do before going to bed.

There was a filmy little curtain hanging in front of the door, so I couldn't see too well. I slammed the door a few times, trying to get it shut. But it wouldn't shut. I said to myself, Maybe the latch is jammed. I felt around in the dark and tried to locate the ridge the latch catches when the door is locked. But I couldn't really tell, so I decided to look for the flashlight I had brought with me. I didn't want

> Sometimes we like to imagine that an individual with a high state of consciousness has a smooth and easy life.

to turn on the lights, because people outside could see in through the filmy curtain. So I kept fishing around, wondering where the flashlight was. A Master is supposed to know *everything*, right?

I finally found the flashlight and shone it at the door. I began to examine the door to see how the frame fit. At the top it looked very tight. I ran the flashlight along the frame all the way to the bottom and discovered that the door was off the track.

By this time, twenty minutes had passed. It'd be very easy just to pull the drape, turn on the light, and do it right—but, you see, I was working with the creative process.

I got down on my hands and knees, put the flashlight in my mouth, and lifted this heavy door. I finally got it on the track. It was level, and it slid. Satisfied with my handiwork, I took hold of the door and slammed it again. The wall shook—but the door still wouldn't lock. Maybe the latch was bent. A screwdriver would fix it.

So there I was in the hotel room, and I needed a screwdriver. On my table, among some flatware, there was a knife. I decided this knife ought to work very nicely as a screwdriver. I used the knife and bent the latch back. I jammed the door shut, and finally it locked. But I couldn't get it open again. So I pried at the latch again with my knife, and soon I got it open.

I learned how to pry the door open and slam it shut. Yet, when I tried to open the door all the way, it wouldn't open very far. It was then I noticed that the management had already put a wooden block into the runner. Nobody could have come into my room—the block had been there all the time!

A half hour had passed, and morning was coming. I had wasted all that time trying to secure my

A Master is supposed to know every-thing, right?

door when nobody could have gotten inside in the first place. I wondered, *Is this an example of creation or manifestation?* It certainly isn't creation, so that just left manifestation. Finally I thought, *What exactly have I been doing here for this last half hour in the dead of night?* I wasn't sure. I thought to myself, *Tomorrow, people are going to expect me to give great wisdom on the subject of creativity, and I can't even lock my door!*

SOLVING IMAGINARY PROBLEMS

I had an imaginary problem, which was the door I thought needed to be locked, when it didn't. We all have imaginary problems. We get upset, sometimes we cry, other times we get angry, and we wonder, *Lord, why me? Why have you done this to me?* This is a period of life we call the dark night of Soul, where everything goes wrong. We ask the MAHANTA, we ask God, we ask anybody who is close, "Please take the burden from me; I can't handle it anymore."

But even if we muster all our creativity and use it to solve our problem, we find that we have actually worked through a false problem. Soul hasn't any problems; we have problems in our mental, emotional, or physical bodies. Soul hasn't any real problems to speak of. It isn't concerned about a whole lot of things. It isn't concerned about how long we live, because Soul is eternal; Soul isn't worried about taxes; It isn't worried about most things. But we in the human consciousness worry about taxes, about our neighbors, our boss, and ourselves. And we wonder every time we face a problem, *What am I going to do now?*

Working with the creative cycle in ECK, when you come up against something, try to put it into a question. Figure out what's wrong, and say, "Something is going wrong. This is the title I've given to

Soul hasn't any real problems to speak of.

what's going wrong. Now I would like an answer for how it can go right."

As we unfold, our potential for solving problems increases. This is simply because we have a closer, more intimate contact with the Light and the Sound of ECK. We expand in our circle of awareness. The Second Initiate ought to have a greater awareness of how to meet his life situations than a First Initiate. So when a Sixth Initiate is viewed by a First Initiate, the First Initiate may think, *Those Sixth Initiates must have it pretty good—no problems.* Yes, they have problems, and some of you can see the problems the Higher Initiates have, and they can see yours—but these problems are of our own individual worlds.

LEARNING THE CAUSE

With the insight of Divine Spirit, we say, "How can I make my load easier? What have I learned while doing this? What have I gained?" Otherwise, why are we here? We ask for healing and to know the future. It's easy for someone else to give it to us—a fortune-teller, palm reader, or anybody who can tell the future—but what have we learned?

Many times the tellers of the future only reveal the obstacle that is coming and how to move to the side of it. They never tell us what put that obstacle in our path in the first place. All they tell you is to run one hundred yards this way, take a quick jump to the left, take a quick jump to the right, and you're safe. You run down the road, and you look back and say, "Thank you; that really worked out great." And then you run into the next boulder, which is just another one of your own creations.

So what do the fortune-tellers do for you if they haven't shown you why this obstacle has come to you?

With the insight of Divine Spirit, we say, "How can I make my load easier?"

And how do we learn the answer to our problem? With the Spiritual Exercises of ECK.

MANIFESTING SOLUTIONS

The trip to the South Pacific was a constant practice of creativity, a manifesting of solutions.

Last fall, two staff members and I went on a trip to the South Pacific. We went to Australia, New Zealand, and Hawaii. The trip was a constant practice of creativity. I'm using the word *creativity*, but actually it's a manifesting of solutions. There are a number of ways to solve each problem that comes along, but you pick the best one that suits you for the moment. We decided it would be a good idea if we could share with other people the kinds of things we face when traveling. People say it must be a lot of fun going on these trips. It is fun if you don't mind being on the opposite side of the clock, enduring jet lag, and going through customs. They want to look at everything, you show them everything, and it's tiring.

On a trip some time ago, I was carrying my own baggage. The international customs offices are sometimes located in remote parts of the airport. My wife was carrying her baggage, which wasn't very much—she packs light—but she was getting tired from walking. So I took her suitcase. Now I had my own baggage, a heavy case in which I carry all my notes and papers, my garment bag, and my wife's suitcase. We walked a little further and saw an elderly lady who could hardly carry her luggage. I offered to carry hers, too, and she accepted gratefully. By then I was actually staggering along, because her luggage was quite heavy. When you are traveling, the less you have, the easier it is.

You learn certain little things when traveling, such as how to creatively get off the plane if you're with several different people. You sit across the aisle from each other, and when the plane lands, the first one out blocks the aisle so the rest in the party can get off.

So on this trip to the South Pacific, we talked about what a good idea it would be to share this experience of creative traveling. I finally said, "Let's not do it." The creative process actually has many kinks in it. We all like to imagine that every idea, every concept, every ad comes out right the first time. It really doesn't; it comes out with a lot of kinks. We like to imagine the creative process would be smooth and orderly if it were done right. I don't think the creative process is ever done right. It's always done in a stumbling, groping manner, where you experiment constantly.

EXPRESSING CREATIVITY

A popular figure of the American Public Radio network, Garrison Keillor, is a good example of creativity. He hosted the program *A Prairie Home Companion* from Saint Paul, Minnesota—an interesting program with homespun music and humor.

Keillor created this mythical town called Lake Wobegon. This town includes true-to-life characters, such as the switchboard operator who listens in on all the calls. Over the years performing on public radio, Garrison Keillor created the entire population of this mythical town. His real creation isn't so much the town of Lake Wobegon; it's the way the people think and the way people who live there act, their weaknesses and their strengths, how they meet life, and what they do when a problem comes up.

Garrison Keillor had, years ago, been a parking-lot attendant. In those days, he said, he never had a problem.

A brilliant man with tremendous insight into human nature, Keillor had, years ago, been a parking-lot attendant—the person who drives your car around and puts dents in it when you let them park it in a hotel parking lot. In those days, he said, he never had a problem; at the end of the day he went home, watched some television, went to bed, and slept well all night. He never had to wonder if things were being done correctly—if, for instance, he could have gotten a Cadillac into the spot where he put a Volkswagen.

A guy who parks cars doesn't really have to make major decisions. You've got so many slots in your parking lot, and you put in so many cars. If you can't fit in any more, you put out a sign that says Full. Then you sit down and just enjoy yourself for the rest of the shift. When the day is done, the day is done.

But it became vastly different as he got further into the creative stream, as radio host for A Prairie Home Companion.

But it became vastly different as he got further into the creative stream, especially as the radio host for *A Prairie Home Companion*. Every week he put on his show. He may have been talking to hundreds of thousands of people. But since he didn't get an instant response, he didn't know if he was doing a good job. Earlier in his career, if he parked a car without getting a dent in it, he had done a good job. Now he would say something, and he wouldn't know until two weeks or a month later if his words and his ideas were having any impact at all.

Those of you who have listened to this man will recognize in him the strong creative element; he fashions these stories out of the air. He'll take a few isolated facts that sound true, and then he'll start weaving them together. It's a very low-key kind of humor. It is really just an interesting outlook on life.

He's an example of the creativity that's going on around us all the time. And it doesn't have a big stamp on it called Eckankar. It doesn't have to. Nor do you have to be studying Eckankar to be expressing your creativity.

UMPIRING LIFE

About three Saturdays ago I attended a Bobby Sox softball game in which my daughter was playing. Up in the stands were the usual smattering of parents, sitting and chatting, having a good time. Next to me was a lady attempting to set her watch.

She said she had just bought it. She worked at setting the watch for an hour and a half.

Watching her struggling with the watch and trying to read the instructions that kept being blown away by the wind, I thought she must have lost her mind from raising two children. At one point I asked, "Do you need the watch?" "No," she said, pointing to her wrist, "I have a watch, but I have to learn to set this one sometime." So I continued to watch her work at her creative plan.

I soon realized she hadn't lost her mind at all. She was actually using time to learn (the hard way) how the watch worked. She had nothing better to do during most of the game. As we talked, I found that she was a very perceptive person. She worked in an office and was very competent. She'd sit for an hour and a half watching her kid play ball while trying to learn how to set the watch. She was growing, she was watching her children grow, and she was fulfilled in her own way.

We talked about a number of things. I said to her, "You're a single parent now, you're working, and you've got two daughters in their preteens. How do you raise your children? How do you handle all of it?"

"With drugs and so many other things going on out there," she said, "the simplest thing I can tell my children—without giving them a whole bunch of rules like the Ten Commandments, which they wouldn't listen to—is this: If what you do doesn't hurt somebody else, it's all right." This was the rule that she made for her children. It cut through a lot of dos and don'ts about what was right and what was wrong. Each time they faced a situation, they had to become thinking individuals who had to make a decision by saying, "I can either do this or I can't, depending upon whether or not it will cause needless injury to someone." This is not to say that if someone attacks you,

Each time her children faced a situation, they had to become thinking individuals and make a decision depending upon whether or not it would cause needless injury to someone.

you can't defend yourself. It simply means not causing needless injury in the normal course of life.

PAUL'S QUEST FOR MASTERSHIP

I've recently been going through some of Paul Twitchell's letters, trying to gain some understanding of how Paul worked with the creative process. The creativity actually comes when we make contact with the ECK, either with the Sound or with the Light in some form. In one of the letters Paul wrote, he said he had made contact with the Cosmic Light at age eight. At that time, a being with a shining countenance, long hair, and a robe came into the room and said, "You are under my charge until you grow up, and at that time your development will be turned over to other Masters."

This little spark in Paul made him a different being.

This was the little spark in Paul that made him a different being. He went out into the world trying to reconcile this experience that he'd had with the Cosmic Light of ECK, or Spirit, and attempted to understand his place in life. At one point in his quest for Mastership, he mentioned that in a way he knew he was a special person. Yet, the Masters had to make sure that, as he went along, his big head shrank in size. It sounds like a funny thing to say, but a person who goes far on his spiritual path has to have a high opinion of himself. I don't mean in the ego consciousness; I don't mean the little self. But his faith and knowingness has to be so strong, even before an individual comes to ECK, so that he can find a solution for most anything that confronts him. And if there isn't a way to solve it, there's a way to control it. In other words, he can always find a way to live in life.

Paul was such an individual. He made the best of what he had. Many things were heaped upon him in his quest for Mastership that the regular person probably would never experience because it's not needed. It will come when the time is right.

PROLIFIC WRITER

Paul was quite an interesting man. In 1940, he won an award from *Writer's Journal* for being the most prolific new writer. He had published a hundred articles and stories, and he wrote this all up in a letter to *Ripley's Believe It or Not*, saying, "Here is more about that fantastic man, Paul Twitchell." When *Ripley's* got it, an editor looked it over and thought it sounded really good. Of course, it was on the letterhead of a man called Carl Snyder, which happened to be one of Paul's pen names. Back in Paducah, Kentucky, Paul had printed himself up some Carl Snyder letterhead, which he used when writing all these blurbs about himself. He wanted recognition so that he could sell his stories easier. Once *Ripley's* mentioned him, for instance, he could include their write-up when submitting another story, and the next editor would see that this Paul Twitchell was really something.

Paul would write stories about himself for publication in a newspaper, and then he would distribute copies wherever he happened to be. He continued to write this constant flow of self-promotional material, because it helped him sell his writings so that he could make a living.

In this particular letter to *Ripley's*, Carl Snyder spoke about the things this Paul Twitchell had accomplished. Paul had a punchy style of writing. It was alive; it just glowed with life. He was drawing on his creativity to survive, so he wrote this promotional stuff. Snyder expanded on all of this talent— "college athletic trainer, swimming coach, track team"—and embellished it even more by adding things like "prizefighter" and "promoter of fights." He worked every angle on every job he ever held, giving each

Paul had a punchy style of writing. It was alive; it just glowed with life.

position all different titles. In addition, he said, "Paul Twitchell reads all the time. He reads a book a night and sometimes doesn't even get a wink of sleep." Paul was good with the word *wink*. You may come across some writings under another name, such as Charles Daniel, another of Paul's pen names. If it seems to encompass the ECK teachings, and the word *wink* is included, you can be pretty sure it was written by Paul.

The *Ripley's* editor read on to find that this Paul Twitchell "once a year reads the Bible from end to end, from Genesis to Revelation. He has read the Bible fifteen times." The editor was impressed enough with this man's talents that he recommended doing an article on him, and he passed Snyder's letter on to the next person.

After reviewing it, though, the senior editor wrote a note underneath the first editor's that said, "I just ran an item on this man—see copy attached." Paul was apparently feeding his material to *Ripley's* too fast. But they did run another article on him three months later.

Paul liked to cause a reaction in a person so he could evoke their creativity.

GETTING A REACTION

Another thing Paul liked to do was to cause a reaction in a person so that he could evoke their creativity. The ECK Masters sometimes do this. They'll set up a reaction in a person by some strange personal habits or conversation.

Somebody wrote to me very recently about a librarian who was working in a library in Washington State. One of the ECKists came in to put up a poster about Eckankar. The lady said, "Oh, Eckankar. Is this anything to do with Paul Twitchell?" The ECKist responded that yes, indeed, it was. And the librarian said, "I used to know Paul Twitchell. I came out of the library one day and saw this man talking to a tree." She walked over to him and asked, "Why are you talking to a tree?"

Paul explained that this was something he had learned in a past life as a Druid. He said that the tree could understand him, and they could communicate.

You can imagine the kind of reaction the woman had to such a statement. Everything in a library fits into a nice, predictable cataloging system—the Dewey decimal system or the Library of Congress classification system—and all of a sudden this woman sees a man standing on the lawn, talking to a tree. Many times Paul would put people on, trying to get a reaction from them, and many times he succeeded.

I came across some articles Paul had written around 1959. For some reason, at this particular period in his life, he wrote some very searching stories about women. If I'd be kind, I'd say they were unkind. I was sitting at my desk, about midnight, reading one of these articles, when my wife came in and asked what I was reading. I said it was a rather dull article that Paul had written about women. "What kind of things did he say?" she asked.

"Well," I said, "one of the points he makes is that this is a woman's world, this is her battleground. She understands it better than men, and therefore she'll use any guile." Now, this was just one particular article. Paul didn't always write like that. He was just working on a point. Then I started adding on to some of the things that Paul had supposedly said. In about five minutes, we were having this nice discussion about Paul's article and the things he actually said, as well as what I threw in.

Pretty soon our very calm discussion—which started when my wife came in to say good night on her way to bed—had turned into a very lively conversation. And in just five minutes' time. "Wasn't Paul a marvelous writer?" I said. "In just a few minutes, he could so inspire us to get creative

The librarian asked, "Why are you talking to a tree?" Paul explained he had learned this in a past life as a Druid.

and really get into life and living." Then, of course, I admitted that I'd added a few words here and there. And it got more lively.

FINDING THE LAUGHTER

The creativity of ECK can be a happy thing. It can be happy even though the clouds come over us. For a while, we may face sorrows and hardships. We are used to our body acting in a certain way, for instance. All of a sudden it doesn't perform the way it used to ten years ago, or we find we have certain illnesses.

The creativity comes in trying to find the correct doctor, or in a spiritual healing if we are ready for it, or in handling whatever comes. This is how we work with Spirit. We look at life and try to find the laughter wherever we can, whenever we can, because laughter is a healer.

We look to find laughter wherever we can, whenever we can, because laughter is a healer.

ECKANKAR International Creative Arts Festival, Boston, Massachusetts, Friday, June 15, 1984

The church tried to prevent Columbus from going on the journey that led to the discovery of America by telling him that if he dared to go, he would fall off the edge of the earth.

15
SOUL TRAVEL: HOW
TO DO IT RIGHT

reedom comes through creativity. The freedom of the individual, and even of countries, has occasionally been stifled by church or political authorities. But, there was usually someone willing to stand up and say, "I believe in this!" They were ready to fight and die for the cause they believed in. Or, if the individual was smart enough, he made his point without needing to die for it.

A LEAP IN CONSCIOUSNESS

In 1492, the world experienced a great opening in consciousness, perhaps the most significant to occur in many centuries. This came about when Christopher Columbus and his fleet of ships came sailing across the ocean to find the New World.

Christopher Columbus was living at a time when the Spanish Inquisition was going strong. Heresy against church doctrine could result in prison or death at the stake. Columbus was shrewd enough to know that if he returned home and claimed he had found a new world and new people, he would be contradicting the teachings of the church—and that could land him in trouble. So he decided to bring back proof.

In 1492, the world experienced a great opening in consciousness, perhaps the most significant in many centuries.

201

When he arrived in Lisbon in March of 1493, he had with him a group of Indians from the Americas.

To realize the importance of this move, you have to understand that the Catholic Church had taught for years that all the people on earth lived in the then-known world, and they were all descendants of Noah.

You'll recall that after the forty days and forty nights of rain, Noah sailed around for awhile. When the waters abated and the earth was finally dry, Noah left the ark with his wife and three sons, Shem, Ham, and Japheth, and their wives. There were all the elements necessary to go forth, multiply, and replenish the world.

The church taught that Shem's descendants were those who populated the Semitic lands which today are known as Israel, Palestine, and Lebanon. Ham's descendants were the people of Egypt, Libya, and the rest of Africa. The light-skinned Europeans were the descendants of Japheth.

The church made everything fit into a nice slot.

Columbus knew he wouldn't be long for this world if he tried to say there were people who didn't fit into this little box that the church had created. So he brought back some of the red men. The Europeans came to see them and, strange as it may sound to us today, some even doubted they were humans. Columbus then wrote a couple of letters to King Ferdinand to assure him that yes, they are human creatures.

Under the circumstances, they couldn't take him before the Inquisition and force him into recanting this heresy, which is what later happened to Galileo when he disagreed with another of the church's long-standing doctrines—that the earth was the center of God's creation.

When Christopher Columbus brought back the Indians, it was hard to dispute that kind of proof. These red men didn't speak any known language; they

When Christopher Columbus brought back the Indians from the Americas, it was hard to dispute that kind of proof.

were completely different—so now what would the church do?

RE-CREATING HISTORY

This is an example of creativity in the negative sense. How was the church going to rearrange their history to make these people fit in? How would they suddenly account for the red race? The church studied the situation for almost twenty years before addressing it. Alexander VI, the pope at the time Columbus presented the Indians, ignored the problem; he had other things to do. But the monks in the monasteries began to ask questions. If there were people not accounted for in Genesis, then maybe the teachings of the Bible were false. This discovery raised great skepticism in the monasteries. So twenty years later, Julius II, the pope who succeeded Alexander VI, decided it was time to come up with a good explanation about the red man. Otherwise the cardinals were going to split the church, and this would cause it to lose control of the people.

The church especially didn't want to lose control of the monks, since they were the educated people in those days. They were, incidentally, the same people who tried to prevent Columbus from going on the journey that led to the discovery of America. They told him the world was flat, and if he dared to go on the voyage, he would fall off the edge of the earth. But when he came back with proof they were wrong, these very same people then said, "Wait a minute. Maybe the Bible isn't correct."

The church had to scramble pretty fast, and in 1512 Pope Julius II presented the findings of the Fifth Lateran Council: The history of Noah and his sons stands true, but just before the flood some wicked Babylonians were cast out and sent to America. This became doctrine, and the question was

How was the church going to rearrange their history to suddenly account for the red race? They had to scramble pretty fast.

resolved. The red men did fit in the Bible; they were the descendents of outcast Babylonians.

Now came the big problem: How did the outcasts get to America? This gave rise to several ideas. One man ventured the theory that God had grabbed them by the hair, carried them across the ocean, and dropped them off in that far land as part of their banishment. Some people actually thought that made sense.

Another person speculated that, even though it wasn't recorded in the Bible, Noah found two of these wicked Babylonians—a male and a female, of course— hiding on the ark. So he took a side trip and dropped them off in America.

Some fairly sensible guy said that perhaps an ill wind blew and caused a shipwreck. Nobody took him seriously.

This is an example of how the church, through its monks, sought complete control. By attempting to stop Christopher Columbus, they tried to keep the people from moving beyond themselves. Columbus's explorations raised more questions than they answered. So in order to keep control, the church started to fiddle with history, and they got very creative at it. We can believe the history books if we want to, but as a teacher once said, "History is somebody's fiction of what actually happened." He generally told the students in his classes, "This is what the books tell you, but if something doesn't seem to quite fit as it should, keep an open mind."

> By attempting to stop Columbus, the church tried to keep the people from moving beyond themselves.

YEARNING FOR FREEDOM

The Church of England grew prominent during the reign of Henry VIII, when the pope said Henry could not divorce his wife. In a move to gain liberation from the Catholic Church, Henry VIII abolished papal authority and established royal supremacy. But this, too, in its own way, was op- pressive—to minority religious groups in England.

The Pilgrims did not subscribe to the teachings of the Church of England. In about 1609, in their search for religious tolerance, they settled in Holland, remaining there for about eleven years. The Pilgrims then made arrangements to go to the New World, but first they stopped in England again.

The *Mayflower* sailed from England in August of 1620, accompanied by another ship called the *Speedwell*. But the *Speedwell* developed a leak and had to return to port while they patched it up. The *Speedwell* was finally abandoned as unseaworthy, and the *Mayflower* sailed on alone carrying 101 pas- sengers, 28 of whom were children.

You have to wonder about some people's planning. By then it was September, and they were facing a voyage of perhaps two months. This would get them to the New World, where no known shelter awaited them, right at the start of winter.

It was a harsh life. Within the first five months after they landed, they buried half their number. But they knew the risk, and they were willing to undertake it for spiritual freedom.

Today this yearning for freedom is sometimes lost on us, because the conflicts and obstacles that face us today are more subtle. There are no people with guns saying, Believe our way, or else! In many countries we have the right to speak up and to fol- low the kind of religion we choose.

There are people who strongly advocate the unification of church and state. Yet history, includ- ing the bit just mentioned, has shown the abuses that take place every time the church is in total control of the people. The abuses against the spiri- tual freedom of the individual did not even stop at

Today this yearning for freedom is sometimes lost on us, because the conflicts and obstacles that face us today are more subtle.

taking away people's physical freedom or their lives. Still, today there are some who try to say the First Amendment didn't mean the separation of church and state. They would like to see the strength of the church grow to the point where it would eventually become the law of the land. And if we haven't learned the lessons of history that show us what happens whenever the church has a stranglehold, then maybe we deserve to have the church stand taller than the state again.

Half of the Pilgrims made it through to April. Then one day an Indian named Samoset came out of the woods. He started his conversation with the Pilgrims not by using sign language or anything like that, but by saying something totally unexpected: "Welcome, Englishmen." Shortly thereafter, Squanto came to meet them. He would become their guide.

These events are history to us. We've heard about them, but we forget. For most of us history has become a dead issue that we take for granted. Yet the area near Boston became the seedbed of the inner yearning for personal, social, and religious freedom. Soul's yearning and striving for spiritual freedom eventually expressed itself outwardly as the American Revolution.

Soul's yearning and striving for spiritual freedom eventually led to the forming of the United States, which was one of the goals of the Vairagi ECK Masters.

CREATING PERSONAL FREEDOM

This morning the ECK children and teenagers went on a bus tour along the Freedom Trail. One of the tour guides said the kids were excited because they had a chance to see some of the history they had been learning about in school. This trip made it relevant, because Boston is the cradle of American liberty. This is where the American Revolution began. It led to the forming of the United States, which was one of the goals of the Vairagi ECK Masters. Seeing all of the historical sites made it very interesting.

At the end of the tour they all met at a park
where there's a statue of Paul Revere on a horse,
representing the midnight ride that he took along
with William Dawes. Soon they were having a little
Satsang class, discussing the American Revolution
and how it relates to the spiritual revolution which
is going on today in Eckankar. They also talked about
how the ECK Master Yaubl Sacabi was shown the
destiny of America in a dream which lasted for ten
days. These teenagers are the future leaders of
Eckankar.

Freedom is a big word. What does it mean to the youth?

Freedom is a big word. What does it mean to
the youth? They think about it more in practical
terms, relating it to their own family and school
situations. Some of the teenagers have trouble at
home or school in doing what they want to do.

They were asked what they did when they encountered situations where they felt depressed or
suffocated. One thing they brought up was the
power of using the Spiritual Exercises of ECK to
help work out certain situations.

HOW TO DO THE SPIRITUAL EXERCISES

We always go back to the Spiritual Exercises of
ECK, because these lead to Self-Realization and
God-Realization, and from this come the attributes
of wisdom, charity, and freedom.

When I first began practicing the spiritual exercises, I was scared. I tried some of the positions that
Paul mentioned—sitting on the floor tailor-fashion,
legs crossed, back erect. I started by sitting in the
middle of the floor, but as soon as I began to put
attention on my contemplation, my body slumped—
and that would jolt me out of the experience.

The next level of experimentation in my evolution
with these exercises was to sit with my back against

a wall. This resulted in a 25 percent improvement: Now I could only fall sideways or forward.

When I found a comfortable position, I could relax, shut my eyes, and look at the inner screen. It was like watching a movie screen. Sometimes it was black, sometimes white, sometimes gray. There were even times when I could actually see a scene or a moving picture.

For a while I looked straight into it. Sometimes that worked, but eventually it didn't. Occasionally I let my inner vision stray to the left about ten degrees or so, and then suddenly I would notice that something had appeared on the screen. This is how I began to look for the Master. In a relaxed way I would look to the side, knowing that my attention was really toward the center. And then I would start to chant *HU* or my word.

My greatest obstacle was fear. Even while I was trying to go out of the body, I was afraid I might really do it!

These were some of the things I tried, but the greatest obstacle that held me back at the time was fear. Even while I was trying to go out of the body, I was afraid I might really do it!

Paul always recommended that we do the spiritual exercises sitting up, but necessity forced me into different positions. While in the service, I certainly wasn't about to sit on the floor with my legs crossed, hands folded, and eyes shut. In the barracks the cubicles were an open area, and there were always a lot of other airmen around. I was with the security service; we had a top-secret classification, and they are very selective of the people who come in there. They like to be sure you're stable. If they see you sitting on the floor, doing strange things, it won't be long before you'll find yourself in some other line of work—without your top-secret clearance. I had a good job, and I wanted to keep it; so I figured if I did the spiritual exercises sitting up, I was dumber than I looked. That's when I started doing them while lying down in bed.

Out-of-the-Body Experience

One of my early out-of-body experiences happened when I was stationed with the National Security Agency at Fort Meade, Maryland. One Saturday night about ten o'clock, after everyone else had left the barracks, I lay down on the bed, pulled up the covers, and stretched out as straight and stiff as a mummy. This position had occasionally brought comments from my friends, such as, "You sure sleep strange." Later I learned how to do the spiritual exercises lying on my side so I didn't look quite so obvious. But at the time, the move from the floor to the bed was a big jump in my spiritual evolution.

While lying there with my eyes closed, doing a spiritual exercise, I began to hear a whirring sound that grew increasingly louder. All of a sudden it felt like I was floating. Not yet realizing I was in the Soul body running the astral form, I thought maybe I was levitating.

It's not like a dream when these things happen; you're right there.

As I started rising higher, I wondered if I really might be floating, so I opened my eyes—and was startled to find myself above the pillow. *This is really neat,* I thought. The next thing, I'm settling back down on the bed. I noticed that as I began to go down, the whirring sound subsided. There seemed to be a relationship between my elevation and the intensity and pitch of the sound. The lower it got, the lower I went. "No, no, no!" I said. "Up! Up! Up!" But I went down, down, down. *Rats!* I thought. *Out of the body, and I couldn't stay there. I blew it.*

When my body settled back down, I decided to get out of bed, but it was very difficult to move. I couldn't understand why. It felt like somebody was holding me down. It took all my strength to get to the edge of the bed. Finally I rolled out, hit the floor,

It's not like a dream when these out-of-body experiences happen; you're right there.

and came bouncing up. I thought, *Boy, that was some experience. I'd better write it down before I forget it.* I didn't yet realize I wasn't back in the body.

I looked around then and saw that the sheets on the bed had spilled out onto the floor. But my perceptions had changed. The vision I had at that point was different than I was used to. My seeing power was like tunnel vision. Anything I gazed at, I could see, and the only thing I cared about was what I gazed at. It commanded my complete attention.

It was when I picked up the sheets that I noticed this pulsing bluish thing that gave off a luminous glow. It was the silver cord, but it looked more like a bluish-white plastic hose. It was actually pulsing with life. The strange thing was, I couldn't tell where this silver cord was attached. I knew it was connected to me somewhere—but where?

As I studied it intently and tried to figure it out, I happened to look over at the bed, and that's when I saw myself lying there. I wasn't impressed at all. One's sleeping body, especially when viewed unexpectedly, isn't exactly the greatest thing in the world to see. In sleep everything shows.

It felt great to be out of the body, but now what?

PROOF OF SOUL'S SURVIVAL

It felt great to be out of the body, but I wasn't sure what to do next. I'd picked up the sheets—done my housekeeping—but now what? You know the saying about how the devil finds work for idle hands. It was that kind of thing, but mostly it was the desire to explore, to try something new, to have an adventure.

I glanced around and saw the television set in the next cubicle, a makeshift room comprised of lockers that were arranged in a semibarrier. But this TV was brown, whereas on the Physical Plane it was white.

If you walk around your home in the inner worlds, you'll find it's a little bit different. The television set might be another color or another size; your house might be bigger or smaller. Don't fight it—it's just a different world than our creation down here. The Physical Plane builders fashioned your house here because there was already an image of it on the Astral Plane, and they got as close as they could. So the TV set may end up white here instead of brown.

Just as I was trying to figure out my next move, I heard somebody walking up the center aisle that separated the cubicles that lined each side of the barracks. The footsteps sounded like he was approaching very quickly. I thought it was one of my roommates and tried to face him, but I couldn't get turned around. The glowing cord seemed to hinder my movements in certain directions. Maybe I was tangled up in it. It occurred to me that if I backed up so that I stood in his path, he would have to walk right through a ghost. Wouldn't that be a laugh! Would he feel a cold wind? I was experimenting and having a good time.

Wouldn't that be a laugh! I was experimenting and having a good time.

All of a sudden a man comes walking right up to me. I was standing in the middle of the aisle, but there was enough space behind me for him to slip into my cubicle. Later, after seeing his picture on a book cover, I learned it was Paul Twitchell, but at the time he seemed like an intruder.

When the stranger walked over and stood in a dark corner by the dresser, my happy mood suddenly changed to fear. *I'm out of my body,* I thought. *What am I going to do if he hurts it?*

There I was in a world that was so much lighter and better, and I found myself worrying about the thing I had been making fun of just a few minutes ago.

The fellow stayed over in the corner, leaning against the dresser, one ankle crossed over the other.

All he did was stand there, calmly observing me. But fear has an interesting effect.

I rushed at him. "No! Don't go near my body!" He wasn't making a move toward it. "Go away!" I shouted, waving my arms the way you'd shoo a goose. "Go away!"

The next thing I knew, I was lying on the bed. There had been no sense of transition at all. At first I couldn't figure out where I was, but I finally realized I was back in the physical body. When I rolled out of bed this time, my body moved quickly. I glanced toward the dresser—nobody was there.

What this experience taught me was that whoever I am, I am me. My Real Self had nothing to do with the physical body or even a body running around on the Astral Plane. This was my proof of the survival of Soul, a greater consciousness that lived outside of and beyond the Physical or the Astral body.

This was my proof of the survival of Soul, a greater consciousness that lived outside of and beyond the body.

I had a friend at the time, a great big fellow named Sam, who stayed in the barracks next door. Sam was with the army; I was with the air force. We were both in this special unit of the NSA that included personnel from the army, air force, navy, and marines. Sam was the kind of person who was well suited to the Society for Creative Anachronism, guys who attend tournaments dressed like knights in shining armor. They ride around on horses and in general enjoy acting out another era. He told me that he had been somebody's squire in a previous life.

Sam also enjoyed studying occult subjects. The morning after my experience, I went over to see him. "Sam," I said, "there really is something to this Soul Travel business. It actually does bring about the expansion of consciousness."

I hadn't had any out-of-body experiences since being stationed in Japan, when I had traveled out of the body back home to my parents' farm. At the time, I thought, *Anybody can do this.* As a result of my big head, the Inner Master wouldn't let me go traveling like that for a couple of months. Now I was more humble: This time I knew better than to take credit for it.

Sam was fascinated. Then he told me about his experience. He said, "A strange thing happened to me too. I was reading in my room last night at about ten o'clock, and all of a sudden this light filled the room." At first he didn't know what was going on. Then he said Paul had come and given him the ECK-Vidya, showing him a prophecy about his future and mine.

A day or two later we went for a drive around Washington, DC, and talked about what he had been told about my future and his own. We were both awed by the power of the Living ECK Master. Paul had said he could give people proof of the survival of Soul, and now we were convinced. It was proof that took away a little of the fear of death. But the fear of death doesn't always go away completely the first time you have a realization. Fear is usually a habit that has accumulated for years, and it sometimes takes a while to get rid of it.

Paul had come and given Sam a prophecy about his future and mine. We were both awed by the power of the Living ECK Master.

A Visualization Technique to Try

If you would like to try a visualization technique later, start by sitting comfortably or lying down. Turn down the lights if you wish. Then shut your eyes and chant *HU* or your own word. From this point on, you're going to work with the imaginative faculty.

Tell yourself, "I'm going to get out of this chair and walk over to the dresser." Go over to the dresser, and study it. Notice all the details. Get really interested in how it's made. Then look at the mirror over the dresser. Study it carefully. Take a walk to your closet. Get totally absorbed in what you see. Watch how the door opens. Check out the hangers. Examine your clothes.

When your interest wanes, walk to the bathroom. Observe the sink, the faucets, and all the other fixtures. Get very interested in what you're doing. Then say, "OK, now I'm going to walk out into the hallway and go into the next room." Remember, you're working in your imagination now.

Go over to the door, and turn the knob. Notice what the doorknob looks like. Before you open the door, say, "On the other side, I'm going to see the Inner Master." Then open the door. Sure enough, he's there, and he says, "Are you ready to go yet? Let's take a walk outside."

You and Wah Z take a walk and look at the sights along the way. Strike up a conversation with Wah Z. Don't bring up heavy spiritual subjects yet; just talk about something more ordinary.

Whenever you're ready to return, say, "Wah Z, why don't we go back to my room now? I'd like to see myself sitting in the chair." Walk back to your room. Throughout this experience, try to remember to chant *HU* or your word every so often.

Open your door, walk into the room, look over at your body, and say, "I'll see you later, Wah Z. I'd better sit down in the chair and get myself together again." Then end the spiritual exercise by moving back to your body and opening your eyes.

TRAINING THE IMAGINATION

The imaginative faculty within yourself is like a muscle; you're going to have to train it day after day. Go to different places. Maybe you'll want to re-create a plane ride: I'm sitting in the airplane seat. What do I see? What do the people look like?

Whenever you're ready to return, say, "Wah Z, why don't we go back to my room now? I'd like to see myself sitting in the chair."

What happens when I walk down the aisle? What is on the food tray? Visualize all the details.

When you go to sleep at night, tell yourself, in a very relaxed way, "I'm not going to worry or think about this kind of exercise. If the Inner Master wants me to take another trip, great, but I'm not going to be trying. I'm just going to get some rest." Then look into the inner vision, and chant yourself to sleep.

What you are actually doing is learning how to become aware and observant of yourself in a different state of consciousness. As you go through the day, you'll find yourself looking at objects and making mental notes, because that physical information about the dresser or the clothes in your closet will be helpful when you sit down in your chair and try to visualize it. If it doesn't work, try it again tomorrow. Keep trying it in different ways.

For some of you this will work, while others of you will find other ways to do your spiritual exercises. Experiment. As you do your spiritual exercises, set up enjoyable things to do on the inner planes. If one technique doesn't work for you, then modify it, adapt it, experiment. Do whatever you can.

May the blessings be.

Experiment. As you do your spiritual exercises, set up enjoyable things to do on the inner planes.

ECKANKAR International Creative Arts Festival, Boston, Massachusetts, Saturday, June 16, 1984

At the end of the Freedom Trail, the teens climbed into
a deserted fountain which they called the Fountain of Youth.

16

A TALK WITH THE TEENS

 y daughter has been staying up later than usual for the last few nights, so she is not in the best of moods when she wakes up in the morning. This morning I lectured her about being crabby. A little while later she said, very sweetly, "Dad, do you know how long you talked last night?"

This morning my daughter said, "Dad, do you know how long you talked last night?"

THE ECK'S SCHEDULE

Of course I know, because I check as soon as I come off the stage. It's easy to lose track of time up here. But I just said, "How long?"

"You talked for a whole hour!" she said.

"I did?"

"Yeah," she said. "And I fell asleep for half an hour."

"I don't mind," I said. "You had a long day." I had to think fast. "By the way, Paul sometimes used to talk longer than an hour."

She said, "He did?"

"Yes. And do you realize that a minister in a church gives one or two sermons fifty-two Sundays every year? In addition to that, he also has all of the religious holidays. So he's got a lot of time to get everything in. But I don't. Sometimes the ECK wants to give certain things to people, and I have to sit there until it's given."

"Well, I guess it's OK then," she said.

She left the room and returned a few minutes later. "You know, Dad, the real reason I fell asleep was because I swam all day yesterday." It was more like a couple of hours, but I just said, "Yes, that's probably why you were tired. I know it was late."

As you can see, when I cross the forty-five-minute line up here, I'm walking into bear country at home.

SPIRIT OF LIFE

I don't try to recite *The Shariyat-Ki-Sugmad* to you from the stage. You can read it yourself. You can always fill your mind with the material in the ECK books. Hopefully it will inspire you and be the catalyst for the spiritual unfoldment to follow.

In my talks I try to show you how to work with some of the ECK principles through stories that demonstrate the spirit of life. I approach it in a number of different ways, and people sometimes wonder if the subject was really spiritual. Maybe our definition of what is spiritual has been too limited.

Maybe our definition of what is spiritual has been too limited.

One of the ECKists told me about the bus tour she took along the Freedom Trail with some of the ECK youth. When I met with the teenagers, they told me there's more they'd like to say.

HK: I'm curious to find out what stood out the most for you on your bus tour. Was it the issue of freedom?

BOND AMONG YOUTH

Teen: We wanted to express the real bond that has developed among all the ECK teens. If this is the base for tomorrow, it's a great one. We finally know that there are other ECK youth out there, and we can talk to them about things that we can't talk about to our regular friends.

Teen: Being a teenager growing up in Eckankar has been difficult because I've had no one to really share my experiences with. Soul is ageless, but in the physical adults and teenagers are still two different types of people. The chance to get together with other ECK youth has given me great inspiration to be able to spread the message of ECK, whereas before I was terrified. I wouldn't even mention I was an ECKist because I didn't know how to express myself.

Teen: At the end of the Freedom Trail, we found a deserted fountain that had no water in it, so we decided to climb in and sit down. We called it the Fountain of Youth. Soon we were doing a contemplation, and you could just feel the bond there. It was so strong that I felt like I didn't ever want it to end. We imagined ourselves as the water in the Fountain of Youth. The ECK that was flowing out of us took the place of the water. It's hard to explain, but it was an incredible experience. We talked about what freedom meant and how the ECK was behind all history.

Teen: At the Fountain of Youth we formed a group consciousness. But when we asked each other what was the most significant thing each of us had experienced, each person had his own particular aspect to talk about. Yet each of us seemed to understand what the others were talking about.

Teen: *It was an incredible experience. We talked about what freedom meant and how the ECK was behind all history.*

Importance to History

When we first got to the park, we looked at the statue of Paul Revere, then everyone drifted over to the fountain. It suddenly occurred to me that it was symbolic that the fountain was right behind this statue which represented a historical event. It seemed to be pointing out the same thing: The ECK is behind history.

Teen: In *The Shariyat* it is said that freedom has to be won and rewon all the time. By getting together and growing stronger, the ECK youth are learning how to carry on the movement of ECK. Eckankar is going to keep gaining new ground, and it's going to be up to us, the youth, to help it keep growing.

HK: The teens were concerned about what to talk about onstage. I said, "You'll be surprised once you get going. It's as if the ECK puts a little light on the one who is supposed to say something." I didn't put it like this, but I knew they'd be like cylinders in a car: each one moves at the right time.

We really don't like to think about renewal—when we leave and someone else replaces us. But it's the fabric of our teaching, and we are making provisions for it as we go. It's the natural order of life. I feel that the future of Eckankar will be in good hands.

OPENING THE DOOR OF ECK

The study plan in ECK is designed to make the teachings more accessible. We are working to open the door of ECK to people who haven't heard about it.

When you first come into ECK, you don't know if anything of a spiritual nature is going to happen or not. As a new student, I wanted time to think about it, and I felt relieved when the ECK writings said you had two years before deciding if you wanted the formal outer initiation. I needed room to think, because by the time you come to the path of ECK, you've likely been betrayed by just about every conceivable path and concept on earth.

We are trying to take into consideration all the different areas of our membership so that if we are careful, the ECK message will be able to come out more fully into the world.

INITIATIONS

It's a great advantage to have an ECK discourse come once a month so that you can absorb it a little bit at a time. You also need time in this world to grow into the initiations. The purpose of the study program is to lead you to the initiations.

At the age of eighteen, a person who has been enrolled under the family plan may begin the adult discourses and receive individual study credit. It will then take approximately four years of study credit to qualify for the Third Initiation.

THE GOLDEN STREAM OF LIFE

I am concerned about the youth, but I want there to be more to the spiritual life than just putting in study time. I'm looking to have living programs for the youth which they have a hand in developing. In this way, while they're growing up, they will have a good way to participate in ECK and become firmly grounded in the principles of Light and Sound as they come to meet life.

This is the way of ECK—we become better in some specialty or interest which helps us not only on the ECK path but also out in the world. There isn't a separation between the spiritual and the physical at all. They work together. Some call it the waking dream. It's the connection, the golden stream of life, that flows through all aspects of living, from the waking to the sleeping.

I'm looking to have living programs for the youth which they have a hand in developing.

As you go on your way home, the blessings of the SUGMAD, the ECK, and the MAHANTA go with you. My love is always with you. May the blessings be.

ECKANKAR International Creative Arts Festival, Boston, Massachusetts, Sunday, June 17, 1984

The custom of taking home food you couldn't eat in the restaurant is actually based on a spiritual principle.

17

THE LAW
OF ECONOMY

he Law of Economy presupposes that everything we do is in harmony with ECK, in harmony with life. This somehow is taken to mean we should also be adroit, coordinated, and do all things with polish.

Somebody wrote me a letter recently and said that he had discovered my deep secret. He now saw very clearly why a talk went in a certain direction and why it sometimes turned out that people laughed.

SECRET OF LAUGHTER

"Some of your stories," he said, "have made me wonder what the subject had to do with ECK. Then one day, while laughing at something humorous you had said, all of a sudden I realized what it was all about: Laughter is a healer, and this is what the ECK uses to open the door to Soul." I thought, *Oh, no! He's found out the secret!*

Laughter is a healer, and this is what the ECK uses to open the door to Soul.

FREEDOM OF CHOICE

Two years ago we went into a restaurant in Amsterdam, and one person asked, "Do you have a salad bar?" The waiter looked at us very strangely. The idea of a salad bar, where the customer serves himself from a large variety of fresh fruits and vegetables, was completely foreign to him. He said, "You mean where a bunch of people attack the salad?"

In Amsterdam again this weekend, we had lunch at a restaurant. They had a salad bar. Now the diner has a choice. Salad bars have sprung up all over Amsterdam. The reason is that the consciousness is changing.

Isn't it wonderful to choose what you want to eat? Spiritual freedom also means freedom of choice.

Isn't it wonderful to choose what you want to eat? When you were a child, your mother put the vegetables on the plate and said, "Eat them." Children don't have much choice about a lot of things. Before salad bars it was much the same for adults. When they went into a restaurant and were given a salad with the meal, it was just like Mother saying, "Eat your vegetables." If you asked for a choice, and you didn't get it, you didn't go back to that place. Instead you found someplace where you did have a choice.

This all fits in with the Law of Economy, because you get what you need. As a child you don't have many choices. As you grow older, you should have more. We look for spiritual freedom, and this also means we must have freedom of choice. The further we go along the path of ECK, and the higher we go into the worlds of God, the more choice we expect to have.

GETTING THE MOST FROM LIFE

"Doggie bag" is a fancy term for food you take home because you couldn't eat it all in the restaurant. In America it used to be considered improper. You wondered about the person who had the audacity to ask the waiter for some kind of container to take part of his steak home. We were living in a time of plenty, which often is a time of waste.

The spiritual principle is that you get the most effect out of everything you do, and everything is turned to a spiritual effect. Through doing the spiritual exercises, the forces are no longer being scattered all over and wasted; they are now aligned in one direction, and that direction is home to God, to the SUGMAD. So you see that the Law of Economy is important. What usually isn't noticed is that the Law of Economy is expressed in everything we do and in the people we meet every day.

Last night about ten of us went to a Greek restaurant. After we finished eating, one of the ECKists decided to ask the waitress if she could provide something to wrap the leftover food in. He came back a few minutes later wearing a big smile on his face. "The waitress will bring something to wrap the food in," he said.

The waitress walked over to our table carrying a huge sheet of aluminum foil. It was enough to wrap up all the food in the restaurant! Our friend began to wrap his food with this noisy stuff, and it suddenly got very quiet in the restaurant. People actually laid down their forks and turned around to watch this marvelous performance: a person carefully and ever-so-lovingly placing half-eaten food in the center of this foil, which first had to be folded over several times to get it down to a size suitable for that small amount of food. And then, finally, the grand deed was accomplished, and the gentleman set the package aside.

People actually laid down their forks and turned around to watch this marvelous performance.

I believe we made a great step forward for the doggie bag. Only time will tell. Perhaps those of you who want to get better use out of your money can go to a restaurant and be able to ask for a doggie bag, knowing there's a spiritual principle behind it. This is the Law of Economy, where you actually make good use of the food instead of throwing it out. So despite the cold stare of the maître d', this gives you the right to do good in the name of some principle that is greater than the uninformed attitude of anyone in the restaurant.

THE LAW OF KARMA

We know that the world economy hasn't been operating on the Law of Economy. America is one of the great offenders. How long can you run without paying your debts? Some governments feel they can always start up the presses and print more money. There is a law against people doing this in their basement, but this is how many national governments operate—because they don't realize how the Law of Karma works.

The life of a country spans many decades, and karma doesn't necessarily come back tomorrow morning; it sometimes takes several years. In the meantime, everybody thinks they are getting a free ride. But they are forgetting the basic Law of Economy, which is the Law of Cause and Effect. You pay for everything you get, both spiritually and materially.

The different countries of the world act like many human beings. They simply don't understand the laws. The ECKist is among the chosen and enlightened; he understands, at least in his head if not in practice, that sometime he must pay his debt—if not sooner, then later.

The ECKist is among the chosen and enlightened; he understands he must pay his debt—if not sooner, then later.

MAKING PROPHECIES

The Law of Economy works in a number of different ways. Spiritual teachers sometimes get into an area they don't understand at all, and this is prophecy. They look at the short-term benefits of this practice, believing it will hold the interest of their followers. By studying financial charts and political trends, they develop a feel for what the experts have to say about future directions. Then, using a pendulum or some other device, they'll make a grand prediction—and it won't come true. If the person were wise, he would make small predictions first and try to establish a track record. But generally when somebody gets started in the field of prophecy, he feels he's got to make big predictions right away.

Often when a master dies, one of the followers quickly jumps to the front and proclaims himself the new master, and then he tries to hold his little band of followers together by giving prophecies. Many of these people have absolutely no idea about spirituality at all, let alone economics or any of the other things that a person needs to know in order to make a good prediction; yet they do it anyway.

Within the last year, someone made a grand prediction: the European economy was going to collapse in June of 1984. It's July, and it hasn't happened. He made the mistake of getting too specific. All of his followers waited and waited for that day in June, but the great collapse didn't occur. And you know what it does to the prophet's credibility when he misses on his prediction. His followers probably went back home, restudied their holy works, and wondered why this teacher couldn't make an accurate prediction. Perhaps they concluded that making a prophecy probably doesn't have anything at all to do with spirituality.

This is a world where people are allowed free rein, to bumble and blunder along, and to do it at their own speed. Maybe this is why most of the prophets miss when predicting the date a disaster is supposed to occur.

Maybe the prophets don't understand that people—the consciousness, the karmic family of earth—have a choice in how fast, how selfishly and greedily, they are going to use up the earth's resources. The spiritual life is tied right in to how we live every day and how well our government does or does not regulate itself. It all ties together. When the law is broken, the debt must be paid.

This is a world where people are allowed free rein, to bumble and blunder along, and to do it at their own speed.

HOW TO HANDLE PROBLEMS

In a crisis of any kind, it is generally not understood why certain people benefit. For instance, when the stock market crashes, there are people who become rich. Why? Because every time a big bubble is created in the regular pattern of human activity, those who understand the laws—whether of economics or politics or anything else—can use the energy to advance their own careers.

If you have problems and catastrophes in your own life, this energy can propel you to spiritual heights.

In a spiritual sense, if you have problems and catastrophes in your own life, this energy can propel you to spiritual heights. Letters come to me from people begging to be spared problems in life. They are looking toward the old concept of God: "If something goes wrong in my life, Lord, please deliver me from it." They are deaf to the question But what will you do in return? They think it is enough to say, "In return I'll love you and worship you." It's not enough.

We have to take full responsibility for our own lives. Once we do, we find that the problems we have are ones we can handle. Not only that, but we can often choose our problems. You may think if there were a choice between problems and no problems, you'd choose to have no problems, and I'd say you would be very wise. Unfortunately, this world doesn't run like that. It works by degrees, not absolutes. You can't say you will or will not have problems. That's absolute, and life doesn't work that way. It works like this: You are going to have problems, but you now have a choice as to how to handle them.

You can choose to take a short-term solution that will make you feel good for a day or two. But it's not going to work out so well in the long run. You have a choice: Should I handle the problem with a good solution or a poor solution? If you don't have self-discipline, you say, "Here today, gone tomorrow; I may not be around in a week." So you take the short-term solution. A week later you're still alive, and you have to pay the piper. And then it's, "O Lord, why me? Why have you done this to me? Someone else must be responsible, certainly not I." Like Job in the Old Testament, you can cry and curse the day you were born. You might even blame the devil for your misfortune.

THE RELATIONSHIP BETWEEN GOD AND SATAN

One of the mysteries the religions haven't been able to decipher is this: If God is more powerful than Satan, why doesn't God stop this foolishness? Why not just unleash the powers of heaven and let Satan have it with huge bolts of lightning? That would fix this evil force for good!

But it doesn't happen. Why not? Because the negative power is an agent for God. You might say the evil force, the devil, Satan—known as the Kal Niranjan in Eckankar—is a hired employee of the SUGMAD. His job is to act as the schoolmaster, following SUGMAD's will. SUGMAD said, "I've got a schoolroom of children here. Make sure these Souls get enough of an education so that when they graduate, they can go into the spiritual worlds and stand on their own two feet. Their destiny is to become Coworkers with God, helping me in the administration of my worlds."

The religions don't understand the relationship between God and Satan, nor the principle behind self-discipline and self-indulgence. So the people have problems they can't handle. We have problems, too, but they are problems we can handle better and better the further we go in ECK.

The guru who made the prediction that the economy was going to crash in June of 1984 may have been right, but his timing was off. There was another guru in Canada who picked sometime early in 1984 as the date for the end of the world. What happened among some of his followers was interesting too. One lady gave up her job—the predictable

Why doesn't God just unleash the powers of heaven and let Satan have it with huge bolts of lightning? That would fix this evil force for good!

reaction if your teacher says the world is coming to an end. Working was a real chore and a nuisance to her anyway, so why do it now? In just a couple more weeks Armageddon would come, and it would all be over. She gave up her job, her security, and didn't worry about paying her rent—because why bother? The Lord would be here soon, and if the landlord wants his money, he's gonna have to go to the big man. Well, it didn't happen.

COMMUNICATION

Followers of the path of Light and Sound should know not to take as gospel the words they hear from any outer source, including me. Recognize also that even if you hear the truth, you may misunderstand it. This sometimes happens in the meetings held at the Eckankar International Office. The manager will give a directive and then find that it was carried out completely differently. Now when he gives directions, he verifies that the people actually understand what he means. If there is still a misunderstanding, he'll go over it again.

Communication is often very difficult, and we have to work at it all the time. When we succeed, it's easier to work together in presenting the message of ECK to the people who have yet to hear it. If we believe our words could never be misinterpreted, then it stands to reason we always blame the person who didn't hear us correctly, instead of learning to communicate more clearly.

When something isn't carried out the way I'd like, the first thing I do is ask, Where's my responsibility in this? Is it possible I didn't communicate this clearly enough? Very often this is true. Working as we do at all the different levels, and with all the different languages we speak, communicating with each other can be quite difficult. As we go higher in ECK, our communication with Spirit becomes

When something isn't carried out the way I'd like, the first thing I do is ask, Where's my responsibility in this?

clearer. And hopefully, as we go further along the path, the communication among initiates should be cleaner and clearer.

An aspect of the Law of Economy is recognizing the weaknesses in any system on earth. This includes recognizing the weaknesses in our own character and makeup and working with them, as well as recognizing the same traits in other people and trying to work with them.

Earth will never be a heaven. Nor should you serve SUGMAD for some cause other than your spiritual growth. The spiritual exercises are given for the purification of Soul and for the self-perfection that you can take upon yourself as you reach the heights of God.

LOOKING AT THE FUTURE

We think of the future as something we're facing, something coming up in front of us. Imagine yourself on a train: The station is in the present where the train is. As the engine starts moving along the tracks, you see the future far off in the distance—like little trees and buildings seen from the train windows. The closer it gets, the clearer you can see the future—until it becomes the present. The station is now past, you can no longer see it very well at all, and soon it's forgotten.

The ancient Greeks regarded the future from a different perspective. They turned it around the other way. They stood on the platform of the caboose and watched the station receding as the train pulled away. The past receded in front of you while the future came up from behind.

Perhaps the ancient Greeks had a better concept of Soul as It operates in the worlds of time and space. As the train pulls out of the station, you can see the past events very clearly. They are very close at hand, and you can describe them well. But as the train picks

The ancient Greeks regarded the future from a different perspective. They turned it around the other way.

up speed and increases the distance between you and the station, you can describe less and less of the past.

Our records of Atlantis and Lemuria are almost nonexistent in human history. The events are so far in the past that we can't see them clearly. Nor can we see what's going to happen tomorrow. It's coming up at the front of the train, but we're facing the back. So this puts a lot of importance on living in the moment, being aware that we are alive, and getting experience right now.

This puts a lot of importance on living in the moment, being aware we are alive, and getting experience right now.

CHOOSING A MASTER

There are people today who are struggling to make up their minds who to follow as a Master. Some want to hang on to the ones that came before. But there's something sound to the idea of not looking to a Master who has passed from this arena. Other people won't look to a Master who is here now—they'd rather wait for the next one. It's a sad thing, because they are in the same boat as those who waited for the last judgment day in the year AD 1000, or those who are going to be sitting around and waiting for the world to end in the year AD 2000.

These people are sitting and waiting for life to begin, and in the meantime, life is passing them by. What they are waiting for will never come, because they do not understand the ways of Spirit. They live in the past, they live in the future, but they refuse to live in the present moment—and they are only cheating themselves. They will leave the path of ECK having convinced themselves that they are following the Light and Sound, and they feel somehow they can do it without a Master.

Choosing a Master is the great gamble of life. You pick right, you pick wrong; you take your bruises or your rewards. But next time you're smarter. Soul has become a little more mature, a bit more able to make a wise decision in whatever world the SUGMAD has stationed It in. It's better qualified to someday take up Its place as a Co-worker and help administer the worlds.

LIVING VEHICLES FOR GOD

Being a Coworker with God means having the highest spiritual consciousness embodied in individuals we call ECK Masters. They go among the people quietly. Except for the few whose job it is to work in the public eye, the ECK Masters very rarely speak about who they are. It's not important to them to be known by a title; what's important to the ECK Masters is giving upliftment to Soul— to even one individual Soul somewhere. If they can do this for one person, that's all they care about.

The ECK Masters are walking among you now, dealing with one person at a time. If you choose to stay blind and not look for the manifestations of the ECK miracles about you every day, you may do so. It may or may not be an ECK Master who brings the principles of Spirit to you in ways so common-place that you might overlook them.

Someone once asked why certain individuals reached the higher initiations so fast in this life. He thought it unfair. He didn't see anything in those people that would justify them having become a Seventh or Eighth Initiate so quickly. In a past life, that Eighth Initiate was the person who came to the fork in the road beyond which he could not go. One more time he had to face the question of that crossroad: Will I go the way of ECK into the heart of SUGMAD, or will I get off the path for some imagined injury to my ego?

The Eighth Initiates of today got off the path of ego lifetimes ago. When they came back this time, the Master recognized them, and he said, "Let's see if we can get you the Eighth Initiation. Do you want it?" You bet they wanted it, because

What's important to the ECK Masters is giving upliftment to Soul—to even one individual Soul somewhere.

now they knew: They had nothing else to live for in this life but to be aware, to be conscious of themselves as living vehicles for God. This occurs in a more enlightening way than could ever be imagined by the followers of the orthodox religions.

Those of you who are willing to give up and let go of the smallness of yourself, to take a risk and go into the other worlds, are the adventurers—the chosen people. When the blessings of God are showered on you, don't expect your neighbor to see it, because it may not show up as material wealth. But it will show up in happiness and in an ability to handle your own life, even through the times when beloved family members have to leave the earth plane. We cry, but we can go on; our life is not destroyed and shattered. Because we know that the Master's promise is true: I am always with you.

Those of you willing to let go of the smallness of yourself, to take a risk and go into the other worlds, are the adventurers—the chosen people.

ECKANKAR European Seminar, The Hague, The Netherlands, Friday, July 20, 1984

You can start in your room tonight and use your imagination to take a short trip into the other worlds.

18

A SHORT TRIP TO
THE INNER WORLDS

reparing these talks is a creative experience. I like to prepare well for a talk: I used to spend months gathering material. But it's the same as any activity—the more you do it, the more you can refine it. You begin to find out the things you don't have to do. Somewhere along the line, a person comes to trust the ECK. You realize what is necessary to do as well as what is a waste of time and energy. You begin to simplify the process.

Somewhere along the line, a person comes to trust the ECK.

KEEPING IT SIMPLE

When you give a talk about ECK, you want to make it as clear and simple as possible. You try to imagine who's going to be sitting in the audience. The right audience for that day will be there, and so as you construct your talk, you visualize them and try to figure out what their spiritual needs are.

During the weeks and months preceding each talk, I make it a discipline to write talk notes on little slips of paper. These include anything out of the ordinary that happens to me that expresses the ECK, whether it's something funny, outrageous, painful, whatever. I'll sketch the gist of the story in condensed form and gather these notes into an envelope.

TAKING CARE OF YOURSELF

Some of our experiences have to do with maintaining good health. What my body needs keeps changing. As soon as I figure out just what it needs, all of a sudden the body has changed and doesn't respond. Then I can either take the time to find out what I have to do to adjust to this new change that prevents the body from running the way it should, or sometimes I'll go to a nutritionist. What's important is the experience of finding out where and how to take care of myself under constantly changing conditions.

I often go to a health food store near my home. It is run by a spry, energetic lady in her seventies and her daughter. One time we got to talking. I told them about a disastrous two-day vacation our family had just taken the previous weekend. We stayed at a hotel that caters to businessmen during the week. There isn't much business on the weekends, so they offer a special rate to try to fill the rooms. The pool was a tiny thing that only held six people, but there were at least twelve kids jumping into the water, having a great time. It was a hundred degrees outside, and we couldn't get near the water to cool off.

A lady at the health food store is always trying to get me to go to her church, even though she knows about my job.

I was at the health food store, telling the two ladies about everything that had gone wrong. The mother is always trying to get me to go to her church, even though she knows about my job. She's very crafty about it. She'll say something like, "At church we have a real good cooking class."

This time she said, "It's too bad about your vacation. I have just the answer for you." *Here we go again*, I thought. She continued, "You can buy yourself a biorhythm meter. They really work!"

I thought about the ECK-Vidya, the ancient science of prophecy, and how dull it would be to know everything that's going to happen before it happens. It would take all the surprise out of life, even for me. I usually don't look into the future unless I get myself in a bit of trouble. Then I take a look and try to figure the quickest way out of the problem I got myself into. People generally assume that I would love to know everything that's going to happen in the next minute or day, but I really don't. That would make it a boring, dull world—and I don't know if I could stand it.

I do my contemplations every day simply because I like to, and because I can get away—go somewhere else and have a good time. Sometimes they aren't such good times, but I do get away, and that's usually how I take a vacation. But sometimes my family likes to get away, too, so we go off on a vacation such as I described.

I like the lady in the health food store; she's a good friend of mine. We have a mutual respect, and in a motherly way she's concerned about my health. But when she starts talking about her religion, I very politely excuse myself.

APPRECIATING ANOTHER'S AWARENESS

There are people who are not ready for ECK. They look to the religion that fits them, often drawn to the emotionalism that Eckankar doesn't have. At a certain level of their unfoldment, some people just need a good, healthy, emotional songfest.

My daughter joined a girls' softball league. One Sunday we went out to practice: She's the batter, I'm the pitcher. The ball field is part of an abandoned school which has been taken over by members of a refugee temple. The school doors were open that day because of the heat, and the whole congregation was singing hymns with all the full

People look to the religion that fits them, often drawn to the emotionalism that Eckankar doesn't have.

power and beauty that some of these songs have. It was wonderful to listen as we played ball outside.

The people who attend this refugee temple are immigrants to the United States. They work hard for very little money, and they build up an enormous amount of frustration trying to support their families in an area with such a high cost of living. But every Sunday they can go to their church and sing, allow all the frustration and anger to pour out, and then go home feeling more balanced.

They would never be drawn to Eckankar because of their state of consciousness. They're happy where they are, and their religion is very good for them. We could only appreciate them, enjoy the music, and let them be in their own level of awareness.

The people who attend this refugee temple are happy where they are, and their religion is very good for them.

REFLECTION OF CONSCIOUSNESS

My wife went to an art museum in Amsterdam to look at paintings of the masters. She noticed that the art illustrated a peculiar thing about the evolution of consciousness that has occurred in Europe since the Middle Ages. Her perception was that during the Dark Ages paintings portrayed people with expressions that seemed to reflect the harshness and darkness of the era, the persecutions by the church, and the lack of knowledge. But then during the Renaissance, many gifted artists came forward.

In the paintings that bridged the period from the Dark Ages to the Renaissance, the painters first began working with religious scenes and figures from the Bible. Later came portraits of the nobles and royalty. As the Renaissance went along, the artists painted common people engaged in their everyday work and activities.

These paintings are perhaps one of our main records of what life was like for people at that time. There were no news cameras getting the life of the man on the street for the six o'clock news. So many of our perceptions of the past depend on the snapshots painted by these great masters.

Hanging on the wall in the hotel room were a couple of reproductions of paintings by the masters. The colors were drab and dull. In the art museum the colors were so alive, so vivid and clear, it's almost as if the light is pouring out of them. My wife concluded that it's impossible to reproduce the vivid quality of those paintings.

EVERYDAY LIVING

In ECK it is the simple things we do that provide a lasting spiritual lesson and demonstrate a spiritual principle. When I give my talks with the little stories about life and living, I am aware of the weaknesses, the things I wish I had said. But perhaps someone will say, Ah, this is how the high theory of ECK translates to everyday living. That story was able to show me how to do something for myself, and how to understand a problem I couldn't live with. If these stories help translate the words of *The Shariyat-Ki-Sugmad* into everyday living and illustrate ways to meet life without being defeated by it, then perhaps they have accomplished something.

When I write an article, if a certain paragraph doesn't read right, I'll begin to cut it down. Sometimes I'll rewrite it three or four times, all for the purpose of saying it more simply and trying to get the images clearer and clearer.

In ECK, if we can remember that Soul is an atom of God, that our relationship with the Divine Being is always one-on-one, then we have made a substantial step. No longer is it important what people think about what we do. Every act has a consequence, and we recognize the consequences of our actions. But instead of weighing each action, we now work with the simplicity of Spirit. We listen to the heart, and then we say, Yes, I can do this, or No, I will not do

When I give my talks with the little stories about life, perhaps someone will say, Ah, this is how the high theory of ECK translates to everyday living.

that. Our life becomes simpler and more straight-forward, even though the events and circumstances around us would appear to another person to be swirling at a thousand miles an hour.

HEARING THE MASTER'S WORDS

There was an elderly woman who had gone through many libraries, reading through the stacks of books in her search for truth. Truth is the one element that is not multifaceted. It is one unit, but it has many applications, depending upon the plane where we live. This woman couldn't find the answers, so eventually she gave up.

One day, by some chance, she came across a notice that said there would be a lecture on Eckankar given by Paul Twitchell. She decided to attend. During the talk, Paul made a statement that she misunderstood. She thought he said old people cannot unfold spiritually. This really upset her. She stood up and asked, "Why do you say that?" Paul replied, curtly, "I never said that" and cut her short.

She left the meeting feeling very dejected. I'll never go and listen to that kind of stuff again, she told herself. As she drove away, she came to a red light at an intersection and braked to a stop. Paul stood on the corner. When he saw her, he smiled and gave her a big friendly wave. Then she understood: He was getting a spiritual principle across to her. What happened at the meeting had nothing to do with the personality; it was the only way the MAHANTA could break through the human consciousness and touch her heart.

In another instance, a man with a heart condition asked Paul if he should have open-heart surgery. Paul advised very strongly against it. "Don't do it," he said. "Your condition will improve in six months." The man went ahead with the open-heart surgery anyway, and

A man with a heart condition asked Paul if he should have open-heart surgery.

through some kind of a miscalculation by the doctors, he turned into a vegetable. In his body he was no longer useful to this world. His condition completely drained the family finances, and there was no hope for recovery.

After a period of time, the man's family found out that if he lingered beyond a certain date, they would lose the insurance money they needed to survive. Some of the family members came to Paul and told him about this. Paul said, "The silver cord has already been severed. It will take a little while for the physical body to cease functioning, but it will happen a week before the insurance policy expires." And so it happened.

Creating Our Own Problems

If someone asked about an intimate problem, there were times Paul would give clear advice; but in this case, the man didn't listen. Perhaps every Living ECK Master has run into this same situation. People make problems for themselves out of ignorance of the Law of Karma. When the pain comes home to them, they say, "Please deliver me from this problem." Once in a while the Master will step in and try to help, but often it won't do any good. The person will ignore the advice simply because he hasn't the state of consciousness to accept it. Sometimes only the pain of the condition can bring about the raising of the state of consciousness to where one can actually understand the Master's words.

The pain or health problem that we suffer is actually a tool to raise us another degree in our state of consciousness. Soul needs the trials and tribulations. The greater we become, the greater our problems; but at the same time, the greater becomes our ability to solve or control them. You will have a greater ability to handle your own life, and with a greater degree of happiness.

If asked, there were times Paul would give clear advice; but in this case, the man didn't listen.

ECK HISTORIANS

We are making an effort to construct a physical history of Eckankar, looking for actual physical records to verify the existence of some of the ECK Masters in a way that historians of the future will be able to accept; something beyond just the words of one of the Living ECK Masters of the past. It will be vital for the survival of Eckankar as a religious teaching in the future.

As we began research in a number of different areas around the world, we got reports that Sudar Singh had lived and really was an ECK Master. Many ECKists have experiences with Rebazar Tarzs, Yaubl Sacabi, Fubbi Quantz, and other ECK Masters, but very few see Sudar Singh. As it turns out, he did live and work in Allahabad. Paul mentioned he died around the 1940s, but it seems to have been around 1955.

The research we do today will someday be pored over by historians. They will get into great debates about this or that crisis, about this or that person. We are living the historical moments today, and whatever later historians want to make of it for their own unfoldment is up to them. For now, we continue to live our lives in the mainstream of Spirit.

We continue to live our lives in the mainstream of Spirit.

PAUL'S MISSION

Paul Twitchell brought together the scattered fragments of truth and put them in one place. He had to work fast, because after he was poisoned in Spain, it was an inescapable fact that he would soon drop the body. He certainly had nothing to gain from continuing to gather this truth, yet he was driven by Spirit to put these writings in one place. As a result, you and I don't have to spend our money on a personal expedition to India, to the Vatican library, or to Tibet. We need not pass our whole life trying to find what has been written about truth in this world in order to further our spiritual unfoldment.

Nothing written in any book is a perfect reflection of truth. If the written words can inspire us, give us a road map to the heavens, open a door to lead us from the fear of death, and release us from the fear of what other people think so we can live this life in full consciousness, then Paul's mission will have been a success.

What we are faced with now is taking the message of ECK out into the world. We do this with the books and discourses we have, while never claiming that they are perfect. No teachings and no bibles on earth are perfect. They can never be so, for this is an imperfect universe. The perfection isn't here; it is in the worlds beyond, and this is what we are trying to reach.

An ECK Miracle

At an ECK seminar in Boston, two Higher Initiates were walking down a hallway, talking about what it means to be a vehicle for Spirit. They came to a lobby area and saw a woman lying flat on her back on a sofa, with two men standing helplessly on either side. The people were guests in the hotel but were not ECKists. Something had slipped in the woman's back, and she was in such great pain that she couldn't move. If she had just been able to get up, the two men could have helped her to a hospital for medical treatment. But every time they touched her, she moaned in pain.

The two ECKists came over to see if they could help. For some strange reason, one of them pointed at the woman and said, "In the name of the Sugmad, get up!" The woman immediately got up.

For some strange reason, one ECKist pointed at the woman and said, "In the name of the Sugmad, get up!"

She said, "I don't know what you did, but thank you." The two men were then able to help her out the door to get medical aid. As the two ECKists continued their walk down the hall, one turned to the other and said, "My God, a miracle!"

Someday this incident will be included in our ECK writings, but time has a way of embellishing the truth. Perhaps when it's retold a few times, someone will have added that the clouds parted and lightning flashed. This is the basis of many stories in the Christian Bible. Whatever actually occurred was turned into a historical event by a good writer. Perhaps in the same way this ECK miracle will someday be spruced up and polished a little bit too.

CREATING SPIRITUAL EXERCISES

Someone spoke of the difficulty he was having with his spiritual exercises. For some reason, this reminded me of the snails in our garden. Last year the snails found my vegetables, so this year I planted flowers. The snails found those too.

Whenever I go traveling, I come home to find that the snails have been busy. They like to hide underneath the railing of the wooden fence in our backyard. I scoop them up with a little shovel, put them in an empty milk carton, and call my daughter. I say, "Find a good place for these snails." They'd eat up the entire garden, but my daughter wouldn't care—she thinks they're cute. So I give her the job of finding someplace away from my garden to put them. I say, "I don't even want to know where you take them—just don't put them in the neighbors' gardens."

The neighbors' cats like my garden too. What the snails don't destroy, the cats get. They find my flower bed a very nice place to dig.

The difficulty someone was having with his spiritual exercises reminded me of the snails in our garden.

There is a spiritual principle involved here: How do you handle things as humble as snails and cats? You use all your expertise, and you do the best you can. Sometimes you win, sometimes you lose; sometimes the snails win, sometimes the cats win.

It's the same with the spiritual exercises. It takes discipline, it takes persistence; sometimes you win, sometimes you lose. Sometimes the inner experiences will come when you use a certain technique, and then suddenly they won't. It means that you have outgrown that technique and it's time to scramble and find a new spiritual exercise.

When we do the spiritual exercises, we are actually working with images created by the mind. I find the mind is a tricky thing to work with; it gets bored very fast. If you do the same exercise several times in a row, especially if you are highly creative, you are going to get bored. So nothing happens—no Light, no Sound, no Inner Master, no nothing. Not understanding this, some people will keep on with the same technique for weeks and weeks until finally they'll give up, thinking the spiritual exercises don't work.

They should have been recognizing that, to get around the mind, you have to constantly devise your own spiritual exercises. You can do interesting things with them. The only limitations are in the use of your imagination.

To get around the mind, you have to constantly devise your own spiritual exercises.

Using the Imagination

The imagination is the God-spark within you. The only gift of God that we can rightly lay claim to in the physical body is the gift of imagination. If you learn how to use the full powers of the imagination and direct them toward the spiritual exercises, you will be able to find ways around the blocks set up by the mind.

One method is to try to take a short trip into the other worlds. Don't try to go to Venus; forget about

God for now—take those on next week. Start humbly. In your room tonight lie down on your bed, close your eyes, chant *HU* or your secret word, and visualize yourself sitting up and getting out of bed. The physical body is lying down, of course, but act "as if." This is Soul operating.

Get really interested in what you are doing in your imaginative body. For instance, say, "I'm getting out of bed. Here's the nightstand. Does it have a drawer in it?" In other words, you begin to watch for details. Examine the nightstand, and maybe you'll find that this one doesn't have a drawer. There's the lamp. Look at it carefully. In your imaginative body you lean over and look underneath. Maybe you say, "I'll push it to the side so I can move my dream notebook closer to the bed."

Then start walking around the room. You can go over to the window and look out at the view; but if you find it difficult to relate to so many details, just look around your room. Notice the chair. What color is it? Maybe you notice that the wooden armrest is battered; somebody has really given this chair a hard time.

Walk over to the door. Ask yourself, "What will happen if I go out into the hallway?" As you grab hold of the doorknob, observe what it looks like. Is it round? Is it a handle? Open the door, go out into the hallway, and walk up and down a couple of times. Then look toward the other end of the corridor. Maybe you'll see a blue light, about the size of a human being, that looks like somebody in the radiant body.

Walk to the far end of the hallway, and try to look through the blue light to see who's in there. If you can't, let your gaze stray to the side. Maybe you can tell who it is by looking indirectly, using your side vision. If you still can't see through it, just say, "That's OK. I know this is the Living ECK Master in the radiant form. I'd better get back to my room now." Remember, this is supposed to be just a short trip, not an epic voyage.

Head back down the hallway with the Master in the light body walking beside you. Go back to your door, walk in, and close the door. When you first opened that door to go out, you were walking into another world. Now you're back. Go over to your bed, look at your body lying on the rumpled sheets, and say, "I'd better get back in bed now. Is the lamp in the right place? The notebook? Yes, they are." Then just lie back down on the bed, and open your eyes.

I've had interesting reports on this technique from some people. But telling you about their experiences would be like putting a box around the technique and making their experiences conclusive; like trying to organize truth. I'd rather have you practice it yourself. If you have any success, maybe it's better to keep it to yourself. Sometimes by talking about it, you feel the great weight of responsibility: Now you have to do it again. But because you've used the energy to talk about it, you can't.

This is one technique you can use to begin working with the imaginative body. It has to start on the inner planes in order to form into a solid world, but first you have to become very conscious of what you are doing. This actually is Soul, perhaps in one of the lower bodies, enlivening the imaginative body.

May the blessings be.

Head back down the hallway with the Master in the light body walking beside you.

ECKANKAR European Seminar, The Hague, The Netherlands, Saturday, July 21, 1984

The checkout clerk's eyes widened, and she stepped back and stared at me. It was the ECK making contact.

19
TEEN PANEL TALKS
WITH THE MASTER

een: Harold, as the Living ECK Master, you have so many duties, and you have to travel so much. Don't you sometimes neglect your daily life with all this?

HK: I schedule things very carefully. I try to make the ECK duties fit in with my family duties. If we are living the life of ECK correctly, somehow it all works together. But sometimes it does go very fast.

THE ECK MAKING CONTACT

Teen: Could you please explain about the Darshan? When does it happen, and how is it possible to recognize it? Is it always recognizable?

HK: An ECKist recently mentioned to me that every so often someone will have a reaction to her. Something passes from her eyes to the eyes of another person, which causes a reaction, and she doesn't know why. It's the ECK making contact.

The Darshan, which is the meeting with the Master, may even be recognized by people who aren't ECKists. About a month ago I went to a store for some bottled water. As I handed my money to the

The Darshan, the meeting with the Master, may even be recognized by people who aren't ECKists.

checkout clerk, all of a sudden her eyes widened, and she took one quick step back. Instead of putting the change in my hand the way she had been doing for the other customers, she laid it on the counter. Then she just stood there and stared at me. It made me a bit uncomfortable. My mind was far away from spiritual things at the time; I just wanted my bottled water.

Often the ECK works on someone else, such as through the Darshan, when I'm not expecting it myself. It's a very interesting learning experience, but sometimes it is awkward. I have no idea what this woman saw. Sometimes people will see an aura or something else they have never seen before, but whatever it is, it can cause a shock.

COMING HOME

Teen: I have not been in ECK for very long, but when I was coming here to the seminar by train, it felt like I was coming home to see an old friend I've known for a very long time, even though we have not met before in the physical. It was so strange how everything worked out so that I ended up here on the stage. I never believed this would happen. It has made me so happy!

Teen: Last night in my room I was doing a spiritual exercise before going to bed. After a while I became aware of the sound of the clock ticking. I'm not used to that, because I have a digital clock at home. It didn't disturb me, but as it ticked away, my attention was drawn to it. I felt it was telling me that it's time now for many new things to start happening.

The programs coming up will be for the youth of the future. The youth in ECK are the future of Eckankar.

Teen: It's a wonderful opportunity. With great joy, I put everything—all my energy, all my love—into the ECK. If I can be a true channel for the ECK, I think it's the best I can do in this lifetime here in this world.

INNER GUIDANCE

Teen: I think I have known the Inner Master for a very long time, even before I came into ECK. I had a very strange dream when I was about seven or eight. I saw some kind of a deity surrounded by a yellow light. This dream recurred for another two nights, but when I told my mother about it, she was not very interested.

After some time, I began to ask things of this being. They came true in anywhere from a few days to a few months, or sometimes years. They involved changing schools, homes, and even moving to different countries.

Teen: In our everyday lives, we can feel the ECK, always pushing and guiding us. This guidance, both inner and outer, is so fantastic. You feel you are helped wherever you go, or whenever you feel helpless. It is always here, and you never need to doubt it. This is a source of great joy for me, every minute of the day.

BRIDGING THE COMMUNICATION GAP

Teen: The youth programs are not meant to separate the adults from the youth; we are trying to bridge the communication gap. We have seminar workshops for parents and youth together. They discuss ways to communicate, share interests, and to better understand each other.

HK: This is real interesting. I just sat here and hardly said anything, so they had to do the talking. The youth were nervous backstage, and I said, "When

Teen: This guidance, both inner and outer, is so fantastic. You feel you are helped wherever you go, or whenever you feel helpless.

you get out there, you'll probably find it easy to speak."
I didn't tell them that sometimes it's not. But it starts
breaking through a barrier, and the next time will
be much easier. You'll be more confident in talking
about ECK.

I'd like to thank the young people in ECK.

ECKANKAR European Seminar, The Hague,
The Netherlands, Sunday, July 22, 1984

The famous painting now known as *Whistler's Mother* was originally mocked by curators of the Royal Academy in Britain.

20
In ECK We Trust

*T*he phrase found on American coins is "In God We Trust." For us it's really "In ECK We Trust." ECK is the Sound that comes from the Sugmad, or God. Carried into the worlds, It is the force that sustains all life, the golden thread that makes life possible in all the worlds of God. Among the names that have been given It are the Holy Spirit, the Comforter, and Paraclete.

Divine Imagination

A certain rabbi was brought before an inquisition for heresy. Because they felt he did not follow the same God as the Catholic Church, the inquisitors grilled and questioned him, but the judge, or grand inquisitor, still couldn't find enough evidence to prove whether or not the rabbi actually was guilty of heresy. The grand inquisitor finally said, "We will write *not guilty* on one slip of paper, *guilty* on another. Then we will let him be judged by his own God."

But the inquisitor wanted the rabbi convicted of heresy. Using a little trickery, he wrote *guilty* on both slips of paper. A guilty verdict meant being burned at the stake. The rabbi was a very sharp man who understood human nature. He knew the

The grand inquisitor said, "We will write not guilty on one slip of paper, guilty on another, then let him be judged by his own God."

inquisitor would pull something like this, but how was he going to get himself out of it?

The two verdict slips were brought into the courtroom. "Pick one," said the judge. The rabbi reached out, took one of the slips of paper, popped it into his mouth, and swallowed it.

"What did you do that for?" said the judge.

"God made me do it," said the rabbi.

"Well, how will we know whether you're guilty or innocent?"

The rabbi said, "I swallowed the true verdict. Read the one that remains, and you will know that I am the other."

We help ourselves through divine imagination. You suddenly get a brilliant idea, but where did it come from?

Sometimes we help ourselves, as the rabbi did, through divine imagination. You suddenly get a brilliant idea, but where did it come from? Necessity has no laws: you get the help as you need it.

ECK PROTECTION

There have been occasions where people have done things, overtly and covertly, against a vehicle for God, never knowing the person was a vehicle. As a result, their karma speeded up, they had a lot of troubles, and they wondered, *Why me?*

In 1970 when I left the farm in Wisconsin, I was already studying the Eckankar discourses. There was quite a feeling against me because of my strange religion. Although it was a difficult thing to do, I had written a note to the council of the small country church where I grew up. It said, "I am resigning from this church because I am now a student of Eckankar, the Ancient Science of Soul Travel." You can imagine what kind of reaction that caused.

Six years later, by which time I had made my way to California, a relative wrote to tell me that one of the neighbors had won a trip to Hawaii for selling a certain amount of fertilizer. On his way there, he would be coming through Los Angeles, and he was just going to stop in for a visit. I lived in the San Francisco Bay Area, which is about four hundred miles north of Los Angeles.

This neighbor and I had never been close friends, so I knew he had but one reason for coming: He intended to put pressure on me. He would say something like, Everybody misses you back home. Give up the ways of the devil, and come back. I didn't know what to do about this, so I said, Well, I'll just trust the ECK.

He and his wife flew into Los Angeles, but before they could arrange to get to San Francisco, he became very ill. This man was a sturdy farmer, almost six feet tall, hale and hearty, always in good health. But he got so sick that he couldn't even go on to Hawaii for their vacation. Nor could he come up to San Francisco to preach to me about God. All his wife could do was put him on the plane and send him back home.

For several months he was unable to run his farm because of this illness. The doctors never found out what caused it, but I knew what had happened. Spirit had chosen to put up a wall of protection beyond which the man couldn't pass. I would not have to be bothered by him just because I follow ECK. It was all right with me if he followed his religion, so why shouldn't he act in kind? This is just another kind of protection that comes from the ECK.

Across the street from the Eckankar International Office in Menlo Park was one of the largest printing plants in the San Francisco Bay Area. The heavy trucks that delivered their paper routinely drove into our parking lot, and this extra weight eventually began to break down the pavement.

We approached the management of the printing plant about this problem. We told them that we didn't mind if they used our parking lot, but we asked them to please chip in so that we could lay thicker concrete to prevent the trucks from destroying our driveway. They acted as if they had no control over this situation, and furthermore, they wouldn't help pay for any damages to the parking lot.

This was just one incident. Every time we turned around, the printing house did something to harass us. And one day, after a particular incident in a series of many, their printers suddenly went on strike against the company's management. The company was shut down for several weeks, which hurt their profits very badly.

The printing company was situated in a business park that wasn't completely built up yet. They stored huge loads of paper, wrapped against the weather, on several adjacent lots. All of a sudden, everybody started to put up buildings in those lots. The printing company was told to get their paper off the adjacent properties. Now if they wanted to grow, they had to move. They made their decision, and in a short time our neighbors moved out. Another company soon moved in, and we had a good relationship with them from the start.

Our former neighbors relocated closer to San Francisco. Because of higher operating costs of that area, they weren't able to continue doing business at the same level as before. It wasn't long before a bigger company bought them out, and their name and operations were completely dissolved. Strangely enough, soon after that, the company who bought them also went out of business. In about three years, that entire enterprise had vanished from the face of the earth.

This is an interesting example of how the ECK protection works. As vehicles for the ECK, we did whatever we could to live in harmony with our neighbors, but they went out of their way to cause trouble for us. As a result, one set of reverses after another began to plague this company, until finally it no longer existed.

Every time we turned around, the printing house did something to harass us.

Preparing for God-Realization

The ECK staff is a group of very sharp individuals who carry an impressive workload. When the employees leave the office and go back out into the commercial field as secretaries, receptionists, printers, and all the other occupational areas of business we utilize, their new employers are always surprised at the amount of work they are able to do. These people are self-disciplined and innovative; they know what to do in order to get the job done, and they get it done fast. The temporary agencies are always soliciting people who worked at the ECK office, because they know they are going to get a good worker.

Because of your level of consciousness, it's the same with most ECK chelas. The higher you go in Spirit, the more you expect of yourself. The Inner Master says to you, "There is always a better way to do it," and so you are gently nudged to bring out the best. This is the preparatory work that is being done for the individual Soul who will one day step into God-Realization.

The Inner Master says to you, "There is always a better way to do it," and so you are gently nudged to bring out the best.

Reaction to ECK

I'd been going to the same barber for over five years. He ran the barber shop with his wife, and she was the one who usually cut my hair. The barber was also a fisherman. His favorite pastime was to take his boat out in the Pacific Ocean and catch fish. But he had a peculiar attitude about his customers: He felt superior to them. He took their money because it fed and clothed his family, but he had no real regard for them. He was often overheard saying very unkind things about them.

Over the years I occasionally mentioned something to him about Eckankar, but as soon as I left his shop, he would make unkind remarks about it. Later, when I would overhear conversations between him or his wife with the other customers, he always talked about unfortunate events that befell him. One time while he was out on the ocean, his boat sank; another time the motor stopped, and he had to drift until the Coast Guard came along to give him a tow; the tax people audited him and made him pay more taxes; and his son broke his arm. It just went on and on.

I used to enjoy chatting with him because he was such an independent person; he bowed to no one. But finally I decided I'd better get my hair cut somewhere else—before that family was destroyed. And for you, too, the responsibility comes. If you see the ECK is having a real reaction in someone's life, you may have to stop talking about It and just quietly live the precepts.

I'm not suggesting you give up your job just because someone else at your workplace is having troubles. But the fact is, you are the vehicles for Spirit where you work and where you live, and the ECK will use you. You're going to see some amazing changes happen around you. People are being uplifted in consciousness; the gossip and negative thoughts that they engaged in before will no longer work. The ECK cleanses Itself of impurities. When these people are around a vehicle for Spirit, their negative attitudes and words flow into this aura that surrounds you and then return out into the world and fall back upon the sender.

You're going to see some amazing changes happen around you.

SPIRITUAL CHARLATANS

Several years ago, before I became the Living ECK Master, a friend and I were asked to investigate a group in San Francisco that was using a form of HU as a chant. We wanted to find out if they were trying to create an offshoot of Eckankar. We decided the best way to investigate this was to attend one of their meetings.

When we arrived, we found a small room with chairs for about thirty people. Behind a podium stood a little gentleman who looked to be from the Far East. As we took our seats, this man began a long, drawn-out speech, the gist of which was the selling of his spiritual services. For $350 he guaranteed that anybody who signed up would have all of his needs taken care of, whether it was someone to love, a new job, a new car, or a new house.

My friend was very tired, and he started to fall asleep in his chair. But each time he dozed off, he would tip over. We were in a prominent place in the audience, where everybody could see this, and it made it seem as if what the speaker had to say wasn't very important. The man started out very confidently, but after my friend inadvertently caused some commotion, he cut his talk short.

"We are now going to do a short meditation," he said. "Now chant whatever word you want to chant." As soon as everyone else had closed their eyes, we happened to notice one of his assistants outside the door putting perfume in front of a fan and blowing it into the room. This was probably designed to inspire the proper mood: As these strange scents and aromas came wafting in, we were supposed to assume they must be from some divine source. The assistant then started to play a tape recording of some of the different sounds that the man said we would hear, very slowly increasing the volume throughout the meditation.

The other ECKist and I had protection against these tactics, because as we went into the meditative state, which for us was contemplation, we chanted *HU* or our own word. So again, the saying "In God we trust" was true.

On the inner planes, my friend and I stood on a plateau surrounded by the Swordsmen of the SUGMAD. Approaching in the distance were huge armies representative of the psychic forces. While the group was

On the inner planes, my friend and I stood on a plateau surrounded by the Swordsmen of the SUGMAD.

in meditation, this man would unleash his psychic
hypnotic power; it was his way of putting his hooks
into them. But as the battling armies came forth, the
Swordsmen of the SUGMAD, who are the ECK Masters,
started waving their swords about. Suddenly, with
an earth-shattering roar, the heavens rolled with
thunder and flashed with lightning, and the armies
of psychic forces melted before these awesome swords.

I don't know what the little man experienced,
but he ended the meditation very abruptly.

Don't go into a bad situation knowingly. If you
know there's trouble, avoid it. It's best not to beg for
trouble, because the ECK just might use it to let you
learn something. The ECKist can find himself in the
worst situations, but if he gets into an area where he
doesn't belong, the ECK will step in to protect him.

SHORTNESSES OF CONSCIOUSNESS

The works of some of the painters of the Middle
Ages caused quite an uproar in their day. The paintings depict ordinary events, such as people doing
housework and other common chores. By today's
standards, these scenes are almost dull; certainly
not shocking.

But in those days, as the consciousness of the
human race was leaving the Dark Ages, the painters were expected to do portraits of their patrons
in a fixed way. The subject of the painting was to
be shown standing very stiffly, the head turned a
certain way, the face painted with either a stony
smile or no smile at all. This was the accepted pose
that the painter had to work with.

When the Renaissance occurred, the painters
began to put life and expression into their art,
slowly breaking away from this set, fixed pose. They
added a little movement, a little change, showing
their subject in a natural instead of a contrived

Don't go into a bad situation knowingly. But if the ECKist gets into an area where he doesn't belong, the ECK will step in to protect him.

setting. This was considered by some as a corruption of art.

Today we wouldn't even think twice about the values of that era. But we still have similar chinks in consciousness. We have certain attitudes about people who do not believe as we do, who don't dress the way we do, or who have a different kind of morality than we do. These are our shortnesses of consciousness.

Around 1872, a painting called *Arrangement in Grey and Black No. 1: The Artist's Mother* was presented by the artist to the Royal Academy in Britain. Something about the style aggravated the curators, and they mocked not only the painting but also the title.

It was a simple picture. With the use of very little color, it portrayed a woman sitting quietly in a chair, hands folded in her lap, wearing a bonnet to cover her hair. Many years later this same painting gained recognition as a work of art, and eventually became known as *Whistler's Mother*.

When Eckankar came out in 1965, it caused a real shock wave.

When a spiritual teaching known as Eckankar, the Ancient Science of Soul Travel came out in 1965, it caused a real shock wave. The years since then have brought about a change in consciousness. Out-of-body experiences are being enacted on television and in the movies. People are getting used to this phenomenon. Even today the term *Soul Travel* seems a little unorthodox. But in another twenty years Soul Travel is going to be a commonplace idea. People of those times will wonder why there was ever a reaction to Eckankar back in 1965.

BLESSINGS OF THE SOUND AND LIGHT

The karmic patterns of the human race are speeding up. As these karmic patterns accelerate, we find ourselves under nuclear threat, the economy on the brink of collapse, and geological changes occurring.

Catastrophes such as these put people in the position of learning lessons with each other, and this causes a rapid rise in consciousness as they become more open to ideas which are different from their own. This is the world into which ECK has come, and this is the world into which you, as the ECK chela, go, speaking and demonstrating the principles of ECK.

I realize that for some of you, quite an effort was made to attend the seminar. But you will find that the blessings of the Light and Sound that come to you will bring a payment for the effort you have made, and this balance will be self-evident.

When you get home, you will find that you are a changed person. You may or may not notice it right away, but your neighbors will see that you are different in some way. The difference may be slight, perhaps showing up through increased thoughtfulness. After a few weeks the shine of this seminar will wear off, but you will integrate into your spiritual body the truths that you have learned today. And then, when you go to another ECK seminar, the ECK will fill even more of your being. This blessing you will again take with you, and give back to the world through your actions and your words.

As you go home today, the love and protection of the MAHANTA go with you. Wherever you go, remember to use your secret word or chant *HU*, quietly or out loud, when you are in trouble, in need, or when the danger is more than you can handle. Do what you can, and at the point where you are unable to do any more for yourself, stand back and let the ECK take over. You are in the hands of Divine Spirit.

May the blessings be.

Do what you can, and where you are unable to do any more, stand back and let the ECK take over. You are in the hands of Divine Spirit.

ECKANKAR European Seminar, The Hague, The Netherlands, Sunday, July 22, 1984

Your spiritual unfoldment will come from what you do
at home. The Light and Sound have entered your heart,
and the changes will come; you will be different.

21

TECHNIQUES FOR PROTECTION

*S*omeone mentioned to me that when he needed to translate the ECK teachings into another language, he would first tell the listeners, "Words are not able to fully express the ECK, so listen to the meaning behind the words." The Spirit of ECK is Light and Sound, and It can never be perfectly spoken by any human voice, including my own.

WALKING YOUR OWN PATH

Many letters come to me from chelas here in Africa who ask for a healing from Spirit. Spirit will begin to heal you if you are willing to first help yourself.

When someone asks for help with money or health or happiness, I try to open his heart to the Light and Sound of ECK. Keep in mind that SUGMAD wants Soul to become strong, able in every way to stand and walk in all Its worlds. One day we want to become as the ECK Masters, who look only to themselves to solve all problems. They do not look for the SUGMAD to solve them. We must learn to be totally responsible for all of our actions, deeds, and thoughts.

SUGMAD wants Soul to become strong, able in every way to stand and walk in all Its worlds.

When you ask the ECK for healing, you must open your spiritual eyes and ears in order to recognize how the divine force is bringing about a change for you.

It is often a struggle to bring home to the initiate in ECK the necessity to become stronger and to walk his own path. When the child is young, the parent watches over him. But as we grow in Spirit, we must one day become an adult in the worlds of God.

Defense against Black Magic

How can one become strong so that no power of Kal can harm him?

The forces of black magic are powerful in Africa. How can one become strong so that no power of Kal can harm him?

First, do not look for trouble or anger anyone who has these powers. But if the powers of darkness are thrown against you, put your full attention on the Mahanta, and chant *HU*. See a shining light around you through which no evil can penetrate, and know that the Mahanta, in the form of a Blue Light, stands by your side.

Study what *The Shariyat* says about how to overcome the dark forces. It is important to understand what in your emotions has opened the door for this power to attack.

Always remember that ECK is stronger than any force in the lower worlds. Only one who surrounds himself with Its presence and knows that the Mahanta is with him will be safe.

Imagination and Soul

A gentleman told me that as a boy, he loved to go to church. There he would sit with the other people and see the statues of saints standing on high platforms all around him. *How wonderful it would be to stand up there beside them,* he thought to himself. And so, while the people all around him prayed, he went in the Soul body and stood near the ceiling next to the statues.

One day he told his mother, "Church is so wonderful, because I can go up there."

"You mean in front by the altar?" she said.

"No, I mean up there by the ceiling."

"Be still," she said. "Don't speak such foolishness."

Yet he could see and feel himself in another place in the body of imagination. And where the imagination goes, there is Soul. He was quite surprised to find that the other people who attended services didn't go up near the ceiling, and he wondered, *What, then, is the point of going to church?*

Where the imagination goes, there is Soul.

By starting with the imagination, you, too, can move into the worlds that lie beyond the physical world. But first, all fear and guilt must be taken away, because they stand between us and our true spiritual heritage. Sometimes it's the religious leaders who put guilt in one's path.

GETTING RID OF GUILT

When this same man was about fourteen years old, he was expected to go to the priest for confession. The priest said, "What have you come to confess?"

"Nothing," he said. "I have committed no sins."

The priest said, "That can't be. Think harder." The boy still couldn't come up with anything.

The priest was persistent; no one had ever before come to him claiming he had never sinned. But the boy felt no guilt, and that is why he was able to Soul Travel above the congregation. The priest said, "Please tell me *something.*"

The boy finally said, "Well, I fight with my brothers, and sometimes I say bad words."

"What words?"

"None in particular." Actually, he didn't use any
bad words. A moment later the boy said, "Forgive
me, but what I just told you is a lie."

The priest was satisfied at last. "That is very
bad," he said. "You must do penance." He directed
the young sinner to walk down the long church aisle
and go in front of the people to do penance.

The boy stood before the congregation. "Dear God,
forgive me," he said, "but the priest made me lie."

At times confession is used in a constructive
way. If talking to another person helps someone by
relieving his guilt and fear, then Soul can take
another step to God. In that case, a proper thing
has been done between the religious leader and the
person who seeks his help.

BUILDING AN AURA OF STRENGTH

We must guard ourselves against those who say
they wish to help us in our spiritual life. We must
ask the MAHANTA in contemplation, "Is what he told
me for my good?" If it is for the good, then follow
it; if not, then don't.

To build an aura of strength in ECK, use the
three declarations of ECK every morning. They are
said upon arising, spoken with humility and sincer-
ity. You also will find this declaration useful for you
as protection from black magic.

It goes like this: *I declare myself a vehicle for
the SUGMAD.* You wait a brief moment while you feel
that certain stream of SUGMAD enter your being.
Then you continue: *the ECK.* Wait another moment
until this flow of ECK fills Soul, and then continue
with the third declaration: *and the MAHANTA.* Let it
fill the world of Soul.

And so it goes like this: *I declare myself a vehicle
for the SUGMAD, the ECK, and the MAHANTA.* Then go

To build an
aura of strength
in ECK, use the
three declara-
tions of ECK
every morning.

forth to meet your day with confidence, because the
MAHANTA is always with you.

A SPIRITUAL EXERCISE

I would like to mention briefly a way to do a
spiritual exercise by using the imaginative body.

At home, sit down on the floor or on a chair, or
lie down on a cot or bed. Make yourself comfortable,
and then say, "I shall go for a short walk in the
Soul body." Close your eyes, and look into the
Spiritual Eye in a soft, sweet, gentle way. Chant
HU for a minute or two, and then imagine yourself
getting up.

Make yourself comfortable, then say, "I shall go for a short walk in the Soul body."

If I were doing this contemplation right here,
I would say, "I will get out of the chair in the Soul
body and walk in front of the table. I will become
very interested in the things around me, such as
the color of the tablecloth, the flowers, and the
vase.

"While the physical body is still in contemplation
with its eyes shut, I will walk in the imaginative
body to look at the curtains. I will touch the curtains
and notice how nice this beautiful yellow cloth feels."

I may become curious and decide to see what's
on the other side of the curtain. I would then observe
the floor behind the curtain, notice the scratched
wood and scuff marks, and pay very close attention
to every little detail.

As you walk around like this, Soul is becoming
used to going beyond the physical body. At first it's
only imagination, but the practice of this spiritual
exercise will strengthen the experience until one
day you will find yourself in a higher state of consciousness exactly as you had seen yourself in your
imagination.

FREEDOM IN SOUL

You will find yourself in the Soul body, and for the first time, you will know that in Soul you are free. You will know that Soul lives always in the present moment. It has no age and can know no death. No longer will fear and guilt hold It in the bonds of slavery. Soul then moves forward into the worlds of God to gain wisdom, power, and freedom.

The Darshan is the meeting with the Master, which can take place inwardly or outwardly. A chela may see the Inner Master years before he comes to meet or see him at a lecture in the physical. The physical form is only a shell used by the ECK to carry an image to those who wish to serve the cause of SUGMAD.

If you wish to walk the path of ECK, you must know that It will come into every part of your being until you are only It.

The Darshan takes place as you sit here in the audience. There is no need to shake hands; the real meeting is as we see each other now. But the greater meeting is with the Master in the inner worlds. This is where I want to lead you.

I can do this only for those who will be faithful with the Spiritual Exercises of ECK, for they are what will strengthen you as Soul.

The Spiritual Exercises of ECK are what will strengthen you as Soul.

CHILD OF THE MAHANTA

Tonight, before you go to sleep, speak to the MAHANTA. Say, "I am a child of thine. Take me where you will, to show me the ways of SUGMAD."

Your spiritual unfoldment will come from what you do at home. The Light and Sound have entered your heart, and the changes will come; you will be different. Every day, every week, every month, Spirit is uplifting and bringing you closer to the high worlds of the Ocean of Love and Mercy. Only he who has seen the Light and heard the Sound will know truth.

The ECK leaders will need your help to plan and find ways to bring the message of ECK to the people here. As you give of yourself—your time, your thoughts—you are growing into the being which you already are but do not yet know.

I am not able to tell you more here, but tonight I will meet in the dream state with those of you who are ready.

And so I leave you for now with the love of SUGMAD. Baraka Bashad. May the blessings be.

You are growing into the being which you already are but do not yet know.

*African Seminar, Lomé, Togo,
July 28, 1984*

The image of what makes a holy man has become so
embedded in us that when an ECK Master comes along to
give truth, he looks and acts too normal to be believed.

22
THE CHOSEN PEOPLE

his afternoon I was throwing a
softball with one of the other ECKists.
We were on the ECK office softball team
a couple of years ago, and it felt good to
be practicing again. I was throwing wild because
of all the open space behind him, but he's a pretty good catcher. At first I threw overhand, then I
got adventuresome and started to throw some
underhand. One got away and headed off into the
bushes—and that's when we discovered the creek.

We tried to reach the ball with a little broom,
but it didn't quite make it. Then we threw a big
ball of mud next to the softball to see if we could
get it to work free. This went on awhile, and we had
a good time.

One softball got away and headed off into the bushes— and that's when we discovered the creek.

THROWING KARMA

A young man with a good, strong arm joined us.
We stood on one end of the field, and he stood at the
other end, and we tossed the softball back and forth.
The two of us had to throw only one time to every
two of his, and we noticed a curious thing. Whenever
my partner made a bad throw to the guy at the end
of the field, then that fellow would throw a bad one

back to me. We kept taking turns. In other words, the karma came back, but it was always one step removed.

Karma is like that. If it came back too quickly after the action, everyone would have caught on and been out of this world a long time ago.

I was reading recently about the difference in beliefs among those of the Jewish, Christian, and Hindu faiths. Each of the religions has tried to answer the question of why the good suffer and the evil prosper. This is a great generalization that certainly doesn't apply to every person within each religion, but basically, there are differences.

The Hindus explain it with their belief in karma and reincarnation, or cause and effect. The Christians, on the other hand, teach according to the biblical saying "Blessed are the meek: for they shall inherit the earth." To some, that means if you don't want to take responsibility for living right, you can consider yourself meek and go through life blaming your misfortunes on the devil, your boss, and just about anybody but yourself. Before you die, if you expect to get your reward in heaven, then you start being nice. And so the Christians actually see it in kind of a mystical way.

The Jewish faith has a pretty down-to-earth viewpoint. They believe if you do something wrong, you'll get your punishment, and if you do something good, you'll get your reward. While some of them may recognize that you come back in other lives, for the most part they believe it all happens in this lifetime.

These religions are all trying to answer the question of why the evil prosper and the good suffer. And what do we say in ECK? We say all of these things and more. One of the ECKists said that since he has been in ECK, he even looks forward to the days of trouble because of all the things he has learned about himself and Spirit. When problems come, we don't feel that life is treating us badly and that it's some-

If karma came back too quickly after the action, everyone would have caught on and been out of this world a long time ago.

thing to be avoided. Sometimes it's very difficult, and you'd like to run and hide from it, but you can't.

THE CHOSEN PEOPLE

We in ECK are the chosen people. That implies a responsibility that is not usually associated with that claim. Someone once said to me that the reason the Jewish people had such a problem for so many thousands of years was not because they were the chosen people, but because they set themselves up as being better than their neighbors. It occurred to me that maybe this was their Achilles' heel. If this is the case, then ECKists must learn something from it if we are going to call ourselves the chosen people.

A lot of people throughout history have considered themselves the chosen people. The Germans under Hitler felt they were the superior race, and the French in Napoleon's day thought of themselves as being above others. Whether or not we call ourselves the chosen people is not the important issue. What matters is what we do and how we go about living our life.

Perhaps the real reason the Jewish people have had such a hard time is that they had it more together than the other religions. Ethically and morally, perhaps they were better than their detractors. Furthermore, since childhood, they were taught by their parents how to organize better. This ability soon earned them a place in the top echelons of government; and once they got into positions of power, it wasn't long before they found themselves in control of a lot of money.

Human nature being what it is, I've never been disappointed in its predictability. We can be the most envious of creatures. You see somebody who's doing well, and you think of a hundred reasons why he really doesn't deserve his good fortune. The guy was either born lucky or he did something

What matters is what we do and how we go about living our life.

dishonest, but certainly he didn't earn it. This goes back to the old Christian idea embedded in so many of us—that you can get something for nothing. It's a fallacy that the followers of Christianity have been stuck with, and as a result, many think the Law of Cause and Effect doesn't apply to them. We in ECK know it does, so we've come to grips with that; but to some extent, a lot of these ideas still hang on.

As the chosen people, we recognize our responsibility. Somehow we are going to have to learn how to work with each other. In my estimation, ECKists stand at the top of their professions. The more you give, the more you get. There is no way that ECK can keep from having an influence in this world, and once It does—as It has—people become envious of us. This means we will draw the attention of those who can't do it as well. And in their envy they will look for laws and rules and reasons why we are not conforming with society, when in truth we are model citizens in our communities.

STORIES ABOUT PAUL

Paul was willing to do whatever he had to do, whenever he had to do it, to get the teachings of ECK out.

I occasionally pass along stories about Paul Twitchell, because they illustrate something about this complex human being who started Eckankar. As we learn more about him, we also learn that the ECK Masters are not gods. Yet Paul was willing to do whatever he had to do, whenever he had to do it, in order to get the teachings of ECK out.

After he was poisoned in Spain in 1970, he had to cancel an appearance at a seminar in Europe. He sent a telegram to one of the Higher Initiates there. It said, "Something has come up to change my plans. I regret I am not able to come. A letter will follow." He was considerate of the people who had made the plans and invested so much time and energy, but at that point he simply couldn't make it. The letter that followed said, "An individual put something in my food, but I caught it quickly enough that there wasn't too much damage done."

A couple from the Midwest sent in some pictures of Paul and Gail when they were first married. They mentioned that he had spent a year studying to be a chiropractor. I can just imagine him sitting there for a year, going through the harsh disciplines of learning all the medical terms. When he had an interest in something, he stuck with it until he learned whatever he needed from it.

The spiritual masters have different ways of working with people. Often we are disappointed if they don't dress in a robe, speak in somber tones, and walk in measured, stately grace. Or when they throw a softball into the creek, we ask, "Why would he do something like that?"

When the spiritual masters throw a softball into the creek, we ask, "Why would they do something like that?"

INITIATION FROM THE MASTER

At one time Paul gave all of the initiations himself, even the Second. Around 1970 he changed the policy. Having advanced a number of people to the higher initiations, he said the Mahdis in Eckankar could now give the Second and Third Initiations.

A Russian woman who worked in Philadelphia as a children's governess wouldn't stand for that. In a very imperial voice she stated to her friends, "I'm not going to have some stand-in give *me* the Second Initiation!" She wanted it from the real source. At a seminar she knew which room was Paul's, so she marched up there and knocked on the door. There he sat at a desk, writing notes for his talks the next day.

Paul just said hello and kept on working. She explained the purpose of her visit: she wanted the Second Initiation from him. "All right," he said. "Your word is such and such. Sit down, chant it for five minutes, and then leave." This woman with the regal manner quietly sat down on the couch and did exactly what he said. Then, just as quietly, she got up after five minutes, slipped out the door, and shut it very softly. Paul never even looked up; he just kept right on making his notes.

When this woman came back downstairs, her friends could hardly wait to hear what happened. She was uncharacteristically quiet. "Did you get your initiation from Paul?" they asked. She said yes and wouldn't say any more. When she finally told them the story, two weeks later, she was really humble about it. That probably was the last time Paul gave a Second Initiation in the United States.

Sometimes people ask, What's the point of the initiation? The initiation is Soul's linkup with the Holy Spirit, to give Soul the power to see the Light and hear the Sound.

THE VALUE OF PERSISTENCE

This summer my daughter joined a Bobby Sox softball team, and I've been showing her how to bat.

This summer my daughter joined a Bobby Sox softball team, and I've been showing her how to bat. She joined the team in midseason. That is a bad time, because by then everybody else feels like they are part of the team, and you don't, but she was able to do pretty well. Now I'm getting her ready for next year, when she goes into another level of play where the pitching is faster.

It's amazing what the pitchers can do in fast-pitch softball. They can throw risers: balls that start out at your knees, cross over by your chin, and cause you to swing wild because you didn't see them rise. You look pretty funny swinging in the air at nothing in particular.

Eventually I figured out how to hit fast pitching. For a while I always hit pop-ups, balls that landed behind second base. But I also consistently struck out. The pitchers on the opposing team were fast. You try to observe the ball as it's coming toward you, and then you swing. Like a lot of batters, I was swinging too late.

When the pitcher is really fast, you have to be brave just to stand where you can hit the ball. If the pitcher sees that you're nervous or that you are standing too close to the plate, he'll throw a fastball right under your chin. He wants to make sure that you're watching. The ball is coming along at ninety or a hundred miles an hour from forty-six feet away. So at first I had to build up the courage to stand in there.

Once I got the pitcher's rhythm, however, I was always ahead of him. As soon as he'd start winding up for the pitch, I'd bring my bat around, so it looked as if I had this nice, easy swing. At that point, if the ball happened to be thrown anywhere in the strike zone, all I had to do was meet it with the bat and push. Pretty soon I started to bat a very high average. It gets to be fun once you figure it out.

This is what I was trying to pass along to my daughter. I used to pitch an easy underhand to her. That helped her for a while, until she got used to hitting. Then I started pitching the windmill very slowly. She's a little kid with a strike zone no more than one-and-a-half feet high. Even so, the pitch was too fast for her. I told her not to worry about hitting the ball. "Just keep swinging," I said. "If you don't mind swinging, I don't mind throwing."

Every so often I'd uncork a wild one and hit her. This was to build up her courage. I'd say, "You've got to stand in there. If the pitcher ever finds out you're afraid, you'll never see another good ball come through again. You'll never be a hitter, and you won't be on the team."

One day when we were practicing, she went up to bat, and at last she got it. Bringing the bat around, she hit a deep fly ball into center field. I pitched a second one; she hit another line drive. She was so happy.

I told her not to worry about hitting the ball. "Just keep swinging," I said. "If you don't mind swinging, I don't mind throwing."

TRUST AND TECHNIQUE

I wouldn't stick
with you and
give you all
these techniques
on Soul Travel
if I didn't know
you could do it.

I wouldn't stick with you and give you all these techniques on Soul Travel if I didn't know you could do it. I've done the same things. When I first tried to learn how to bat, I did it wrong, but by working at it persistently, I finally figured it out. The same thing happened with my daughter. If she hadn't gone out there and put up with a few weeks of batting over and over again, and just trusting Dad, she wouldn't have made such progress.

She had the heart to get out there and stand in the way of a couple of fastballs. They come along at a pretty good clip, and she had to be tough enough to take the inside pitches. At first, when she saw the ball coming at her, she'd run away from it. Then she got a little smarter, and she started to just step back. Now I'm showing her how to get hit accidentally on purpose, because that gets you to first base, and that counts too. I like to get mileage out of everything, even a bad pitch. I showed her how to turn so that the ball would spin off, but I cautioned her: "Don't let it spin off your head. Get it out of the way." So now she knows how to get extra mileage out of a bad pitch—to draw a walk without hurting herself.

This is how we do it in life. And this is what will help in your efforts to Soul Travel. First you learn the techniques. Paul gave a lot of them in the discourses. Now I'm going to show you how to make them work for you. In other words, I've shown you the techniques for hitting, but it's up to you to go to bat. As long as the ball is coming anyway, I'm going to show you how to get mileage from an inside pitch.

What happens when you have a Soul Travel experience or a dream experience? How do you learn to evaluate it so you can understand what the ECK is giving you to use in your life? How can you start using it to make your life better? How can you use it to start moving into self-awareness and on to the God Awareness states? This is what I want to show you. I can tell you, but talking isn't going to do it; you're still the one who has to go out there, pick up the bat, and learn how to use it.

THE PURIFYING SOUND

The spiritual exercises require that we use our creative imagination. This is our gift from God. The imagination is the God-spark, the part of us that makes us like God. And you can direct it toward whatever needs improvement in your life.

To do the spiritual exercises, you shut your eyes, look to the Third Eye, and chant *HU*, an old and secret name for God. It is one of the most powerful words for spiritual upliftment that I can give you.

As you chant *HU*, look inwardly for the Light—which is usually seen as white or yellow or blue—and listen for the Sound. The Sound may be heard in any number of different ways. It can be like a train going by, a bird, buzzing bees, sometimes a flute, or even guitars. The way you hear It just depends on where you are. These sounds are the action of the Holy Spirit, the ECK, as Its atoms vibrate in the invisible worlds. The Sound you hear is the vibration at the particular level to which you are attuned at the time.

This Sound that comes from the ECK has a purifying element which removes the impurities of Soul. It brings an understanding of how our actions have caused our problems. It also gives an indication of what we can do to unfold, and how to figure out the way to do things right. Even if you did something wrong five or ten times, that's OK. If you learn to work with the spiritual exercises, through one method or another—whether it's in the dream state, Soul Travel, or by the inner knowingness—somewhere along the way you're going to find out

You can direct creative imagination toward whatever needs improvement in your life.

how to do it right, so that you can go on from this problem to tackle the greater ones.

This is all we're doing in life. When a problem comes up, we don't say, Oh, no! We look to see the reason or the lesson behind it. What can I learn from it? How has it made me stronger? We are interested in becoming the mature Soul that can go on to become a Coworker with God.

GOD CONSCIOUSNESS

Somebody once wrote a brochure for a workshop on God Consciousness. My question was, How can you do a workshop on God Consciousness unless you've experienced it? Until you do, you are actually promising something you can't deliver.

The brochure talked about how to merge with the God Consciousness. The idea of merging with it is not correct. The God Consciousness is a state of awareness that we enter—and there is a difference. I can enter a room, but it's not likely or logical to say that I'm going to merge with it. We become one with the ECK, but the God Consciousness is something that we enter. It's a fine distinction.

ECK MASTERS

The ECK publications include stories from people who have met Rebazar Tarzs and some of the other ECK Masters. Their role is to bring spiritual upliftment. You may meet an ECK Master on the street, and even though you won't know who it is at the time, you will notice a feeling of lightness and happiness either while you're with him or shortly after you've left. He will have brought a blessing to you. And as a result, somewhere down the road you will be able to see the truth that is around you. Perhaps some people will find it in ECK.

The ECK Masters' role is to bring spiritual upliftment. You will notice a feeling of lightness and happiness.

Shortly after a couple from Canada had joined Eckankar, the man asked his spouse, "Since the ECK Masters often come in the Soul body, and very seldom in the physical body, is it OK with you if we open our home to them?" She said, "Sure, it's OK with me." He soon forgot about that conversation, but what they had done was give permission to Divine Spirit and Its agents or messengers to come into their consciousness.

One night around midnight, he sat down on the cedar chest and did a contemplation before going to sleep. He had a strong love for the ECK Masters, and as he lay down in bed a while later, his thoughts were on them; he felt light and happy as he drifted into sleep. These happy, spacious thoughts are important if you expect something to work for you in Soul Travel or in the dream state.

All of a sudden he opened his eyes in the dream state, and there in the room was Rebazar Tarzs, the Tibetan ECK Master. Rebazar Tarzs is just under six feet tall, and though he's quite old, he has a youthful appearance and a full, rich black beard. He sat there looking at the twenty-five-year-old dreamer who was trying to grow a beard. It was six weeks old and looked pretty scraggly, coming in with patches of gray. Rebazar kept looking at it and laughing. "What a scraggly thing that is," he said. They talked about other matters for a while, and then the man dropped back into a regular sleep.

By the time he woke up in the morning, he had just about forgotten his visit from Rebazar Tarzs, until his wife asked him, "Did you see anyone in our room last night?" He answered, "No, why?" She said, "Because a man with a beard was sitting on the dresser." At first he said, "That was me. I was doing my contemplation." She said, "No, you were sitting on the cedar chest. This person was on the dresser, and it was after you went to bed." When

The man asked his spouse, "Since the ECK Masters often come in the Soul body, is it OK with you if we open our home to them?"

she described him, her husband remembered his visit with Rebazar Tarzs.

The ECK Master had come to show them that once you open yourself to Spirit, the messengers of the ECK will come to you and bring you the blessings of God, of SUGMAD. This is the spiritual law.

If it doesn't happen the first time you pick up the bat, you might have to work at it. You might have to spend a little time practicing the technique. But if others have learned how to hit fast pitching, you probably can too. And if others have learned how to get outside of the body, meet with the ECK Masters, and get the truth directly for themselves, then you can too. You've been given the techniques, and now you just need to learn how to do it.

If others have learned to get outside the body, meet ECK Masters, and get truth directly for themselves, then you can too.

GETTING THE DREAM MESSAGE

When you do the spiritual exercises, generally the Dream Master, which is the Inner Master, will begin to work with you in the dream state. It often starts out this way. If you were to begin by working directly with Soul Travel, it might be too much of a shock for you. The dream state is the preparation for it. But in the beginning the dreams are often jumbled and distorted, and it's hard to make heads or tails out of them. You might think there's no point to writing something down in your dream journal that you can barely remember. So how do you work with this?

What happens in the highest spiritual levels is that the Dream Master is trying to get a message to the human consciousness. Unfortunately, this pure message of truth has to go through a series of checkpoints in the Mental world, and this function of the mind is called the dream censor.

When the Dream Master tries to get this message to the human self, the dream censor acts like a doting

mother who is very protective of her son. The Dream
Master gives the straight truth, but the dream censor stands in between truth and the human consciousness. "Oh, no," it says. "That would shock the
human self. It can't handle that." So the dream
censor, like the good mother, dresses up the message
and makes it nice. Unfortunately, by the time the
message gets to your waking self, it's so jumbled up
that it often no longer resembles the original. The
censor thinks the logical order of truth itself might
knock you over.

The function of the dream censor—those checkpoints built into the mind and the subconscious
part of ourselves—is to prevent the pure truth from
coming through as Light. If the Light comes through
too strongly and directly, one can get burned.

This is what happened to some of the saints in
early Christianity. They got too much Light, had
this great experience, and by the time they woke
up the next morning, they were no longer fit for the
society of man. They couldn't even figure out how
to put one foot ahead of the other, but they spouted
words of goodness and kindness. In the meantime,
they ran off and let someone else feed and support
their families. What good did this amount of Light
do them? Not much.

WHAT IS A HOLY MAN?

In our Christian background and training we
are told that these saints were men of God, ones
you should look up to. Yet, because many of them
got the Light before they were ready for It, It left
them social and spiritual misfits. They have been
given to us as saints, but many of them were quite
strange. The only way they could exist in the world
was behind monastery walls where someone else
fed them and cared for them.

> The Dream
> Master gives the
> straight truth.
> "Oh, no," the
> dream censor
> says. "That
> would shock
> the human
> self. It can't
> handle that."

This image of what makes a holy man has become so embedded in us that when an ECK Master comes along to give truth, he looks and acts too normal to be believed. People are expecting somebody who walks and dresses differently. When a man comes around in a suit and seems pretty ordinary, they forget to listen to what is behind his words.

I am all too aware of my limitations to get across in words the things I want to convey to you. Even when I say, "If you hold the bat like this and swing it like that, it's going to work," you still can't get the real experience unless you do it yourself.

KEEPING A DREAM JOURNAL

When you have inner experiences—probably in the dream state at first—the original clear, true message from the higher worlds is jumbled up. It's turned inside out, mixed with a little bit of coloring, tossed to the floor, stomped on a couple of times, put back together in a little package, and thrown at your feet.

In ECK you learn how to slip past the dream censor to read the hidden meanings behind your inner experience.

What we are trying to do in ECK is to show you how to get past the dream censor. If the dream censor puts up a block, you learn how to slip past it to start reading the hidden meanings behind your inner experience.

The way to begin doing this is to keep a dream journal. If you wake up in the morning feeling unsettled and upset, especially if you don't have a way to work this out, it can undermine your courage in ECK. It doesn't matter that you don't remember exactly what happened in the dream state; you can write whatever you do remember. Because once you start, you begin to work it out through the writing. This is one of the functions of the dream journal.

Soon you'll notice that the dream messages begin to make more sense. When you see an earthquake in the dream state, you'll come to realize this inner experience doesn't mean the earth is going to have a big earthquake. The message might be that a big change is coming in your own world. All too often one likes to start reading the grand picture before he has even solved the problem of the little world.

You start by trying to relate the inner experience to your everyday life. It's not trying to tell you how the United States and Russia are going to fare in the next decade. It isn't concerned about the big world problems.

You have to first make the connection with the Dream Master, which is the Inner Master. The way to start is by writing down anything significant that happens. Write down the experience as well as you can remember it, and try to fill in the gaps. If you can't actually identify the ECK Masters in your dreams, but you have a feeling about who they might be, just write that down. Then see what comes of all this.

DREAMS TO SOUL TRAVEL AND BEYOND

As you study and check your dream journal, you're going to find you remember your dreams better and better. Soon after that, you'll move on to the next step, which is Soul Travel. This is a level of consciousness above the dream state.

As you study your dream journal, you're going to find you remember your dreams better and better.

The difference between a dream and Soul Travel is as great as the difference between imagination and a dream. Once you begin to Soul Travel, you'll continue to do it until about the time you become a Fifth Initiate, established on the Fifth Plane. At that point, you generally don't Soul Travel anymore. Instead, when you do the spiritual exercises, you move directly into the Soul Plane; or if you're going to work in one of the lower worlds, even someplace here on earth, you are there instantly.

There are different levels of learning that you are going to undergo on this spiritual path, and the first step is to use the creative imagination.

FACING YOUR PROBLEMS

One of the ECKists told me of an article he read about a business consultant who conducted workshops on creativity. One of his techniques was to ask the people in his audience, "When was the last time you had a really good creative idea?" Each participant would write his answer on a sheet of paper, and generally the responses ranged from a day ago to a week ago. But one person wrote that it was a little more than a year ago.

The consultant couldn't help being curious. He went over to the man who had given that response. "I notice you wrote that you had a real creative inspiration about a year ago," he said. "I can't help wondering what it was." The man lit up like a lightbulb. He said, "I found a shorter way home from work!"

Instead of using his imagination to be a better businessman, this man's big interest was in how quickly he could run away from his job. How can you be a successful businessman when you're using your energy to come up with better ways to get away from the business?

It's the same with us. How are we ever going to be successful on the spiritual path if we run away from ourselves, from our problems? I won't expect you to cheer when you have bad problems, but you can turn around and bravely face them head on. Instead of running from trouble, you can charge right at it.

One of the ways to begin working out the inner tangles and knots, where the communication lines between the higher worlds and the physical have been twisted by the censor, is to work with the dream

I won't expect you to cheer when you have bad problems, but you can turn around and bravely face them head on.

journal. And as you write, you will find that the tension in your stomach goes away. If the dream journal can help to do this, it's done something.

A STEP AT A TIME

First the imagination, then the dream state, then Soul Travel, and then direct projection. But take it a step at a time. Eventually you go into spiritual realization, and then on into God Consciousness, into the Heart of God.

If you want, the connection with the MAHANTA, the Inner Master, can be made. You need only open your heart in loving kindness and acceptance to it.

A step at a time, eventually you go on into the Heart of God.

*Montana Campout, Avon, Montana,
August 25, 1984*

ABOUT THE AUTHOR

Award-winning author, teacher, and spiritual guide Sri Harold Klemp helps seekers reach their full potential. He is the MAHANTA, the Living ECK Master and spiritual leader of Eckankar, the Path of Spiritual Freedom. He is the latest in a long line of spiritual Adepts who have served throughout history in every culture of the world.

Sri Harold teaches creative spiritual practices that enable anyone to achieve life mastery and gain inner peace and contentment. His messages are relevant to today's spiritual needs and resonate with every generation. *Kirkus Reviews* comments, "The powerful optimism of these teachings should resonate with all readers, even those unacquainted with ECK."

Sri Harold's body of work includes more than one hundred books, which have been translated into eighteen languages and won multiple awards. The miraculous, true-life stories he shares lift the veil between heaven and earth.

In his groundbreaking memoir, *Autobiography of a Modern Prophet*, he reveals secrets to spiritual success gleaned from his personal journey into the heart of God. Find your own path to true happiness, wisdom, and love in Sri Harold Klemp's inspired writings.

NEXT STEPS IN SPIRITUAL EXPLORATION

- **Browse our website: www.Eckankar.org.**
  Watch videos; get free books, answers to FAQs, and more info.
- **Attend an Eckankar event** in your area.
  Visit "Find a Location" (under "Engage") on our website.
- **Enroll** in an ECK Advanced Spiritual Living course.
- **Read additional books** about the ECK teachings.
- See **"Contact Eckankar"** page 302.

ADVANCED SPIRITUAL LIVING

Go higher, further, deeper with your spiritual experiences!

Eckankar offers enrollment in Advanced Spiritual Living courses for Self-Discovery and God-Discovery. This dynamic program of inner and outer study unlocks the divine love and wisdom within you. It offers step-by-step advances in enlightenment through initiation.

From the first day of membership, you can have direct experience with the God Current and begin to meet life's challenges on the highest possible ground.

You will enjoy monthly discourses from the spiritual leader of Eckankar, Sri Harold Klemp, creative spiritual practices for daily life, and the quarterly *Mystic World* publication. Optional classes with like-hearted Souls are available in many areas.

Here's a sampling of titles from the first course:

- In Soul You Are Free
- Reincarnation—Why You Came to Earth Again
- The Master Principle
- The God Worlds—Where No One Has Gone Before?

BOOKS

You may find these books by Harold Klemp to be of special interest. They are available at bookstores, from online booksellers, or directly from Eckankar.

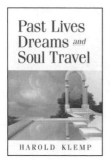

Past Lives, Dreams, and Soul Travel

These stories and exercises help you find your true purpose, discover greater love than you've ever known, and learn that spiritual freedom is within reach.

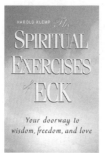

The Spiritual Exercises of ECK

This book is a staircase with 131 steps leading to the doorway to spiritual freedom, self-mastery, wisdom, and love. A comprehensive volume of spiritual exercises for every need.

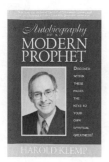

Autobiography of a Modern Prophet

This riveting story of Harold Klemp's climb up the Mountain of God will help you discover the keys to your own spiritual greatness.

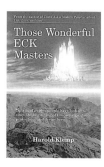

Those Wonderful ECK Masters

Would you like to have *personal* experience with spiritual masters that people all over the world—since the beginning of time—have looked to for guidance, protection, and divine love? This book includes real-life stories and spiritual exercises to meet eleven ECK Masters.

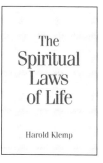

The Spiritual Laws of Life

Learn how to keep in tune with your true spiritual nature. Spiritual laws reveal the behind-the-scenes forces at work in your daily life.

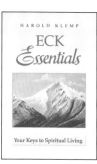

ECK Essentials

Your keys to spiritual living. These ECK essentials from the Master nourish, guide, uplift, heal, reveal and strengthen the desire and resolve of Soul to reach Its sacred goals. Open your heart to the Master, and you will hear inner, secret whispers of truth.

CONTACT ECKANKAR

For more information about ECK or ECK books or to enroll in ECK membership, you may

- visit ECKBooks.org,

- enroll in Advanced Spiritual Living courses at Eckankar.org > Engage,

- call Eckankar (952) 380-2222 to apply, or

- write to
ECKANKAR, Dept. BK156
PO Box 2000
Chanhassen, MN 55317-2000 USA.

GLOSSARY

Words set in SMALL CAPS are defined elsewhere in this glossary.

Blue Light   How the MAHANTA often appears in the inner worlds to the CHELA or seeker.

chela   A spiritual student, often a member of ECKANKAR.

ECK   The Life Force, Holy Spirit, or Audible Life Current which sustains all life.

Eckankar *EHK-ahn-kahr*   The Path of Spiritual Freedom. Also known as the Ancient Science of SOUL TRAVEL. A truly spiritual way of life for the individual in modern times. The teachings provide a framework for anyone to explore their own spiritual experiences. Established by PAUL TWITCHELL, the modern-day founder, in 1965. The word means Coworker with God.

ECK Masters   Spiritual Masters who can assist and protect people in their spiritual studies and travels. The ECK Masters are from a long line of God-Realized SOULS who know the responsibility that goes with spiritual freedom.

ECK Rite of Passage   One of the Four ECK Celebrations of Life. This ceremony is for youth on the threshold of becoming adults, at about age thirteen. It celebrates a personal commitment to the ECK teachings, to accepting the presence of the MAHANTA, and to becoming more aware of one's true spiritual nature.

Fubbi Quantz   The guardian of the SHARIYAT-KI-SUGMAD at the Katsupari Monastery in northern Tibet. He was the MAHANTA, the LIVING ECK MASTER during the time of Buddha, about 500 BC.

God-Realization   The state of God Consciousness. Complete and conscious awareness of God.

Gopal Das   The guardian of the SHARIYAT-KI-SUGMAD at the Temple of Askleposis on the Astral PLANE. He was the MAHANTA, the LIVING ECK MASTER in Egypt, about 3000 BC.

303

HU *HYOO*   The most ancient, secret name for God. It can be sung as a love song to God aloud or silently to oneself to align with God's love.

initiation   Earned by a member of ECKANKAR through spiritual unfoldment and service to God. The initiation is a private ceremony in which the individual is linked to the Sound and Light of God.

Kal Niranjan   The Kal; the negative power, also known as Satan or the devil.

Karma, Law of   The Law of Cause and Effect, action and reaction, justice, retribution, and reward, which applies to the lower or psychic worlds: the Physical, Astral, Causal, Mental, and Etheric PLANES.

Klemp, Harold   The present MAHANTA, the LIVING ECK MASTER. SRI Harold Klemp became the MAHANTA, the Living ECK Master in 1981. His spiritual name is WAH Z.

Lai Tsi   An ancient Chinese ECK MASTER.

Living ECK Master   The spiritual leader of ECKANKAR. He leads SOUL back to God. He teaches in the physical world as the Outer Master, in the dream state as the Dream Master, and in the spiritual worlds as the Inner Master. SRI HAROLD KLEMP became the MAHANTA, the Living ECK Master in 1981.

MAHANTA   An expression of the Spirit of God that is always with you. Sometimes seen as a BLUE LIGHT or Blue Star or in the form of the MAHANTA, the LIVING ECK MASTER. The highest state of God Consciousness on earth, only embodied in the Living ECK Master. He is the Living Word.

Mahdis *MAH-dees*   The initiate of the Fifth Circle (SOUL PLANE); often used as a generic term for all High Initiates in ECK.

Peddar Zaskq   The spiritual name for PAUL TWITCHELL, the modern-day founder of ECKANKAR and the MAHANTA, the LIVING ECK MASTER from 1965 to 1971.

planes   Levels of existence, such as the Physical, Astral, Causal, Mental, Etheric, and SOUL Planes.

Rebazar Tarzs   A Tibetan ECK MASTER known as the Torchbearer of ECKANKAR in the lower worlds.

Satsang   A class in which students of ECK discuss a monthly lesson from ECKANKAR.

Self-Realization   SOUL recognition. The entering of Soul into the Soul PLANE and there beholding Itself as pure Spirit. A state of Seeing, Knowing, and Being.

Shariyat-Ki-Sugmad   Way of the Eternal; the sacred scriptures of ECKANKAR. The scriptures are comprised of twelve volumes in the spiritual worlds. The first two were transcribed from the inner PLANES by PAUL TWITCHELL, modern-day founder of Eckankar.

Soul   The True Self, an individual, eternal spark of God. The inner, most sacred part of each person. Soul can see, know, and perceive all things. It is the creative center of Its own world.

Soul Travel   The expansion of consciousness. The ability of SOUL to transcend the physical body and travel into the spiritual worlds of God. Soul Travel is taught only by the LIVING ECK MASTER. It helps people unfold spiritually and can provide proof of the existence of God and life after death.

Sound and Light of ECK   The Holy Spirit. The two aspects through which God appears in the lower worlds. People can experience them by looking and listening within themselves and through SOUL TRAVEL.

Spiritual Exercises of ECK   Daily practices for direct, personal experience with the God Current. Creative techniques using contemplation and the singing of sacred words to bring the higher awareness of SOUL into daily life.

Sri   A title of spiritual respect, similar to reverend or pastor, used for those who have attained the Kingdom of God. In ECKANKAR, it is reserved for the MAHANTA, the LIVING ECK MASTER.

SUGMAD *SOOG-mahd*   A sacred name for God. It is the source of all life, neither male nor female, the Ocean of Love and Mercy.

Temples of Golden Wisdom   Golden Wisdom Temples found on the various PLANES—from the Physical to the Anami Lok; CHELAS of ECKANKAR are taken to these temples in the SOUL body to be educated in the divine knowledge; sections of the SHARIYAT-KI-SUGMAD, the sacred teachings of ECK, are kept at these temples.

Twitchell, Paul   An American ECK MASTER who brought the modern teachings of ECKANKAR to the world through his writings and lectures. His spiritual name is PEDDAR ZASKQ.

vairag   The spiritual virtue of detachment.

Wah Z *WAH zee*   The spiritual name of SRI HAROLD KLEMP. It means the secret doctrine. It is his name in the spiritual worlds.

Yaubl Sacabi   Guardian of the SHARIYAT-KI-SUGMAD in the spiritual city of Agam Des. He was the MAHANTA, the LIVING ECK MASTER in ancient Greece.

For more explanations of ECKANKAR terms, see *A Cosmic Sea of Words: The ECKANKAR Lexicon*, by Harold Klemp.

INDEX

acceptance, 66, 162
acting, actions, 70
  as if, 250
  assessing Mastership by, 186
  karmaless, 130
  seeds of, 95
  of Spirit, 287 (*see also*
    Sound(s))
active(ity)
  being, 2, 3
  refining an, 239
acupuncturists, 71
Adam and Eve, 32–33
adventure, 210
Age
  Bronze (*see* Bronze Age)
  Golden (*see* Golden Age)
  Iron (*see* Iron Age)
  Silver (*see* Silver Age)
agnostic(s), 33
American Revolution, 206, 207
Anami Lok, 128
angel(s), 108
  fallen, 36
anger, 101, 109, 110, 162, 188
animism, 55
air force, 208–9, 212
airplane(s), pilot(s), 25–26, 190,
  214
ambition, 48
animal(s), 47, 248–49
Arawak Indians, 98, 202–4
architect story, 121–22
art(work), 109–10, 242–43,
  266–67

ashram(s), 37, 160
Askleposis, Temple of, 164
Astral
  body (*see* body(ies): Astral
    (emotional))
  Plane (*see* Plane: Astral)
  travel, 95
  world (*see* Plane: Astral)
Atlantis, 17, 19, 90, 234
attachment(s), 3, 62
attacks, 194, 272
attention, 62, 122
  on MAHANTA, 135, 272
  and outside world, 160
  during spiritual exercises, 208,
    210
attitude(s), 23, 96, 99, 163, 227,
  264, 267
Audible Life Stream (Current),
  1, 25, 44, 64, 82, 89, 110, 112,
  130
aura, 27, 94, 264, 274
Australia, 108
authority, 31–32, 46, 91
  challenging, 34, 92, 113
  and freedom for individual,
    201
  papal, 204
aware, awareness, 44, 45. *See
  also* consciousness
  becoming more, 189, 215, 236
  of God, 287, 288 (*see also*
    God-Realization)
  lack of, 77
  levels of, 47, 242

cycle(s) (*continued*)
life runs in, 49, 116
in terminal illness, 162

Daniel, story of, 123
dark night of Soul. *See* Soul:
dark night of
Darshan, 40, 253, 254, 276. *See
also* Living ECK Master:
meeting
Dead Sea Scrolls, 98
death, 93, 125
fear of, 62, 117, 125, 126, 213,
247
of an ideal, 162
MAHANTA helps at time of, 6
process of, 154–55
sorrow at, 116
Soul knows no, 26, 63, 73, 276
debts, 228, 229. *See also*
karma(ic)
decisions, 192, 193, 234–35
declarations. *See* ECK: declarations
delegating, 122
depression, 49, 162, 182
destiny, 70, 207. *See also* mission: of Soul
detachment, 117, 182
detail(s), 121–22, 250, 275
Devil, 126–27, 210, 261, 280. *See
also* Kal Niranjan
as secret agent for God, 127, 231
direct projection, 295
disciple(s), 39, 91
of Jesus, 24
discipline, 1, 72, 239
of learning, 283
self-, 65, 230, 231, 263
and spiritual exercises (*see*
Spiritual Exercises of ECK:
and discipline)
doctor(s), 11, 58, 64, 71, 76, 77,
80, 198, 245
doggie bag story, 226–27
door, sliding glass, story, 186–88
dream(s), dream state, 70, 123,

255, 289, 290–91, 295
censor, 290–91, 292, 294
experience(s) in, 26, 28, 66, 92,
111, 113, 286, 292–93
initiation, 154 (*see also*
Initiation(s): First)
journal, 250, 290, 292–93,
294–95
message, 290, 291, 292, 293
seeing Master in, 55, 277
Soul Travel and, 209
truth taught through, 17,
97–98, 100
waking, 172, 221
Dream Master, 26–27, 55, 133,
277, 290, 291, 293
drugs, 193
Drums of ECK, The (Twitchell),
140

earthquakes, 140, 160, 292–93
Easy Way, the. *See* technique(s):
the Easy Way
ECK
becoming one with, 288
is behind all history, 219, 220
being ready for, 241
commitment to, 181
contact with, 60, 194
declarations, 274
disagreement about, 175
gifts from, 218, 286
as golden thread, 259
identifying, 157
influence of, 282
Initiates (*see* Initiate(s))
message of, 40, 111, 156, 219,
221, 232, 247
path of, 7, 11, 13, 14, 21, 22,
104, 107, 115, 116, 129, 147,
158, 221, 226, 235, 276
power of, 22, 44, 156
proof of, 9, 11, 22
as Spirit, 5, 114
theories of, 243
trusting the, 239, 259, 261
tuned into, 44, 109–10

world(s) (*continued*)
  influence of ECK on, 282
  inner, 63, 93, 211, 276
  invisible, 287
  of knowing, 25
  lower, 3, 58, 96, 157, 161, 170,
    174, 272, 293
  physical, 273
  of pure Light, 82
  starry, 78 (*see also* Plane:
    Astral)
  of time and space, 117
worship
  of God, 230
  of Living ECK Master, 46
  of Moloch (*see* Moloch)
  of nature spirits (*see* animism)
  of personality (*see* Moloch)
wristwatch story, 193
write, writer(s), writing, 4–5, 161,
    247, 293. *See also* poetry
  absence of, 18, 91
  correcting, 243
  and editor, 4–5
  techniques used by, 56
  work out problems through, 292

Yaubl Sacabi, 128, 207, 246
youth, 253–56
  bond among, 218
  discourses, 178
  enjoying, 136
  follies of, 48
  freedom and, 207, 218
  programs for, 221, 255
  at seminars, 153, 218

Zoroastrianism, 103